Dear Dad,

I hope you enjoy this book as ~~~~~~
read this book I thought of you beca~~~ ~~~~ ~~~~ ~~~~ much
of FDR!

Happy Father's Day Bapu!

All our love,

Johny, Vickie & Kate

A
THEOLOGICAL
INTERPRETATION
of
AMERICAN
HISTORY

by

C. GREGG SINGER

Revised Edition

PRESBYTERIAN AND REFORMED PUBLISHING CO.
Phillipsburg, New Jersey 08865

Library of Congress Catalogue Card Number 64-13205

Printed in the United States of America

Second Edition 1981
ISBN 0-87552-426-5

To William Childs Robinson

The Author

C. Gregg Singer is a graduate of Haverford College and received his Ph.D. from the University of Pennsylvania. He has been the chairman of the History Departments at Wheaton College (1944–1948), Salem College in Winston Salem, N. C. (1948–1954), Belhaven College, Jackson, Miss. (1954–1958), and Catawba College, Salisbury, N. C. (1958–1977). He has served on the summer graduate school faculties of Furman University, Greenville, S. C., and of the University of Pennsylvania. He has also taught at the summer institute of Young Life in Colorado and at the Pensacola Institute of Theology. Since 1977 Dr. Singer has been professor of church history and theology at the Atlanta School of Biblical Studies.

The author of *Toynbee* in the Modern Thinkers Series of the International Library of Philosophy and Theology, *Calvinism: Its Roots and Fruits, From Rationalism to Irrationality: The Decline of the Western Mind from the Renaissance to the Present, The Unholy Alliance,* and *South Carolina in the Confederation, 1781–1789,* he is a frequent contributor to *Christianity Today* and the *Presbyterian Journal,* as well as numerous other periodicals.

A
THEOLOGICAL
INTERPRETATION
OF
AMERICAN
HISTORY

Contents

Introduction

It is not the purpose of these essays to present a history of the United States nor of American Christianity, but rather to portray the influence of theology and the changing doctrines in the life of the church on the pattern of American political, constitutional, social and economic development. This book is born of the conviction that ideas in general do have consequences and that theological ideas have tremendous consequences in the life of a nation. Indeed, it is impossible to understand completely the history of a nation apart from the philosophies and the theologies which lie at the heart of its intellectual life.

Historical scholarship, if it remains true to its purpose, is characterized not only by the necessity of finding the facts of history, but also of achieving a correct interpretation of all the data which it has in its possession. The quest for meaning in history has been no less characteristic of American historiography than for the historians of other nations. In fact, it is increasingly recognized that it is the duty of the historian to present a meaningful interpretation of the data which he is discussing. In recent years this aspect of the task has become an increasingly important pre-occupation of leading historians; Arnold Toynbee's *Study of History* is a monumental effort in this respect.

In American historiography there have been many schools of interpretation, some of which have been applications of general theories of history to the American past, while others have been more genuinely native in their origin. In addition to the Marxian approach to history which has not lacked adherents in this country, there have been important modifications of this philosophy which have made much greater headway than is generally recognized. Some scholars, aware that in its original form the Marxian view of history would not fit into the New World pattern, sought to adapt Marx to the facts of American experience. One of the most popular and influential of these modifications, although not widely recognized as such, was the thesis suggested by Frederic Jackson Turner that the key to the meaning of America was to be found in the determinative influence which the frontier had exercised on the political, social and economic development of the nation from the earliest days of the settlements until the closing of the frontier about 1890. Essentially this theory was simply an affirmation that the culture of the American people was, to a great extent, the result of the influence of the frontier environment in which it had developed. Even apart from the historical objections which have been brought against Turner's position, it is open to severe criticism because of its subtle denial of the Christian view of human personality in favor of one which is basically materialistic in outlook. This appeal to the frontier as a frame of reference for the interpretation of the American past was only a thin disguise for a Marxian point of view. Although this thesis no longer commands the unquestioning loyalty which it received some fifty years ago, there are still many historians who rise to its defense and who still look to it, even when they change it in the light of more recent findings.

Still other historians have been much impressed with the growth of democracy and the rise of the common man as the most important phenomenon of the whole sweep of our national development. They see in it the one thread of unity which relates the events of 1776 to those of our own day; for them the gradual, yet steady, unfolding of that American Dream, which Jefferson enunciated in the majestic phraseology of the Declaration of Independence, is the dominant note in the drama of American history. The members of this school would not necessarily rule out from their consideration the importance of the frontier, and many of them would even claim it to be an ally of the democratic movement, but they would insist that the real meaning of America is to be found in the ultimate realization of the democratic philosophy in all aspects of its national life.

For other historians, Charles A. Beard set the pattern of thought with his economic interpretation of the writing of the Constitution and the period of Hamilton and Jefferson. In his insistence that economic factors were the determining influence in the formation of the American tradition, Beard also had Marxian overtones which could not be denied.

In recent years there has been a renewed interest in the intellectual forces at work in American life and with it has come an increasing recognition of the role played by the American mind in our political, social, and economic development. Such scholars as Merle Curti, Perry Miller, Henry Commager, Ralph Gabriel, and Richard Mosier have rescued intellectual history from its long period of neglect and have rendered a tremendous service in restoring it to its rightful place in historical scholarship.

Although each one of these schools may rightfully claim to have laid hold on some aspect of historical truth, they have generally done so in such a manner as to neglect, or even deny, other equally necessary approaches to historical problems. In spite of the serious distortions of which the Marxists have been guilty, they have served to remind historians that economic facts are important and that they do play a role in history which cannot be neglected. Beard was likewise correct in his insistence that many men are willing to sacrifice other values in life for the sake of economic gain. Even though Frederic Jackson Turner made extravagant and unjustifiable claims in behalf of his frontier thesis, claims which later scholars have been forced to modify, it cannot be denied that the westward movement holds an important place in the history of the nation up to 1890; this also cannot be neglected. Likewise, those who profess to find the key to the understanding of America in the growth of political, economic, and social democracy are also correct insofar as they bring to our attention the fact that democracy lay at the very heart of the American dream as it was envisaged by Jefferson and his colleagues. But this attempt to interpret our history in terms of this philosophy is quite unsatisfactory at certain points, for it fails to answer certain basic questions: why did Jefferson look to Locke and the other philosophers of democracy rather than to the Puritan political heritage, and why did the Founding Fathers of 1787, in turn, take such elaborate precautions to set up a form of government which would guard against the rise of democracy? A third question which has also largely been ignored concerns a closely related problem: why has the Constitution been increasingly used to promote this same democratic form of government which it was designed to prevent from gaining a foothold in the new nation? What are the circumstances under which this document has been changed so that it might become the instrument for ushering in a kind of government which the Founding Fathers regarded as a type of enemy to the liberties of the people? The drastic change from a constitutional republic to a democracy is certainly one of the major events of American history, and historical scholarship must deal with it adequately. It is unfortunate that those historians who have recognized its importance have, at the same time, failed to answer some very basic questions which are intimately related to it; unless these are answered, the simple recognition of this momentous event tends to raise more questions than it solves.

In like manner, we are greatly indebted to those historians who have recognized once again the importance of intellectual developments for a proper understanding of history. However, too often their efforts have largely concentrated on depicting those intellectual changes which have taken place in American life, but they have failed to analyze them as to their inner meaning. As valuable as these studies are, they lose a great deal of their effectiveness as guides to the understanding of history because, all too frequently, they are not presented in the light of the predominant theological and metaphysical issues of the day. Too seldom have these historians given theology its proper place as a determining factor in intellectual life. The recognition of the importance of intellectual forces in the stream of history must be followed by one other step, namely, the realization that the intellectual development of a people is not an entity in itself, but, in turn, depends upon their theology, or lack thereof.

To acknowledge that there are germs of truth in these various approaches to an understanding of American history does not bring with it the admission that they are, singly or collectively, adequate as keys to its meaning. They must certainly be less than satisfactory to the Calvinist, for, without exception, they approach the problem of history either in terms of the achievements and aspirations of man as a sovereign and self-sufficient being, or in terms of some form of economic or environmental determinism. Whether the meaning of history be sought in man himself, or in his physical environment, the result must be disappointing. In neither one of these approaches can either meaning or purpose be found for the historical process; it must remain an inexplicable mystery to those schools of historical interpretation which look to either man himself or to nature as their ultimate authority and frame of reference.

The great weakness in the major schools of historical interpretation of the present day lies in the fact that they have adopted either humanism, or some form of scientific naturalism, as the source of all the necessary presuppositions for their philosophies of history. By many, if not most, of the professional historians of the present day, the world and life view of the Scriptures is frankly rejected as having no possible authority, or value, for them in their intellectual endeavors. Whatever may be their personal convictions toward the biblical message of redemption, they refuse its claims of authority in the world of scholarship.

The unfortunate consequence of this refusal to allow the Scriptures to have their rightful place and to furnish a frame of reference for their interpretation of historical data has been their inability to recognize the tremendous role which the Scriptures have played in the formation of the American tradition, and the very great influence which theology has exercised in the political, social and economic development of the American Republic, as well as in its cultural and intellectual life. Not only is it impossible to understand the colonial era apart from the Puritanism of the day, but the essential nature of the American Revolution, the rise of Jacksonian democracy and abolitionism, the coming of the War between the States, the rise of big business, and the development of modern liberal and radical movements will elude successful analysis by these historians who fail to see all these developments in the light of their theological significance and their philosophical connotations. Transcendentalism, the Social Gospel, Social Darwinism and dialectical materialism have been, at one time or another, or still are, dominant influences in American political and economic life, but they cannot be understood unless they are seen in their proper theological perspective.

This book is written in the light of the conviction that only in the light of the Christian revelation can American history be brought into a proper perspective; that the intellectual, political, social, and economic trends of the past and the present can be rightly interpreted only in the light of the scriptural norm. Only on the basis of the historic Christian faith can the various schools of historical thought, now in sharp disagreement on essential points, find a common ground for agreement. This must not be in such a manner that the particular emphasis of any, or all, the other schools of historical research will be declared totally in error, but that the contributions of all of them will be carefully weighed and evaluated as they are subjected to the authority of the Scriptures. Thus, as they are brought into harmony with this biblical frame of reference, they will gain a new validity which they could not otherwise possibly command.

The Puritan Mind and Dream

Puritanism, the prevailing theological and philosophical system, not only in England, but in most of the colonies founded during the seventeenth century, is the key which unlocks the meaning of colonial history as a whole. It pervaded not only the religious life and thought of most of the early colonists, but their political, social and economic life as well. Nothing could be more misleading than the contemporary notion that Puritanism was little more than a "Sunday" religion which had little or no influence on the daily life of those who professed it. The direct opposite was actually the case, for it permeated colonial life to an amazing degree, not only in New England but in the colonies to the South as well; and Puritan influence was not lacking in the founding of Virginia and the Carolina Colonies. For most of the colonies along the Atlantic seaboard Calvinism was a kind of theological common denominator which gave great consistency and coherence to colonial life as a whole.

The predominance of Calvinism in New England has been generally recognized by historians and, almost as frequently, lamented. Less frequently has much attention been paid to its significant influence in the other colonies. Instead, it has been greatly overlooked that Calvinism had strong roots in the Church of England during the early half of the seventeenth century and that it was quite natural for Calvinism to appear wherever this church took root in the New World. The popular impression that Calvinism was largely, if not totally, confined to the Congregational Churches of New England is quite erroneous and misleading for, as its strength was sapped by the growing Arminianism of the Established Church after 1650, it found new roots in the coming of Presbyterianism to the middle and southern colonies.

The question then arises: Why were the early settlers of Virginia, and some of the other colonies, not as articulate in their devotion to Calvinism as the Puritans of New England? There are several answers to this question. In the first place, they never had the local autonomy over their own affairs which marked the early history of the New England colonies. While they had a commendable degree of self-government, they never had the experience of a practical independence which characterized life in New England during its first fifty years. It must also be remembered that while many of them were Calvinists, they were not necessarily as "Puritan" as their fellow settlers to the north; neither had they come with the same enthusiasm for forming a biblical commonwealth. They had not virtually seceded from the Kingdom of England as had the Puritans, nor from the Church of England in the manner of the Separatists of Plymouth. They were content to remain in both, but to say this is not to cast doubt upon their devotion to Christianity. They were content with a Christian society under the Crown and were less interested in striking out on new and untried paths of ecclesiastical and political independence.

In the third place, it must be remembered that within a relatively short time, other groups came to Virginia who were not religiously motivated to the same extent as the earlier settlers had been, and they did not share the Calvinistic convictions of many of those who had promoted the London and Virginia Companies. The Carolina Colony could not claim even that degree of Calvinistic influence, and the religious life of this colony was quite different in its complexion almost from the very beginning. Thus, the Calvinistic influence in the southern colonies was diluted at an early date and it was never the dominant influence in the life of the people that it was in New England; for here it lay at the very heart of the "Holy Experiment." When Calvinist refugees later came to Virginia and the Carolinas, they found a somewhat different pattern of life already established there and the political situation did not allow them to express their own convictions until the American Revolution brought about the disestablishment of the Church of England.

The Puritans of New England went there for the express purpose of setting up a commonwealth which would give full expression to that world and life view inherent in their Calvinistic theology. This was to be reflected not only in their political activity, but in the economic and social life as well. At the heart of their political, social, and economic philosophy lay a theology— Calvinism. Puritanism was thus a theological interpretation of life, and, in Calvinism, the Puritans found the guide for their economic, social and political conduct. Thus it was necessary that its content should be clearly defined and widely understood, not only by the ecclesiastical and political leadership of the colony, but by the church members at large who were, at the same time, the voting citizens of the state.

The widespread knowledge of, and appreciation for, the theological foundations of the Puritan way of life was absolutely necessary if the biblical commonwealth being erected in Massachusetts Bay were to endure. Those who had the responsibility for choosing the leadership in both church and state must clearly recognize the importance of their role and clearly discern those who were properly qualified to serve in these capacities. This necessity lies at the center of the often ridiculed, but seldom understood, requirement that only church members in good standing could vote for those who would lead both the church and the state. A theologically enlightened electorate was as vitally necessary for the state as a biblically oriented membership was for the Church. Orthodoxy of religious belief was, therefore, a prime requisite for participation in this way of life because theology lay at the very heart of their entire system.

It was this conscious application of a Calvinistic theology to the whole structure of life which gave to New England its dominant position in the intellectual life of the colonies. Calvinism gave to this section a character which would survive to some degree even after the passing of three centuries. While the rise of heresies, and the incessant attacks of many of its enemies, would cause it to lose its lofty dominance, traces of its influence would still be discernible in the mid-twentieth century.

Puritan Theology

For the Puritans the biblical doctrines of God, creation, man, sin and redemption were not regarded as simply vehicles for the salvation of the individual soul, important as that was, but they spoke to the whole of life. In Puritanism the doctrine of God was not merely a philosophical necessity, the final step in a finely worked out metaphysical system. God was a Being who was to be worshiped on the Sabbath, and to be reckoned with on the other six days of the week as well. In their theology, he was a Sovereign Being who had not only created the Universe and man, but who continuously governed his creation as well. His sovereignty was not only expressed in the decrees of redemption, but in his complete control of his creatures and all their actions. Thus, the Puritan was to live every aspect of his daily life in the constant consciousness that God was sovereign and that he was responsible to him. This consciousness of the sovereignty of God must be reflected in all that man thinks, says, and does. His political, economic and social life was to be consciously fashioned in the light of this truth, for it spoke to him concerning the form which government should take, the conduct for his economic activities, the kind of education he should provide for his children, and the proper social relationships he must have with the fellow-citizens of this biblical commonwealth.

In like manner, the doctrine of the fall and total depravity guided Puritan thought. Man was not only created in the image of a sovereign God and subject to him, but he was a sinful creature, totally unable to do the will of God, and under a just sentence of eternal condemnation for his sins apart from the mercy of God. In his fall Adam lost for the whole race that original righteousness with which man had been endowed at creation, and, in his total depravity, man was unable to do anything to please God, or be worthy of eternal salvation.

This doctrine of original sin was no less important in Puritan thought than their view of divine sovereignty. It spoke directly to every aspect of life. Human sin made human government necessary; as a sinner, man is to be educated, and, as a sinner, he enters into economic activity and social relationships. The Puritans were under no illusions about human nature and there was no room in their philosophy of life for a doctrine of inherent goodness or inevitable progress for the race. Complete realism characterized their view of man and every sphere of his activity on earth. Their political, social and economic philosophies were beholden to the doctrine of total depravity as much as they were to the sovereignty of God. Both the nature and functions of government were articulated by Puritan writers in the light of the fact that man is a sinner. Likewise man, in his economic activities and in his social relationships, must be viewed in the same light; therefore, all attempts to formulate economic and social thought must take this fact into account.

Of no less importance in Puritan thought and life was the doctrine of redemption. Man, as a sinner, stands in need of redeeming grace if he is to be saved and the great truth that in Jesus Christ, God had provided this salvation was also a dominant theme. The Puritans recognized the distinctive role of sovereign grace in the redemptive process and they never expected human political, social and economic institutions to usurp the place of the Church in society, or, to accomplish for man, either here on earth or in the future life, that salvation which comes through the Gospel alone. No one who seeks to understand the Puritan mode of thought can escape the conclusion that these doctrines of sin and grace were an integral part of that frame of reference which the Puritans consciously used in the formulation of their political, social, and economic policies.

Contemporary liberals should not allow their repugnance and hostility to this colonial intellectual outlook blind them to its real meaning. Puritanism is seldom understood by its many passionate critics; its grandeurs and enduring qualities are too seldom appreciated even by those who claim to be its heirs. Its real essence is often overlooked by both its friends and its foes alike; too frequently it is attacked for being what it was not, and, almost as frequently, it is claimed as the progenitor of movements in contemporary life which the Puritans would have spurned in their own era. The Puritanism of early New England was the rugged Calvinism of Calvin, Knox, and the Westminster divines who brought it to a new home in a new land; to an environment and under circumstances very different from those which confronted Calvinism both on the Continent and in Great Britain. It cannot and must not be denied that both time, and these frontier conditions, brought changes into that Calvinism which came with the first settlers. Neither must it be forgotten that Calvinism came with those Puritans and that it was the dominant element in the forging of a colonial culture not only for the New England colonies, but for most of the others as well. The real wonder of its history in this country is not that it aroused great opposition and bitterness and that it was subject to change, but that it has had a great influence in an intellectual environment essentially hostile to its teachings and spirit, and, that its influence has survived for nearly three and one-half centuries even in those sections of the country where the revolt against it was most bitter. Many of its most articulate critics have, on more than one occasion, paid it something of a compliment when they have attempted to reclaim its basic ideas and set them forth in a secularized version as a guide for a democratic state.

Puritan Political Philosophy

The necessity for a political philosophy which would be in accord with their basic theology was brought home to the Puritans long before they left England. Indeed, differences of political opinion lay at the heart of their quarrel with the Crown under the Stuarts; and, it is impossible to understand the long and drawn-out quarrel between Parliament and James I and Charles I apart from its theological implications. Both parties to the contest were well aware of the fact that beneath the constitutional issue over the nature of Parliamentary power lay a profound theological cleavage which brought forth two very incompatible political philosophies. It may very well be said that the first product of the Puritan theology was a Puritan philosophy of government. It was the clear recognition of the nature of the political conflict in England which induced the leaders of the exodus to the New World to set up a state which would conform to the dictates of the Puritan theology and which would be a fitting home for the church which upheld it. Apart from the recognition of this fact, it is impossible to understand or appreciate the history of the Puritan colonies. This is not to infer that their economic and social thought were less important, for they were both implicit and explicit in their writings. And, to a certain extent at least, the Puritan state was created to make it possible for them to realize these aspects of their world and life view, as well as their conception of the Church and the people of God.

Puritan political thought is a lasting monument to their appreciation of the Scriptures as the whole counsel of God and their desire to realize it in every aspect of their corporate life as well as in their individual experiences. The idea that the state was beyond the reach of the claims of the Bible was as abhorrent to the Puritan as were the claims of Rome that the state was subject to the church. In the Scriptures they found the origin, the form, the functions and the power of the state and human government. This resort to the Scriptures as the exclusive norm for human political organization and activity clearly differentiated them from both the Roman Catholics and that rising group of secularist writers who were finding the origin of the state and the source of its powers in a vaguely defined source known as the social compact or contract. In the Puritan view of life man could no more create the government under which he would live and endow it with its just powers than he could effect his own salvation.

Basic in Puritan political thought is the doctrine of divine sovereignty. It was the sovereign God who created the state and gave to it its powers and functions. The earthly magistrate held his position and exercised his power by a divine decree. He was a minister of God under common grace for the execution of the laws of God among the people at large, for the maintenance of law and order, and for so ruling the state that it would provide an atmosphere favorable for the preaching of the Gospel. He was to so rule that the people of God, the elect, could live individually and collectively a life that was truly Christian.

In Puritan political theory the magistrate derived his powers from God and not from the people. Human government was divinely ordained for the realization of the purposes of God in history. His powers did not come from the people, nor was he primarily responsible to them for the stewardship of his office. It is true that these magistrates were elected by the people and the people had certain definite powers in the legislative process. They were not absolute in their power and were amenable to certain constitutional and elective checks which were placed in the hands of the voters. This is all true, but it must never be forgotten that both the voters and the magistrates were to look to the Scriptures as a guide for the general conduct of their government. The rulers and the people were thus subject to the revealed will of God, and the will of the people could never take precedence over the divinely ordained powers and functions of human government.

It was inevitable that this conviction, that the Scriptures were to be the ultimate guide for political conduct, would raise the question of the relations of church and state. The charge has frequently been made against the New England colonies that they simply exchanged one type of theocratic government for another. And, at first glance, it would seem to be easily sustained. However, the majority of those offering this criticism have overlooked several salient aspects of the situation obtaining in these colonies. It is quite true that at one level there was a kind of theocracy there, but at another level the charge is unjustified. Puritan political theory assigned quite different roles to church and state. Both were divinely ordained for certain definite purposes, but the purposes were not identical, and the Puritans never confused these two institutions, or their respective roles, in their society. Because of their Calvinist heritage, the Puritans were concerned with a proclamation of the whole counsel of God to man, and for the subjection of the whole of human life to the Kingdom of Jesus Christ. They never expected the state to perform any duty which the Scriptures assigned to the church, and they were never willing to allow the church to take to itself those functions which were "secular" in nature. Both church and state had their own spheres of action and neither was to transgress the domain of the other. The state was concerned with the earthly life of the people of God and the unregenerate who might live in their midst. It was concerned with the enforcement of the Ten Commandments, not for the purpose of bringing people to a knowledge of salvation, or to force them to a kind of external righteousness as a means of earning redemption, but for the purpose of maintaining the sovereignty and holiness of God for his own glory. The state, on the other hand, had no power or right to intrude on the domain of the church. The state is an instrument of common grace, while the church is an instrument of redemptive grace. Both institutions had a common theological foundation, but their spheres of activity were quite different and must remain so. In the area of their practical operation in the everyday life of the commonwealth there was not to be a union of the church and state as institutions.

In short, the Puritans of the seventeenth century adapted for their own use, and placed in a Calvinistic context, the Gelasian theory of the two swords (enunciated by Pope Gelasius I in 494). It was well expressed by John Davenport:

> These two different Orders and States, Ecclesiastical and civil, be not set in opposition as contraries that one should destroy the other, but as co-ordinate states, in the same place, reaching forth help mutually to each other, for the welfare of both according to God, so that both Officers and Members of Churches be subject in

respect of the outward man, to the Civil Power, of those who bear rule in the Civil State according to God and teach others to do so; And that the Civil Magistrates and Officers in regard of the inward man subject themselves spiritually to the power of Christ in Church Ordinances and by their Civil Power preserve the same in outward Peace and Purity.[1]

The Church and State were to cooperate in the attainment of their respective goals, for they were both subject to the same God. It was for this reason that the State was to punish blasphemers and heretics. The magistrate, in the discharge of his office, was a steward unto God and he was to be found faithful in this responsibility. It was not the role of the magistrate to proclaim the Gospel, but it was his duty to establish such civil conditions as to enable the Church to perform this function. Neither was it the responsibility of the Church to manage the civil life of the people, but a faithful preaching of the Law of God was bound to have a healthy influence on the community at large.

It must be admitted that this theological conception of the relationship which should exist between Church and State was susceptible to violation in the area of actual practice, and it cannot be successfully denied that the Puritans were not always successful in maintaining a separation between the two institutions in their application of this theory. The fact that there were violations should not be surprising, for the Puritans were not exempt from the influences of that doctrine of original sin and total depravity which they preached so forcefully. Neither did they claim such an exemption. This conflict between theory and practice stalks every aspect of the Christian effort to realize the whole counsel of God in the daily life of the community. In their zeal for maintaining the true religion as a necessary basis for their biblical commonwealth, they were guilty, at times, of forgetting

[1] John Davenport, *A Discourse About Civil Government*, Cambridge, 1663, pp. 8-9 quoted in Joseph Blau, *Men and Movements in American Philosophy*, pp. 6-7.

that the true union lay in the realm of theology and not on the institutional level.

These basic considerations and important ramifications were in other areas of political theory. The Puritans held to a very different conception of liberty from that which is so prevalent in contemporary thought and governmental theory. For the Puritan, liberty was in no way associated with the doctrine of natural law and natural rights, but found its origin and meaning in that covenant which God had made with his people. Liberty was not a natural right, but a God-given right and privilege to be zealously guarded from despots, to be sure, but also subject to precise biblically-defined limits. Their view of liberty received its classic definition in an address which John Winthrop gave to the General Court of Massachusetts in 1645.

There is a two-fold liberty, natural (I mean as our nature is now corrupt) and civil or federal. The first is common to man with beasts and other creatures. But this, as man stands in relation to man simply, he hath liberty to do what he lists, it is liberty to evil as well as to good. This liberty is incompatible and inconsistent with authority and cannot endure the least restraint of the most just authority. The exercise and maintaining this liberty makes men grow more evil and in time to be worse than brute beasts. . . . This is that great enemy of truth and peace, that wild beast, which all the ordinances of God are bent against, to restrain and subdue it. The other kind of liberty I call civil or federal, it may also be termed moral in reference to the covenant between God and man, in the moral law, and the political covenants and constitutions among men themselves. This liberty is the proper end and object of authority and cannot subsist without it; and it is a liberty to that only which is good, and just, and honest . . . . This liberty is maintained and exercised in a way of subjection to authority, it is the same kind of liberty wherewith Christ has made us free. . . . Even so, Brethren, it will be between you and your magistrates. If you stand for your natural corrupt liberties and will to do what is good in your own eyes you will not endure the least weight of authority, but will murmur and oppose, and be always striving to shake off that yoke; but if you will be satisfied to enjoy the civil and lawful liberties such as Christ allows you, then will you quietly and cheerfully submit unto that authority which is set over you, in all administrations of it, for your good.[2]

It need hardly be emphasized that Puritan political theory was far from being democratic but it is quite obvious that nothing could be farther from the Puritan political ideal. Nor is this a mere inference from their writings on government which lacks positive statements as to their contempt for this philosophy of government. John Cotton gave a very clear statement of the Puritan attitude.

Democracy, I do not conceive that God ever did ordain as a fit government either for church or for commonwealth. If the people be governors, who shall be governed? As for monarchy and aristocracy they are both of them clearly approved and directed in Scripture, yet so as referreth the sovereignty to Himself and setteth up theocracy in both as the best form of government in the commonwealth as well as in the church.[3]

The whole conception of government that would later be proclaimed by John Locke and others, which placed the sovereignty in the hands of the people and which found the origin of government in a human compact was utterly unknown to the Puritans. They did not believe in a government by the people, but they did believe in government for the people.

Was this contempt for democratic rule the result of snobbery and an aristocratic mode of life and thought? There have been those historians who have come to such a conclusion, but such an evaluation of Puritan thought is quite superficial and betrays a tragic failure to comprehend the Puritan mind. Writers of Cotton's and Winthrop's caliber were not arguing for an aristocracy per se, certainly not one of a secular nature based upon wealth or social status. Rather did they sense that in the democratic philosophy, with its emphasis upon the sovereignty of the people, lay a fundamental contradiction to the biblical doctrine of the

[2] Quoted in Perry Miller, *The Puritan Mind,* Vol. I, p. 427.
[3] Quoted in Miller and Johnson, *The Puritans,* p. 209.

sovereignty of God. They clearly perceived that democracy was the fruit of humanism and not the Reformation concept. John Winthrop also reminded his fellow-citizens of Massachusetts that a doctrine of civil rights which looked to natural or sinful man as its source and guardian was actually destructive of that very liberty which they were seeking to protect. True freedom can never be found in institutions which are under the direction of sinful men, but only in the redemption wrought for man by Jesus Christ. Christ, not man, is the sole source and guarantee of true liberty. This two-fold indictment of the democratic philosophy of government is one of the enduring testimonies to the keen insight which these leaders of Massachusetts Bay had into both the theological and practical aspects of an effective type of government.

Puritanism as a continuing influence in American political life would have much to say to those who in 1787 sought to erect a constitution for the young republic, but it could only sit in judgment upon those who seek to transform that republic into a democratic state under the banners of a secular humanism that would mock every tenet of the political thought of those who forged the first governments for Massachusetts Bay and the other colonies. Indeed, American history is characterized, in its political aspects, by a continuing conflict between the Puritan political philosophy on the one hand, and the rise of a democratic conception of the state and human liberty which has emanated from non-biblical sources. The insistence that God is truly sovereign and that his sovereignty must be recognized in the political affairs of mankind is an anathema to those modern schools of thought which seek to enthrone man as a sovereign in his own right.

In the area of political thought and practice Puritanism left a legacy of the idea of a government of law rather than of men, and furnished many of the ingredients for the Constitution of 1787. In fact, it lies at the heart of constitutionalism as a way of government.

Puritanism not only gave birth to a political philosophy, but it was the foundation for an equally sturdy social and economic philosophy by which the Scriptures would speak to man in these aspects of life as well. There was a strict regulation of economic life in New England which differed from the laissez faire conceptions later made popular by Adam Smith. John Cotton vigorously denounced this doctrine that a man should sell as dear as he can, and buy as cheap as he can. The Puritans held to the Medieval idea of the just price, even though their definition of it was somewhat vague. Wages and prices were both regulated in the interests of justice. It must also be observed that in this Puritan regulation of commerce and industry, there was nothing doctrinaire about it and socialism found no place in their thinking. The right of private property and of free enterprise was clearly recognized. But economic freedom, as political freedom, was given a biblical setting. It had its source in that freedom wherewith Christ has made men free. The regulation of economic life was not for the purpose of ushering in some kind of a man-made utopia or humanly achieved millennial period, but for the honoring of the law and glory of God in human affairs.

This is a very vital distinction which modern commentators are prone to overlook. Puritan economic thought had no place for an economic individualism which knew no limits except those that the entrepreneur might be willing to impose upon himself in the interests of expediency; neither did it believe that every man in helping his own advancement would also do that which would aid the community at large. The doctrine of sin was too much a part of the Puritan outlook to permit such an indulgence. For this same reason they did not expect that any kind of governmental regulation of the economic or social life of man would radically change human nature and solve the problem of sin. Government had no redemptive quality or ability. Its function was to restrain the expression of human sinfulness, but it could neither remove the sin from human nature nor redeem the sinner. There was in Puritan economic and social philosophy a biblical realism which is too often lacking in contemporary approaches to the perennial problems of society.

Work was a positive virtue to the Puritan, commanded by God as one of the means of common grace for the practical disciplining of a sinful race. It was one of the necessary consequences of our total depravity and, at the same time, it offered a kind of temporal therapy and restraint for the minimizing of the worst expressions of sin in man. This concept of work underlay the Puritan approach to practical politics. The poor and the destitute, the sick and those unable to earn a living, were the responsibility of the colony (through the townships), but the modern idea of the welfare state was quite foreign to their political and social outlook. Labor was a form of worship and was to be encouraged, not discouraged. Every man was a steward and responsible for the particular talent, or talents, which God had given to him. It is most unfortunate that R. H. Tawney, and other writers, in their failure to understand and appreciate this aspect of Puritanism in New England and in England, have so seriously misrepresented it at this point.

It is not surprising that this very high conception of economic activity and the sanctity of work in the everyday lives of Christian people should have produced a high standard of living for that day in the colonies. Neither should it be a surprise that this very prosperity, the result of their fidelity to the injunction of Scripture, could become a snare to later generations who saw only the economic reward of hard work and frugality, and whose eyes were not turned toward the biblical inspiration which lay behind these economic achievements.

The Decline of Puritanism

The decline of Puritanism as a theology and a world and life view, both in New England and the other colonies where it had been an influence, is one of the most significant events in the colonial period of American history. Its dethronement from a position of supremacy has cast its shadow over every succeeding epoch and generation; its effects are seen not only in the life of the churches but in American political, social and economic development as well. In a very real sense the passing of Puritanism brought to an end a very important epoch in our national past, and, at the same time, it ushered in a permanent change of direction for the development of the colonies.

There are several reasons for this decline and consequent lack of influence and prestige. Historians are not of one mind in their answers to this problem. Historians who are hostile to it find in its own restrictive measures the seeds for its own dissolution. Others take the position that the very purposes of the experiment, and the theology which underlay the movement, could only bring about the ultimate failure. Their argument is that the Puritan ideal was not possible of realization even in the New World except for a few years when the early zeal and inspiration of the Puritan leadership could give the needed inspiration for the biblical Commonwealth which they had created. There are some elements in this argument which must be considered. Phrased in different terms, it simply means that all great endeavors of this nature face such difficulties and constant conflict with an unfriendly environment that they often yield to the forces of disintegration. History testifies that even the Church itself is not immune to these forces.

To deal in such generalizations, however true they may be, throws little light on the specific problems of Puritanism, unless some specific applications are made to their situation. Although the second and third generations of the movement produced great leaders like the Mathers, it is also true that there was a lessening of that zeal which characterized the early days of the experiment. By 1660 the situation was serious enough to cause apprehension on the part of the Puritan leaders. As an attempted remedy they proposed in 1662 the Half Way Covenant which allowed baptism to the grandchildren of the members of the Puritan Church even though their parents were not communing members. There can be little doubt that this compromise with reality contributed to a decline which was already under way.

By 1700 other forces were at work which intensified the Puritan departure from their historic orthodoxy and hence undermined their entire world and life view. John Wise was an important factor in this development when he expressed his views in his *The Churches Quarrel Espoused* (1710) and his *Vindication of the Government of the New England Church* (1717), which he wrote in opposition to an attempt by some of the leaders of Massachusetts to save Puritanism by the adoption of a form of church government closer to Presbyterianism than to Congregationalism. In fact, Herbert Schneider in his *History of American Philosophy* insists that John Wise gave away the whole Puritan case when he showed that covenant theology and its concept of Christian liberty could be paralleled by the secular doctrine of the social contract, provided that the doctrine of total depravity be pushed to one side. That such a parallel did exist, and was known to the Puritans, cannot be denied. By 1700 there were intellectual forces at work which were to induce an increasing number in New England to modify and even do away with original sin in their own theology. The advent of Newtonian physics, and the increasing number of scientific discoveries and technological advances, had enhanced the role of science and tended to reduce the importance of theology in colonial intellectual life. By 1730 this condition was very apparent; however, the dominant influence in this intellectual and philosophical transition from the Puritanism of the seventeeth century to the increasingly secularized colonial outlook of the eighteenth century was the arrival of Deism in the colonies.

2

Deism in Colonial Life

That Deism had a revolutionary influence in the political, social and economic life of colonial America during the eighteenth century is increasingly recognized by historians of many schools. Ultimately it provided that political philosophy which would produce the American Revolution, and at the same time, brought in its wake a new theological outlook which was quite conducive to revolutionary activity. Indeed, it is not too much to say that the separation from England could not have taken place unless there had first been a revolt against the Puritan world and life view in the colonies. Richard Mosier correctly stated the case in his *The American Temper* when he wrote that the struggle against the absolutism of the King of England had its corollary in the struggle against the sovereignty of the Puritan God: "the 'Revolutionary' could no more admit a sovereign God than he could a sovereign king."[1] Thus, Deism provided the motivation for not only the American Revolution, but also for the rise of Democracy in America (as distinct from that type of representa-

[1] Richard Mosier, *The American Temper*, Berkeley, 1952, p. 70.

tive government which had characterized the Puritan movement in the seventeenth century). Deism had its origin in the rationalism of Descartes, and in England in the philosophical and religious works of Lord Herbert of Cherbury who probably gave the first formal statement of the Deistic position in his *De Veritate* in 1625. According to Lord Herbert, true religion could be reduced to a very few simple and elementary truths which man must believe if he is to achieve happiness here in this life, and in that life which is yet to come. He taught that God did create the world and man, and that man must live according to that which he knows to be good and true. God punishes those who fail to do so, and rewards those who do. But this knowledge of God, and what he requires of man, is rationally perceived, and the Bible is binding only to the extent to which its teachings correspond with the dictates of right reason.

Deism, as it unfolded, proved to be a revolt against evangelical orthodoxy at practically every major point. Even when there was an apparent agreement, such as in regard to divine creation, it was only apparent and not actual. Deism denied the Scriptures as the only infallible rule of faith and practice and subjected the content of revelation to the demands of reason. It denied the doctrine of the Fall, total depravity, redemption through Jesus Christ alone, predestination, effectual calling, and nearly every other doctrine of the Scriptures. Its principal target, of course, was Calvinism.

Deism underwent considerable change in its epistemological and ethical outlook toward the close of the seventeenth century as a result of the philosophical writings of John Locke with his emphasis upon an empirical epistemology, rather than the rationalism of Lord Herbert of Cherbury, and the scientific discoveries of Sir Isaac Newton, which gave rise to a belief in the infallability of natural revelation, and to the conception of the world as a vast machine governed by natural law, mathematically discerned and explained. It was in this latter form, as it had been influenced by Locke and Newton, that Deism made its greatest and most enduring impact on American theology and intellectual life. Although it was not unknown to the colonies in its earlier rationalistic form, it did not gain any great stature as a philosophical and religious system until after 1700, and when it did arrive, it came in the new format supplied by the scientific discoveries of Newton and the empiricism of John Locke. It was the harbinger of the coming of the Enlightenment to the colonies, and the two movements soon coalesced and became almost indistinguishable so far as their effect on Puritanism was concerned.

Locke and Newton were both studied in the colonies during the eighteenth century, but there is some disagreement as to their popularity and influence. Blau is probably correct when he states that Locke was more important because of his political philosophy than for his psychology.[2] Yet Jonathan Edwards read Locke's *Essay Concerning Human Understanding* in 1716 when he entered Yale at the age of thirteen, and Newtonian physics was taught there as early as 1714. Here, Samuel Johnson, Edwards, and other later leaders of colonial intellectual and political life were introduced to these new intellectual and scientific ideas.

Basic to the Enlightenment, as it developed in Europe and as it came to this country were three ideas: the inherent goodness of human nature, the perfectibility of man, and the inevitability of progress. This latter was not taught in the deterministic sense in which Marx later formulated it, but rather that the very benevolent nature of man, and the goodness of man, demanded such a meaning of the historical process; nothing less could be expected. These three concepts became the foundation for a whole new world and life view which would gradually become the means of rewriting the whole fabric of American life, and furnish an entirely new concept of the American dream which would make it quite different from that envisioned by the Puritan Fathers. The Enlightenment looked back to the Renaissance rather than to the Reformation and was a protest against any reliance on

[2] Joseph Blau, *Men and Movements in American Philosophy*, New York, 1952, pp. 10-11.

ecclesiastical authority in either religion or political life. It assumed the competence of human reason to find the truth of God.

It is obvious that such doctrines as the inherent goodness of man and the perfectibility of human nature through education, and other human means, were a violent contradiction of the Puritan theology at its very center. These doctrines constituted an essential repudiation of the entire Puritan system: theological, political, economic and social. It may be a question as to why a system of thought so diametrically opposed to that of Puritanism could ever have found acceptance in the colonies. There can be little doubt but that the luster of the names of Newton and Locke gave it an advantage which it would not otherwise have possessed. The very grandeur of the Newtonian world scheme, the seeming infallibility of its high priest, and the popularity of Locke as a political philosopher who seemed admirably fitted for the political aspirations of the colonists gave their respective systems a wider audience among the colonists than might otherwise have been expected. The ascent of the power of the Enlightenment in the intellectual life of the colonies did not come at once, but was of gradual growth. It has been argued by a few historians that the germ of some of the Enlightenment can be seen in the thought of Cotton Mather, but this is questionable. However, some glimmerings of the later movement can be detected in the work of John Wise, pastor at Ipswich:

> Right reason, that great oracle in human affairs, is the soul of man so formed and endowed by creation with a certain sagacity or acumen whereby man's intellect is enabled to take up the true idea or perception of things agreeable with and according to their nature.[3]

While Wise was using these doctrines primarily in an ecclesiastical controversy over the proper form of church government, it is nevertheless true that he regarded reason and revelation as equally valid sources of knowledge for man, and he made this

---

[3] Merle Curti, *Growth of American Thought*, N.Y., 1943, p. 108.

assumption the foundation for his theory of democracy. It was but a short step from the use of such doctrines in a dispute over church government to their inclusion in the theology of the body which placed such a value on them.

A much more radical thinker was Cadwallader Colden (1705-1776), who served as the lieutenant governor of New York for fifteen years. In his *First Principles of Action in Matter,* he defined both matter and spirit as types of activities and assumed a position in his psychology which was perilously close to modern Behaviorism. He insisted that all knowledge is the result of action or activity and its effects. His extreme radicalism attracted a very small following in colonial America, and in his own day he had very little influence, although Dr. Benjamin Rush held to a similar position at certain points.

Of greater significance in the spread of the Enlightenment was the predisposition of some evangelicals toward a position which favored it, and the willingness of others to adopt Locke and Newton for the defense of the evangelical cause. In his opposition to the Puritan hierarchy of Massachusetts, and his theological pronouncements, Roger Williams could be called a true forerunner of the Enlightenment, even before John Wise. But however much influence he had in bringing about a partial downfall of Calvinism in Rhode Island, it is extremely doubtful that he had any great influence in Massachusetts. Of much greater importance was the willingness of Jonathan Edwards to claim John Locke in his defense of the faith. In the attempt to utilize Locke in the defense of the evangelical cause, Edwards ultimately made such important concessions to Locke's empiricism that he brought about a permanent change in the whole structure of Puritanism, and unwittingly aided the triumph of the Enlightenment. Edwards developed a metaphysical idealism which was quite foreign to the historic Calvinism of Puritanism. Declaring that bodies have no existence of their own, and that all existence is mental, he reinterpreted some basic aspects of Calvinism in a manner which was quite destructive to its biblical foundations. In his own theology he labored to remain true to the Calvinism which he believed, but he sowed the seeds of its later rejection in New England, and of the later rise of Arminianism and Arianism. Mosier is quite correct when he says that Edwards took the first steps in asserting the sovereignty of man, and that in furnishing an empirical philosophy of religion he made possible a kind of democracy in redemption that was quite contrary to Calvinism.[4]

There can be little doubt that the idea of the benevolence of God in the Edwardian theology was a contributing factor in the rise of liberalism among the Colonial clergy after 1730.

Although Jonathan Mayhew, a Deist and Unitarian, was the first outspoken critic of Calvinism among the Puritan ministers, the rationalistic theory of the more liberal element had made considerable headway among the upper classes of the towns of many of the colonies, and Deism had made its way as far south as William and Mary College in Virginia, and even into Georgia. This fact alarmed Charles Wesley during his visit there. It seems quite likely that its appeal was limited to the upper, and more educated, classes and that its progress among the middle and lower classes was brought to a halt by the Great Awakening in which Edwards had played such a prominent role. Its strength among the upper class is a matter of conjecture, but it exercised a commanding influence during the period of the American Revolution among those who were the architects and leaders of this movement.

The Democratic Revolt Against Orthodoxy and the American Revolution

There have been many schools of thought as to the causes, the character, and the meaning of the American Revolution. Some historians have regarded it as basically an economic revolt on the part of the colonists against British taxation and repressive economic policies, while others have looked upon it as basically a constitutional movement in which the colonists used the Brit-

[4] Mosier, *op. cit.* pp. 79-81.

ish constitution against the government of George III. Some historians have seen it as the beginning of modern democracy and representative government. Others, like Franklin Jameson, have viewed it in an even broader perspective and insisted that the separation from Great Britain was essentially an attempt, on the part of the colonies, to establish not only a political democracy, but a democratic way of life which would bring about a revolution in every aspect of colonial society. Carl Becker saw it as the American expression of that stream of philosophy which ultimately produced the French Revolution; for him, it was part and parcel of a major revolution in western thought, a revolution which was a secularization of that world and life view inherent in the Christian Gospel.

There can be no doubt that economic, political and constitutional forces played an important role in bringing about the American Revolution, but it is also true that those schools of thought, which viewed it as a democratic social revolution and the product of eighteenth century philosophy, have brought to light some important aspects of the movement which other historians have failed to see. John Adams had this fact in mind when he reminded his fellow-patriots that the revolution was over before it began in 1775. He was referring to that revolution which had already taken place in the colonial mind and without which it is unlikely that the economic, political and constitutional factors could have brought about a separation of the colonies from the mother country.

It was this deeper philosophical and theological development among the colonies which gave to the economic and political controversies of the day an importance which they would not otherwise have possessed.

The recognition that the American Revolution and the rise of democracy in this country are integrally related is an important stepping stone toward a better understanding of the implications of this event. Too many historians who have come this far have, for various reasons, failed to take the next step: the investigation

of the philosophical and theological background of the democratic philosophy as it took shape in the colonies during the
eighteenth century. This failure has led to a serious lack of understanding of the American Revolution as a revolution rather
than merely a separation, in a political sense, from Great Britain.
In a very real sense the secession from the Empire on the part of
the American colonies was not really the revolution which many
of the American Whigs had in mind at all, but was a necessary
prelude to it. Undoubtedly there were many American colonists
who did not regard separation from Great Britain as an end in
itself but simply as the means of achieving a social revolution.
There is a vast amount of evidence which makes it abundantly
clear that Jefferson, and the other radical leaders, had much
more in mind than a mere separation from the mother country.
They regarded this step as the necessary prerequisite for the reconstruction of American society according to the pattern inherent in the democratic philosophy which they were espousing.

To say that the American Revolution was the product of the
rise of the democratic philosophy in colonial thought is not sufficient to explain the nature of that movement. We must go much
further and evaluate the democratic philosophy itself. At this
point many historians have stopped and, as a result, have failed
to accurately set forth the real nature of the movement for independence. It is at this point that the studies of Herbert Morais,
John Orr and Richard Mosier assume great importance for these
authors, each in his own way, have brought forth not only the
vital relationship which existed between the American Revolution and the democratic philosophy, but the equally important
connection between the democratic philosophy and Deism and
the Enlightenment. That John Locke was the philosophical inspiration for the rise of modern democracy and the American
Revolution is admitted by nearly every school of historical
thought, and emphasized by most. His *Two Treatises on Government* were a major contribution to the development of modern
political thought taught in the west, and their importance in

Europe and in America can scarcely be exaggerated. All too often the philosophical and epistemological context in which Locke wrote is overlooked by historians who see him chiefly as an oracle of democracy, and who fail to take into account both the philosophy which motivated him and the purposes which lay behind this philosophy.

It has been a widely debated question as to whether Locke was a Christian; evangelical scholars of great repute can be found on both sides of this question. There can be little question that his philosophical system was at serious variance with the Scriptures at many important points. He not only subjected the truths of Scripture to the scrutiny of reason before they were to be accepted, but he also set forth a view of man, and of the learning process in man which denied evangelical Christianity in general, and Calvinism in particular. The best that can be said for Locke at this point is this: if he remained an evangelical Christian, he did so in spite of his philosophy which was inherently a dangerous enemy of Christian orthodoxy.

It should not be surprising that Locke's political thought was a far cry from the biblical declarations concerning the origins, nature and power of human government. He declared that all government was originated by mankind in terms of a social contract for the preservation of those human rights which nature had conferred upon man. From man through the compact, or contract, government derived all its just powers and hence "all government exists by the consent of the governed." When any human government failed to observe the terms of the contract, or failed to protect those rights which it had been created to defend, its citizens had the undoubted natural right of revolution.

The secular nature of this political philosophy is quite obvious. The sovereignty of God was replaced by that of the people and the decrees of God under common grace for the government of his world were replaced by a nebulous, unhistorical and humanistic concept known as the social contract. The ruler was no longer responsible to God for his administration of government, but responsible to the people. The law he enforced was no longer the revealed will of God for men, but the announced will of the majority which was now sovereign. Even the rights which Locke declared that man possessed did not come to him from a sovereign Creator whose image he bore, but from an impersonal nature deistically conceived.

Locke not only furnished the English Whigs of his day with the justification for their own successful revolt against James II of England, but he also was a powerful stimulant to French political thought, and particularly did he influence Rousseau. But his influence was no less among the colonists who saw in his political philosophy the answer they needed to the English interpretation of the British Constitution, and their own justification for the separation from the mother country. Locke was the philosophical inspiration for the American Revolution, and, without him, the Declaration of Independence could scarcely have been written. Jefferson, Franklin, Thomas Paine, and many others, all looked to him for the answers to the problems of 1776.

Immediately the question must arise: Were not these men aware of the context of Locke's political thought? Were they not aware of its Deistic affinities? Were they not aware of how it undercut the Scriptures at many important junctures? Were they not aware that in claiming Locke they were breaking with the early political philosophy of New England, and of most of the other colonies as well? The answer to all of these questions must be in the affirmative. They were fully aware of the nature of the step they were taking and they were quite conscious of the radical break between Locke and the biblical view of government. Even though they failed to see the fatal weaknesses in Locke which would eventually turn those democracies which rested upon his views into totalitarian states, they were fully conscious of the role he would play in the quarrel with Great Britain. Even though they failed to recognize that his doctrine of human rights rested on the flimsiest of foundations and would ultimately be destroyed by the very weapons which he had forged for their defense, they were very much alive to the appeal which he had for those who had come under the influence of the Enlightenment, and those who looked to the Natural Rights Philosophy for their political insights. Of this there can be no doubt. Why then did they accept such a philosophy of government which was so diametrically opposed to that which they had inherited from Puritanism?

Locke was accepted by the leaders of colonial thought because he could be used to justify a revolution against England which many of them believed to be necessary after 1770. However, this is not the whole story. His conquest of the colonial mind was made much easier because his philosophy was part and parcel of that Deism and appeal to natural law and revelation which characterized the growth of religious liberalism during the eighteenth century. Beginning with John Wise, the rationalism of the Enlightenment began to make inroads into the strongholds of Puritan orthodoxy in New England and gained a strength and foothold among the educated classes of Pennsylvania and the southern colonies, particularly in Virginia.

The result of the growth of Deism and the breakdown of Calvinism was quite a different intellectual temper from that which had characterized Puritanism and colonial thought in general during the seventeenth century. Its basic postulates were a reliance on human reason to discover all truth necessary for man's enjoyment of life here on this earth, and for his eternal bliss in heaven; the conviction that natural law, mathematically interpreted, would yield to reason these necessary truths; and that happiness on this earth, rather than the glorification and enjoyment of God, was man's chief end. In theology it brought drastic changes of doctrine. Believing that man was inherently good the Deists, and their Unitarian allies, insisted that the real source of religious knowledge was nature and right reason, rather than the Scriptures. The truths of Scripture were only to be considered as such if they conformed to the rules of right reason. In this system of thought there was little or no room left for the miracles, for the substitutionary atonement of Jesus Christ, for justification by faith, and the other great doctrines of evangelical Christianity.

This intellectual and theological radicalism inherent in the Enlightenment went hand in hand with an economic and political radicalism which furnished the ingredients for the emerging democratic philosophy. Mosier has well observed that this revolutionary age demanded that both the absolute God and the absolute king must "henceforth rule by the consent of the governed. The God of Puritanism, stripped of His antique powers, had no recourse but to enter as a weakened prince into the temple of individualism and there to seek refuge."[5] This sovereignty which he once claimed, and was accorded by the Puritans, was now claimed by man himself.

This was the philosophical and theological outlook of many of the leaders of the Revolution. It would be misleading to say that they were of one mind in their acceptance and understanding of Deism, or that they all equally agreed in their rejection of historic Christianity. But it is quite obvious that theirs was a secular political philosophy and that its roots are to be found in the Enlightenment in general, and in Deism in particular.[6] Most of the Revolutionary leaders desired to retain the Christian ethic, but to separate it from the biblical revelation and to find a new basis for it in natural law.

The beginnings of the rise of this religious liberalism can be seen in the position of Jonathan Mayhew of the West Church in Boston who applied rationalism to theology and, accordingly, not only modified such doctrines as predestination, but went much further than this in his insistence on the unity of God and the subordination of Christ to the Father; in so doing, he came very close to a Unitarian position. Charles Chauncey of the First Church, Boston, carried on this revolt against evangelical the-

[5] *Ibid.*, pp. 69-70.
[6] For a very valuable discussion of this point see John Orr: *English Deism: Its Roots and Fruits,* Grand Rapids, 1934.

ology setting forth a doctrine of the benevolence of the Deity in such a fashion as to virtually teach a doctrine of universal salvation. It must be admitted that this doctrine of universalism was a fitting and logical conclusion to the basic liberal premise that man was inherently good and potentially perfectible.

The natural fruit of this line of theological endeavor was Unitarianism, and by 1776 this development had taken place. Arianism had taken possession of King's Chapel in Boston (the Anglican Church there), and in 1782 it openly repudiated the creedal statements of the Church of England and called itself Unitarian. Under James Freeman it rewrote its liturgy in accordance with the Unitarian theology. However, this was not an isolated case, neither was the rise of Unitarianism and radicalism in theology confined to New England, for it took place, in varying degrees, in all of the colonies. It seems to have made its greatest inroads where the Anglican and Congregational Churches were the strongest. After 1740 it was making considerable headway among the educated classes in most of the colonies. It was found at Harvard, King's College (Columbia), the University of Pennsylvania, and at William and Mary in Virginia. John Adams (for a time, at least), Benjamin Franklin, Thomas Jefferson, Ethan Allen, Thomas Paine, and other leaders were Deistic and Unitarian in their outlook. Indeed, it is not too much to say that many, if not most, of the leaders of the Continental Congress of 1776, who drafted and signed the Declaration of Independence, were greatly influenced by the Enlightenment and were, to varying degrees, self-conscious Deists. It must also be observed that this document is grounded in this appeal to natural law and to Deism.

It has been increasingly recognized by historians of American culture and thought that behind the political philosophy of the American Revolution, as it found its expression in Locke and the Declaration, there lay a view of God and of human nature which was not Christian but Deist, which was not orthodox and conservative but radical. It thus follows that the American

Revolution in its basic philosophy was not Christian, and the democratic way of life which arose from it was not, and is not, Christian, but was, and is, a Deistic and secularized caricature of the evangelical point of view.

That the chief architects of the Revolution were motivated by this philosophy of life cannot be successfully denied by the most ardent advocates of democracy; neither can it be denied that in pressing for the political separation from England they had in view the creation of a society which would reflect their basic philosophy of God and Man, of human destiny. Like their contemporaries in France, they were chiefly interested in rebuilding society according to a pattern dictated by their Deism. The French methods differed and they engaged in the bloody orgy that was the French Revolution, but this should not blind us to the fact that their aims were essentially the same, identical in outlook and ambition. Neither should the fact that the leaders of the American Revolution were less violent in their attacks on the Church blind us to their essential hostility to Christian doctrine and practices. Two facts in this connection must always be kept in mind: the dominant Protestant churches in the colonies had not been guilty of those practices which had aroused such hostility in France and, in the second place, the Deist philosophy never gained an ascendency in American political life which its counterpart obtained in France.

Thomas Jefferson, the architect of the Declaration of Independence, and the guiding spirit of the whole movement which we call the American Revolution, is at the same time the embodiment of its philosophy and purposes. In him those currents of thought emanating from Locke, the Deists, and the Unitarians come into a full blend of radicalism. Jefferson, perhaps more than any other man of his day, saw very clearly the total implications of the Revolutionary philosophy and was willing to carry them to their ultimate conclusion. Franklin was a kindred spirit, but he never stood on the same pinnacle with Jefferson to look down through the ages toward the realization of his new American Dream. John Adams was with him in agreeing to the necessity of the separation from England, and for a time shared his Deism, but Adams finally recoiled from Jefferson's religious radicalism and looked on the growing democratic movement with something akin to both horror and panic. Standing with Jefferson, but lacking his wide influence, was his fellow-Virginian, Richard Henry Lee. Deism had many adherents in the Carolinas, also, but Jefferson was the personification of the Revolutionary Spirit and the prophet of the new order in the new nation.

Thus, to understand the thought of Thomas Jefferson is to understand the philosophy of the American Revolution. That Jefferson was a Deist is almost universally admitted, but it is a curious fact that not too many historians have seen the intimate relationship existing between his Deism on the one hand and his political and social creed on the other. In fact, Daniel Boorstin in his *The Lost World of Thomas Jefferson* goes so far as to say the Jeffersonian liberal tradition in this country has remained largely unconscious of the philosophy which it has adopted, yet he also maintains that Jefferson accomplished for American civilization what Augustine provided for the Middle Ages. By which, Boorstin means that as Augustine saw the City of God marching on earth to its heavenly destiny, Jefferson had a vision of an earthly city yet to be built, which is now known as the American Dream. It is true that this vision captured the loyalty of many in this country who had little or no real comprehension of the philosophy which lay behind it. It would come as a sad shock to many Americans and to many Christians if they were to recognize the true nature of the democratic philosophy which they so often, and so erroneously, identify with the Christian way of life.

In a very real sense, Jefferson was the full expression of the Enlightenment in colonial life, and was a man of fascinating and varied interests. Although he was in no sense of the word a systematic philosopher, he was, nevertheless, tremendously influenced by the intellectual currents of his day; but he was also eclectic, using such aspects of the previous modes of thought as best fitted his own interests and needs of the moment. So far as his theology was concerned, he was rather consistently a Deist, believing in God as the Creator of the universe. But so far as the government of the universe was concerned, Jefferson looked to natural law rather than to the providence of God, a sovereign God. He denied the Trinity and the deity of Jesus Christ. He placed much less emphasis on the necessity of repentance than did many of the English Deists, and seems to have felt that good works were more acceptable to God than sincere repentance. Jefferson had a high regard for the moral and ethical teachings of Jesus Christ, but he did not regard him as a final authority. Although Jefferson tended toward materialism in his metaphysics, he managed to hold to a belief in the immortality of the soul.

Toward the Scriptures he held the rationalistic view common among the Deists. Nature, rather than the Bible, was man's best source for the knowledge of God.

> Do we want to know what God is? Search not the book called Scripture, which any human hand might make, but the scripture called creation.[7]

For Jefferson the material creation was the ultimate expression and revelation of deity. He completely denied the doctrine of the divine inspiration of the Scriptures. He disliked the religion of the Old Testament, charging Moses with corrupting it. Although he held a much higher appreciation for the New Testament, particularly the Gospels, he nevertheless insisted that the writers of the Gospel were ignorant men who corrupted the pure teachings of Christ, and he denounced the Apostle Paul as the corruptor of the pure religion of Christ. Of particular importance was Jefferson's hatred for the clergy, and, in this respect, he went much further than his fellow-Deists in the colonies, except for Ethan

---

[7] Thomas Jefferson, *Writings* (Age of Reason), IV, p. 46. Quoted in Daniel Boorstin, *The Lost World of Thomas Jefferson*, New York, 1948, p. 32.

Allen; it seems likely that Jefferson was the most anti-clerical and anti-ecclesiastical of all the leaders of the Revolution.

Not only did Jefferson consciously hold to this Deistic Unitarianism as his religion, but it was for him a frame of reference which served as guide for his political and social views, furnishing the immediate background for the Declaration of Independence. It is this very same Jeffersonianism which lies at the very heart of the democratic philosophy so prominent in American life. The fact that John Witherspoon and other evangelicals of the day were willing to sign the Declaration should not blind us to its essentially anti-Christian character, or to the basically anti-Christian character of Jeffersonian democracy.

It was this democratic philosophy, proclaimed most clearly in the Declaration of Independence, which was to be the foundation for the new America which Jefferson hoped would emerge after the war with England, and for the realization of which the war was a necessary prerequisite. This Jeffersonian democracy rested on the denial of the sovereignty of God for Jeffersonians, as Boorstin has observed: "put God at the service of their earthly American task." A creator, God had abdicated his throne to his creation, and his role was to be one of cooperating with men in the realization of the American Dream. In this Jeffersonian scheme of things, sovereignty was now in the hands of man, and he was to use it as he saw fit, being guided by the dictates of right reason. The doctrines of the evangelicals of original sin, total depravity, atonement through Jesus Christ alone, and regeneration were replaced by new emphases on the inherent goodness of man, and his perfectibility through education. Salvation, for both the individual and the race, would be through education rather than regeneration and conversion.

These negations of Christianity were the inspiration for Jefferson's social and political thought. They would serve as the means for revolution within colonial society; in fact, Jefferson planned for a rewriting of American life as he knew it in terms of this frame of reference. This revolution, Jefferson fondly believed, would bring to this country what Carl Becker has well called the "Heavenly City of the Eighteenth Century Philosophers." It was, at almost every point, a conscious and even deliberate secularization of the biblical eschatology. It was the firm conviction of the Jeffersonians that man could, and would, achieve this for himself without the aid of God, or of the Church. In fact, he seemed to feel, at times, that the Church was a distinct hindrance to the realization of this humanistic goal, and that God himself would have to learn to cooperate with this revolutionary goal if he planned to retain the allegiance of the American people.

That the Jeffersonian democracy was founded on Christian principles and simply reflects the social implications of the Gospels is one of the most deadly, and at the same time one of the most persistent errors of contemporary America. The reference to God in the Declaration of Independence, and the apparent submission to his will, should not blind us to the tragic misuse of biblical ideas to convey Deistic principles for the realization of a society which would be essentially humanistic and anti-supernaturalistic in character.

Many sincere evangelicals are unwilling to accept this fact, apparently in the fear that in so doing they are conceding too much ground to those who, in our own day, wish to carry this process of secularization to even further excesses than occurred in the early days of the Republic. Their motives are most worthy, but the ground they have chosen on which to defend the evangelical cause, and the cause of a truly biblical conception of the American state, is faulty. They must choose higher ground and that higher ground is the Puritan conception of our destiny, the Puritan Dream for America. Puritanism did not lack for defenders and while their voices were stilled to a great degree during the excitement and full bloom of the Revolution, they would still be heard, and that Puritan heritage would rise again to give health and vigor to the new nation under the Constitution, for in the Convention of 1787, it would gain a hearing that it had been denied in that earlier assembly. An evangelical strategy which overlooks the clear testimony of history in regard to the nature and purposes of Jeffersonian democracy in the interests of preserving the essential elements of a Christian patriotism is doing a great disservice both to the Gospel and to the very patriotism it is seeking to preserve.

Such a low ground for the defense of the state is not necessary. Although the Revolutionary philosophy was in full swing, and would remain so for at least a decade after the signing of the Declaration of Independence, the Puritan view was not dormant; its voice was lost in the popular clamor of the day, but it was not stilled, and it would yet emerge with new vigor and new popular support within four years after the end of the war. As a matter of fact, not all of those who followed Jefferson among the masses were aware of the implications of the philosophy which he had been proclaiming in his public documents and his private letters. It must also be remembered that, according to reliable estimates, about one-fourth of the people remained Loyalist, more or less, in their sympathy throughout the war. Not all of these refused to support the colony cause for theological and allied reasons, but it is probably true that the great majority of the Deists, and their Unitarian allies, were to be found among the patriots. Their entire outlook on life would naturally lead them to such a decision. The revolutionary temper in political and social outlook, was the product of a similar temper in theology and attracted those who were of this frame of mind.

The political thought of the Revolution was much more adapted toward bringing about a separation from England, and a dissolution of the old political ties between the colonies and the mother country, than it was for creating a new government. The Articles of Confederation, finally put into effect in March, 1781, were the conscious application of the views of Locke and Jefferson to the rebuilding of a central government for the new nation. Although some contemporary historians have questioned the accuracy of John Fiske's description of the era between 1776 and 1789 as the "Critical Period," there can be no doubt that the period of the Confederation was something less than a success; the financial and social radicalism sent chills down the spines of many who had supported the separation from England, and they entertained grave doubts as to its merit. The turmoil of these years cast a shadow over democracy and its leadership. By 1787 there was a distinct turning of public opinion away from that leadership, and the principles which they had espoused. The democracy of 1776 had lost much of its appeal; its glittering promises now lacked the luster which they had once possessed.

Deism, however, maintained its hold on the educated classes and Unitarianism was still popular with them. But among the people at large this was not the case. No matter how attractive the thesis may be, it cannot be proved that the writing of the Constitution of 1787 was the result of a mass evangelical revival. Calvinism had not come into its own again. Radicalism in theology continued to prosper, drawing new recruits as literary mouthpieces until 1800 when new evangelical revivals somewhat stunted its growth.

In 1787 no revival had yet taken place and Calvinism did not command the loyalty of the majority of the classes over the states as a whole. Thus, it is not possible to find the origins of the Federal Constitution in a popular return to the Bible as the infallible rule of faith and practice. Neither is it necessary to explain the events of 1787 in such a way in order to understand the theological aspects of that document, and the differences which exist between it and the Declaration of Independence.

The basic philosophies of these two documents were not compatible. It was apparent to those radicals of 1787-89 who opposed the adoption of the new frame of government, and it was as clearly insisted upon by those who saw in the Constitution a remedy for all the ills of the day which they attributed to the radicalism of Jefferson and his followers. Liberalism from that time on has been aware of the gulf which exists between Jefferson's American Dream and the Constitution; there has been in liberal movements, from the time of Jefferson to our own day, a basic hostility to the Constitution and a continuing desire to remake the government under the Constitution into something that more nearly conforms to that political pattern implied in the Declaration of Independence. Many extreme radicals, in theological and political outlook, have breathed hatred against the Constitution and have declared it to be an enemy of human freedom. Enigmatically, conservatives have been less conscious of the cleavage existing between the two documents and have, at times, been willing to place them side by side as the two great citadels of political freedom for the American people.

If the essential differences existing between the two documents can be traced to the triumph of Calvinism in American life, what then is their source, and how are they to be explained? Several important factors form the answer. There can be little doubt that the membership of the Philadelphia Convention was more conservative, politically and theologically, than was the membership of the Continental Congress of 1776 which adopted the Declaration. The demand for an end to the radical excesses of the Confederation made such a change in the complexion of the convention an absolute necessity. Just eight of the signers of the document of 1776 were chosen to sit in the Convention of 1787; this is a fact of great significance. But even this is not the whole story. Of even greater significance is the fact that very few of the radicals of 1776 found their way into the Philadelphia meeting. Franklin was there, to be sure, but a subdued Franklin in contrast to the philosopher of 1776. Conspicuous for their absence were the most forceful of the liberal Deist leaders: Jefferson, Richard Henry Lee and Thomas Paine. There is abundant evidence that evangelical Christianity was held in much higher respect by the majority in the Convention of 1787 than it had been in 1776 when the majority seemed to be Deists and Unitarians.

The Christian world and life view was accorded greater weight by the delegates than it had been given in the councils of 1776.

This accordance by the delegates was given, in part, because of the very nature of the task to which they had been called. Their calling was not for the initiation, or carrying on, of a revolution for the realization of the American Dream; it was their duty to bring the excesses of a democratic revolution to an end. The very detestation which Madison, Hamilton, and other leaders in 1787 held for the democratic philosophy of government brought them, and many others, to a point in their thinking where they were willing to accept the benefits of the Gospel in the political and social life of the American people, even if they did not subscribe to the evangelical, or Calvinistic, theology in principle. The Convention of 1787 displayed a consciousness of the meaning of the doctrine of sin, and was far less given to illusions about the perfectibility of man and the inevitability of progress. Christian principles and virtues were given a greater hearing than they had been given eleven years earlier. The necessity for a return to political conservatism brought with it a theological orthodoxy which many of the members of the Philadelphia Convention were willing to accept. The number of Calvinists, or evangelicals, cannot be accurately stated, but it is conceded that a more Christian philosophy permeated the thinking and actions of the members. One of the continuing characteristics of theological conservatism has been its adherence to the Constitution as the proper philosophy and form of government for the American people, rather than to the Declaration of Independence and the democratic way of life. This does not mean that all Calvinists and evangelicals were solely in the camp of political conservatism and "orthodoxy"; neither is it accurate to say that all theological liberals have been consistently liberal in their political outlook, for there have been notable exceptions in both groups. William Jennings Bryan was intensely conservative in his theology and, at the same time, was quite liberal in his political and economic thought. On the other hand, John Adams was conservative politically but liberal in his theology for the greater part of his life.

Differences in religious outlook did not play a definitive role in the creation of the first political parties, nor in the continuing political differences between the forces of Hamilton and Jefferson. The formation of the first political parties in the Washington era cannot be so easily resolved and described in such terms. Orthodox Scotch Irish Presbyterians of the Pennsylvania frontier could more easily be found in the ranks of the Democratic Republicans under Jefferson than they could be found among the Federalists, who were the bulwark of political and economic conservatism of the day. Conversely, some religious radicals were more loyal to Hamilton's conservative program than they were to Jefferson's political philosophy, and became staunch Federalists. This was particularly true in New England. Staunch evangelicals who were convinced of the necessity for a strict construction of the Constitution for safe-guarding the economic interests of their own particular state, or section, had little difficulty in joining Jefferson's Democratic Republican Party, in spite of his theological radicalism. In spite of conflicting loyalties and the criss-crossing of religious and political interests, the religious outlook, in these early days of the Republic, did play a part in determining the difference between these first two political parties: a greater part than is generally recognized by American historians thinking in terms of the economic forces. There was in Jefferson's religious radicalism a certain compelling attraction which drew to his cause many of the liberal leaders of the day who found in his democratic religion the support they needed for their own liberalism. There was also a deep kinship between political and economic conservatism and orthodoxy in theology which drew conservatives of varied interests together in the Federalist Party. Indicative of the differences between the two parties are their reactions to the radicalism of the French Revolution. The Jeffersonians applauded the new French regime, looking upon the upheaval in France as another manifestation of that same spirit of liberty which had motivated the American Revolution; the Federalists drew back in horror from the atheism and anarchy of the movement after 1791. An ideological conflict in France had ideological reverberations in this country which reflected the difference in the major theological tempers of the two parties. These differences, to some degree, were not without their effect in the area of domestic policy. Timothy Dwight preached a sermon on the text: "Come ye out from among them, and be ye separate" in what is regarded as an effort to justify the secession of New England from the recently formed Federal Union because of the religious radicalism of Jefferson which appeared to Dwight to be a great threat to the religious purity of New England. Dwight's case was weakened by the strength of religious radicalism in New England itself. There is some indication that the most virulent form of religious radicalism had found a home among the Democratic Republicans in New England rather than among the Federalists. The attack on Dartmouth College which brought Daniel Webster to the defense of his alma mater appears to have been the result of a theological cleavage between the Jeffersonian governor of New Hampshire and the orthodox board of trustees who were administering the affairs of that institution.

By 1820 Deism had had its day and heresy was now to take on a new form; a form more in keeping with the intellectual temper of the American people in the age of Jackson and the common man. The decline of Deism did not deal a mortal blow to the Unitarianism it had nurtured, for heresy never dies so easily. However, the Unitarianism of the first half of the 19th century was not the same as that of the latter part of the 18th. The decline of Deism forced the movement to find a new inspiration and source of support. The mathematical character and coldness of Deism began to repel many for whom Unitarianism remained as their way of life. But Unitarianism must disengage itself from its Deistic affiliations if it were to remain a vital expression of religious opinion among those who had long since rejected historic Christianity. A Unitarianism that was too closely tied to Deism as a philosophic frame of reference might very well suffer the same fate as that which ardent Unitarians had envisaged for an evangelical orthodoxy which looked to the Scriptures as their ultimate source of authority.

There were rumblings of a revolt before 1800 among European liberals against Deism as a philosophy, and as a foundation for religion. The implications of Hume's epistemology, and the extreme skepticism of the French materialist and revolutionary philosophers, were not lost upon those leaders of the Enlightenment who looked with fear, and great misgivings, on the tidal waves of unbelief and atheism which had wrought such havoc during the radical period of the French Revolution, and seemed to threaten the political and social stability of Europe as a whole. Evangelicals and many of the more conservative Unitarians in this country were alarmed by the reverberations of this European radicalism which were observable on the American scene.

The revolt against Deism in America was a two-pronged movement. For some, it meant a return to evangelical Christianity and a New Awakening, which had its center in the newer states of the frontier, particularly in western Pennsylvania, Kentucky and Tennessee; it also had much strength in the East where its greatest exponent was Timothy Dwight, the president of Yale College. However, this evangelical answer to eighteenth century Deism never carried as much weight in New England as the philosophical protest was able to achieve. The blighting effects of Deism were too much a part of the New England religious outlook to give way easily to the enthusiasm of a religious revival in conservative terms. In many segments of New England Congregationalism unbelief was in the saddle and Unitarianism had too long been the accepted mode of thought for Puritan orthodoxy to recover its lost position. Though it could no longer look to eighteenth century Deism to supply its frame of reference, Unitarianism was so well entrenched in the New England mind that it would survive the passing of eighteenth century thought, joining hands with the new intellectual developments of the 19th century. Thus it was that, in Transcendentalism, Unitarianism found a new ally, a new source of inspiration, and a new frame of reference which would enable it to outlive Deism, its original ally, and to gain a new religious, political and social prominence in America.

If Transcendentalism rescued the Deism of Jefferson and his compatriots of 1776 from obscurity, it also gave to it a new form and a new direction. Both systems commonly denied many evangelical doctrines, but there were also very great differences between them which made it virtually impossible for the Unitarianism of the earlier era to retain its original form and outlook. The rationalism of Lord Herbert of Cherbury, and the empiricism of Locke, gave way to the intuitionalism of the romantic era; the vast distances which the Newtonian world view placed between God and his creation were replaced by the warm glow of a pantheistic conception of the universe: the universe in its totality is God. Such drastic changes in the inner spirit of Unitarianism as a religious and theological movement could only bring equally important changes in its political, social and cultural outlook and goals. The belief in the inherent goodness of man and the possibility of human improvement, held by the earlier Unitarians, was brought into sharper focus by the pantheism inherent in the Transcendentalist philosophy. This optimism in regard to human nature, in turn, gave to Transcendentalism and the Unitarianism of the nineteenth century an unquenchable zeal for reform; the Unitarian leaders of the nineteenth century became leaders in almost every area of that reform movement which marked the middle decades of nineteenth century American history. Their penchant for reform can hardly be over-emphasized. There is little doubt that the alliance between Unitarian theology and Transcendentalism is one of the most important intellectual developments in American history, for it had profound implications on the political, social and economic history of America in that era which came to a close about 1865. The rise of the common man, the age of Jackson, the rise of the abolition movement, and the Southern reaction to these developments in the North, cannot be understood apart from their relationship to Transcendentalism, affecting, as it did, every aspect of American life. Transcendentalists and Unitarians had important ideas and their ideas had even greater consequences for the history of the American people, for the intensified theological radicalism inherent in this intellectual movement would soon manifest itself in an intensified political and social radicalism which made the Age of Jackson a prophetic forerunner of the Age of the New Deal. The radical movements of present day America were foreshadowed, with few exceptions, by those of the Transcendentalist era, the current democratic philosophy of life having its counterpart in Jacksonian democracy. The clue to the meaning of many of the social and political struggles of our own day is to be found in the intellectual foment of the Jacksonian era, and in the Transcendentalist revolt against the older Unitarianism.

3

Transcendentalism and the Rise of Modern Democracy

Although Transcendentalism in part, at least, grew out of the Unitarianism and even the Deism of the eighteenth century, its development filled many of the Unitarians with horror. Professor Andrews Norton of the Harvard Divinity School, a convinced liberal in theology, openly labeled the Transcendentalists as infidels and, in apparent desperation, called on the Calvinism of Princeton Seminary to refute Emerson and the other prophets of the New Order. It was quite evident that this new radicalism of the early nineteenth century was a distinct threat to the established order of the older Unitarian liberalism which had its stronghold in Harvard College and many of the Congregational pulpits in and around Boston. Not only was Transcendentalism more radical in its theology (or lack of it), but it was also much more radical in its social and political outlook than the older Unitarianism had been. This new movement constituted a distinct threat not only to the established religious order so dear to the liberals, but it also endangered the whole political and social structure which was New England. The fears it engendered among its liberal and conservative opponents were by no means unfounded, for the very nature of Transcendentalism conferred upon it a peculiar affinity with, and sympathy for, the various radical movements which were part of the Age of Jackson, and it was largely through this relationship to Jacksonian democracy that the movement was able to exert such a profound influence upon the political and social development of this country from 1830, or so, until the era of the Civil War. The vitality and distinctive characteristics of this era are not to be found in the rise of the common man, nor in the westward movement, nor in the rise of a self-consciousness within the laboring class, nor in the extension of the franchise among the male population of the country (as important as all these may be), but in the fact that all of these developments were vehicles through which Transcendentalism made itself felt in American life. The Transcendentalists were greatly interested in these various movements and made them their own; in so doing they gave to them a quality which they would hardly have possessed otherwise. What then was Transcendentalism? The point has already been made that in part it grew out of the Deism and the Unitarianism of the previous century. At first glance it may well be asked: How could Deism nurture what seems to be its very opposite? The answer is not as difficult nor as unreasonable as it might seem at first glance. Quite frequently in the history of thought a philosophical system, whether it be Stoicism or Deism, which posits a great gulf between God and his creation is replaced by a system which is virtually pantheistic in nature; this is exactly the case with Deism. Its very coldness and reliance upon rationalism proved to be quite unsatisfactory for those who wanted a warmth in their philosophical outlook and religious quest; this need was met by Transcendentalism.

The question concerning the relationship between the older Unitarianism and the more radical theology of Emerson and his group may be explained in similar fashion. It is most reasonable to state that the triumph of Unitarianism in New England theology made the later conquest of Transcendentalism both logical and necessary. The eighteenth century rejection of the supernatural in Christianity was not total; Deism insisted upon certain beliefs which were not rationally apprehended, but which plainly depended upon the biblical revelation. The frequent claims that such beliefs as heaven and a future life were in accord with right reason were simply concessions to certain remnants of the biblical revelation which these Unitarians found too dear to surrender. They were equally insistent upon the retention of the biblical ethic on the same ground, namely, that it was in accord with the demands of right reason. Eighteenth century Unitarianism was not creedless and was highly ethical in character; but its creed and ethical system rested upon the flimsy foundation of rationalism and naturalism rather than on the Scriptures as an infallible revelation. This rejection of the uniqueness and authority of the biblical revelation proved to be a most unsatisfactory epistemological situation, and the Unitarian movement, in spite of its good intentions to preserve those aspects of Christian doctrine and ethics which met the demands of right reason, was left without any answer or defense against the logical implications of its own inner perplexities in regard to the nature of religious authority and knowledge.

However, it would be quite misleading to give the impression that Transcendentalism was a home-grown movement, having its roots in eighteenth century colonial intellectual life without any reference to those great changes which had taken place in European thought. Indeed, it is very doubtful that there is any intellectual movement which is entirely American in its origins, and only a very superficial reading of our national past can yield such an impression. To interpret the development of American thought simply in terms of our own history is to miss the depth and real meaning of our intellectual history and, even more important, it is to fail to grasp the essential meaning of our history as a nation. Thus Transcendentalism must be studied not only in its relationship to the Deism and Unitarianism of eighteenth century America, but also in its relationship to the new intellectual currents which were arising in Germany, France and England, for it cannot be understood apart from its European background.

The European Background of Transcendentalism

The solutions offered by eighteenth century intellectuals to religious and philosophical problems were no more acceptable to the peoples of Europe than they were to the people of this country. They felt the need of a god who was close to them, whom they could experience without the necessity of approaching him through the treacherous paths dictated by Deism. The god of the Deists had little or no appeal to a generation that was craving for a god it could know in a very personal manner. The first evidences of a reaction against the coldness of rationalism are to be found in Rousseau and, by 1800 the revolt was well underway bringing in its wake philosophical idealism on the Continent (particularly in Germany), and the romantic movement in English literature. Beginning with Kant, German idealism came into its own in the philosophy of Hegel and it wrought a profound revolution in all areas of human thought. Arising out of the debris of a Germany brought low by the Napoleonic conflict, this new philosophical movement, to a great extent, spread over Europe and conquered the minds of those nations which had fought on German soil. When it came into contact with French, English, and ultimately American culture, it underwent various transformations according to the cultural milieu in which it found itself, but underneath these differences superficially imposed, there was an underlying unity to the movement which gave birth to a set of commonly held philosophical assumptions and to a religious outlook which was largely pantheistic in content. This Hegelian philosophy is quite marked in the writings of the English Romanticists, and it is equally apparent in the works of contemporary American writers such as Thoreau and Emerson. American Transcendentalism is thus partly a product of native intellectual influences and partly an echo of those philosophic and religious currents which emanated from England and the continent of Europe. Theodore Parker openly acknowledged his indebtedness to European thought: "Kant gave me the true method, and put me on the right track."[1]

Transcendentalism was not a return to Christian orthodoxy. It was not a repudiation of the Unitarianism of the earlier period, and it most certainly was not a return to the God of Christianity or to the Scriptures as his infallible revelation of what he would have man to do and believe. Like Hegelianism, to which it was greatly indebted, Transcendentalism was probably further from historic Christianity from an orthodox viewpoint than Deism had been. The radical nature of Hegel's system was clearly recognized by the left wing Hegelians in Germany who saw that their master's efforts to integrate his philosophy with Lutheranism were doomed to failure and who were willing to take his system at face value and surrender the last remnants of Lutheran theology. Hegelianism, in the hands of this left wing element, became the spawning ground for an ideological revolution in Europe which would eventually rewrite the political, social and economic life of most of the Continent in terms of that system, the ultimate fruits of which would be communism and existentialism.

Transcendentalism was the heir of the radical nature and thrust of the Hegelian philosophy and its English counterpart. Its pantheism appealed to those minds who were tired of the remoteness of the God of the Deists, and of the logical character of natural religion which was singularly lacking in warmth and fervency. Its general outlook on God and man, and their relationship to one another, also proved to be very congenial to the democratic philosophy of the Jacksonian era and the rise of the common man. The appearance of new democratic processes and practices in the state brought about the need for a suitable philosophical defense and, at the same time, Transcendentalism could not long remain an isolated philosophy, locked within the walls of an ivory tower

[1] Quoted in Mosier *The American Temper*, p. 191.

kind of existence without avenues of expression in the life of the American people. Thus it was that the Jacksonian democracy of the frontier, and that emerging democracy of the East, found in Transcendentalism a philosophical justification for the emerging political, economic and social democracy of the Age of Jackson; and the Transcendentalists found in this movement a highly effective vehicle for expressing the implications of their philosophy in the life of the nation. In the hands of the Transcendentalists then, the Hegelian emphasis on freedom and its corollary, that this freedom can only be found in the state, became an important, if not dominant, factor in the thinking of those who were to become leaders in many phases of American life in the first half of the nineteenth century. It is thus impossible to understand the American literature of this era, Jacksonian democracy, and the many reform movements which emerged between 1820 and 1860 and, above all, the abolitionist movement, without an adequate comprehension of Transcendentalism as a philosophy and its relation to European thought and evangelical orthodoxy. In short, it is well nigh impossible to properly evaluate American democracy apart from its kinship with Transcendental thought, for while it undoubtedly is the product of the rise of the common man, and while it found its strength in the extension of the franchise and those other developments in American political life favorable to popular government, it would not have become the power that it is today if it had not found a philosophy which would nurture and guide it into becoming a "way of life."

The Essence of Transcendentalism

What then was Transcendentalism? It was primarily a religious philosophy, a revolt against the Enlightenment of the eighteenth century, and a reaction against the unrestrained devotion of that era to the scientific method. Its source was post-Kantian German thought as it was interpreted by Samuel Taylor Coleridge. It was, at the same time, a revolt against the last vestiges of Calvinism which its leaders professed to see in New England life. If the

Transcendentalists were discontented with the Deist view of God who was little more than the Author of nature and nature's laws, they were equally dissatisfied with the Calvinistic view which posited a God who ruled his creation and creatures according to the dictates of his own will and for his own glory. Transcendentalism was a revolt against reason as that term had been understood by Calvin, the rationalists and the Deists. It called on man to forget the sensationalism of Locke, to forsake the mechanism of Deism and to achieve a new and more noble view of man and his nature. In this connection Theodore Parker drew up an indictment of mechanism which expressed the view of nearly all Transcendentalists:

> The sensational philosophy has no idea of cause except that of empirical connection in time and place, no idea of substance, only of body or form of substance; no ontology, but phenomenology. . . . Its physics are a mere materialism; hence it delights in the atomistic theory of nature and repels the dynamic theory of matter. . . . Life does not transcend organization, nor does mind, nor God. All is matter.[2]

The Transcendentalists consciously sought a new epistemology and a new metaphysics which would recognize man for what he truly was and which would free him from that slavery to Reason and nature to which the Deists had subjected him. But in their unwillingness to return to Christian orthodoxy for their view of nature and their theory of knowledge, they could only reinterpret the Deist position. They looked to nature, as did the Deists, but they viewed it as the permanent abode of an immanent cosmic mind. This was well expressed by Emerson in his famous essay on the Over-Soul which he described as an impersonal spirit and the reality of all nature:

> Standing on the bare ground—my head bathed in the blithe air, and uplifted into infinite space—all mean egotism vanishes. I be-

[2] Theodore Parker, *Works*, Centenary Ed., Boston, Beacon Press, 1907, 1913, VI, pp. 9-10.

came a transparent eye ball; I am nothing. I see all the currents
of the universe being circulated through me: I am a part or parcel
of God.[3]

For Emerson, man is the very essence of this Over-Soul which is
the essence of all reality:

Within man is the soul of the whole; the wise silence; the universal
beauty to which every part and particle is equally related; the
Eternal One. All men are different. Each in his own peculiar way
expresses the Over-Soul within him.[4]

Theodore Parker gave a particularly clear insight into Transcendentalism in the following description:

The problem of the Transcendental philosophy is no less than
this, to revise the experience of mankind and its teachings by the
nature of mankind; to test ethics by conscience, science by reason; to try the creeds of the churches, the constitution of the states
by the constitution of the universe; to revise what is wrong, supply what is wanting, and command the just.[5]

Thus Deism with its profound separation of God and man
gave way to a pantheistic metaphysics which virtually made God
and man, God and nature, one form of being. This opened the
way to a new epistemology—intuitionalism. The Transcendentalists insisted that man had an innate intuition of God and that
man is not limited to his senses in the quest for knowledge. Emerson held that there is a Universal Mind of God which is the common property of all men and each man is the incarnation of that
Mind. For human knowledge there is no logical or rational basis,
but only intuition. Because God is uniquely present in each man,
man, therefore, has an innate intuition of him which is independent of the senses. Although the Kantian background of this theory
of knowledge is obvious, it came to New England through the

[3] R. W. Emerson, "Nature," *Complete Works* (Riverside Edition), 1883, Vol.
I, pp. 15-16.
[4] R. W. Emerson, *"Over-Soul," op. cit.,* II, p. 253.
[5] *Works,* Centenary Edition, Boston, Beacon Press, 1907-13, VI, pp. 37-38.

works of Samuel Taylor Coleridge, particularly in his *Aids to Reflection*.

It was inevitable that Transcendentalism should have a tremendous influence on Christian thought in this country, for the movement was hostile to historic orthodoxy at almost every point and to the church as an institution. In their efforts to free religion from the dictates of natural law, the Transcendentalists declared their independence from all objective norms of truth and made the individual the ultimate authority and judge of what was true or false in religion. Some of them went so far as to declare that the earlier Unitarian reliance on natural law was more degrading to the spirit of true religion than that of the Calvinistic emphasis on the infallibility of the Scriptures and the sovereignty of God. George Ripley severely criticized the Unitarians at this and other points, and Emerson found himself at such odds with them that in 1832 he felt obliged to resign the Unitarian pulpit which he had accepted just three years before.

The Transcendentalist answer to the problem of religious knowledge was intuitionalism. William Ellery Channing held that we do not know God through nature or natural law, but only through his likeness which we find in ourselves. Theodore Parker insisted that the ideas of God, morality and immortality have an a priori foundation in human nature itself, and that true universal religion is found wherever there is sincere piety and morality. The result could only be a religious subjectivism, the ultimate result of which would be doctrinal and moral anarchy. Parker tried to avoid this conclusion to his system by making piety the subjective form of religion and morality the objective. This was an artificial distinction since both piety and morality had their residence in man, and man himself was not subject to any check on his religious thought or action imposed upon him by either the natural law of the Deists or the authoritative Scriptures of the Calvinists. Because man had a spark of the divine in him, the Transcendentalists argued that when man speaks and acts religiously, he is speaking and acting as God speaks and acts. There is an immediate relationship between God and man which needs, and indeed allows, no mediating agencies such as the Bible or natural law. Man by his very nature transcends such paraphernalia in his religious quest.

This revolt against historic orthodoxy carried the Transcendentalists a much greater distance along the path of reform than the earlier Deists and Unitarians had been willing to travel. Their untrammeled individualism placed no measurable limits on their speculative activities and doctrinal vagaries and this pantheistic subjectivism allowed for theological and institutional anarchy which shocked the older Unitarian movement. Theodore Parker clearly represented the revolutionary attitude of Transcendentalism in regard to religious belief when he asserted that Christianity was not the ultimate form of religion but was only one stage of development in religious thought. Thus there were transient and permanent elements in Christianity and the permanent truths which could be found in the Christian system derive their value and authority from this transcendental quality and not from the religion of Jesus. The ultimate authority for all valid religion is to be found in human experience, in man, and not in any divine revelation from God apart from the human spirit. Emerson, Ripley, Parker, and their followers were convinced that Unitarian Christianity needed to be purged of its remaining dependence on supernaturalism and to this they devoted their energies. George Ripley gave a classic expression to this point of view:

> The time has come when a revision of theology is demanded. Let the study of theology commence with the study of human consciousness. Let us ascertain what is meant by the expression, the Image of God in the soul of Man. Let us determine whether our nature has any revelation of the Deity within itself. If we then discover a criterion of truth, as we firmly believe we shall, we can pass judgment on the Spiritual and the Infinite, we shall then be prepared to examine the claims of Divine Revelation in history.[6]

[6] George Ripley, *The Christian Examiner; XXI*, pp. 225-254, quoted in Miller, *op. cit.*, pp. 130-131.

Thus, the religious man was one who studied human consciousness for in it was all the revelation of God that he needed. Again Ripley supplies us with the Transcendentalist answer:

> The religious man is, indeed, conversant with invisible objects. His thoughts expatiate in regions which eye hath not seen, but which God has revealed to him, by his spirit. He reposes a firm faith in those ideas which are made known to him by his Reason, as in those facts which are presented to his notice by the senses. He has no belief that human nature is so shackled and hemmed in upon in its present imperfect state, as to be confined to the objects made known by the eye of sense, which is given to us merely for the purpose of our temporal existence and is incapable of ascending to those higher spheres of thought and reality to which the eternal elements of our being belong.[7]

It becomes obvious that in spite of its apparent insistence on the transcendental quality of religious experience and its frequent reference to God, this religious philosophy was in its essence a religion of man. It was humanistic to the core. To the Transcendentalist mind God had no existence outside of the human consciousness. William Ellery Channing made this quite clear:

> The idea of God, sublime and awful as it is, is the idea of our own spiritual nature, purified and enlarged to infinity. In ourselves are the elements of divinity.[8]

> The only God whom our thought can rest upon, and our hearts cling to, and our consciences recognize, is the God whose image dwells in our own souls.[9]

The Transcendentalist reconstruction of all previous theology, Calvinist, evangelical and Unitarian, resulted in a man-centered system of thought and humanistic conception of life. In a very real sense man was both the source of his religious knowledge

---

[7] George Ripley, *Discourses on Philosophy of Religion,* quoted in Perry Miller, *op. cit.,* p. 133.

[8] William Ellery Channing, *Works,* pp. 291-302, Boston, 1880.

[9] Quoted in Miller, *op. cit.,* p. 23.

and experience, and the sole judge of their validity. If he did not create God in his image, he at least was a co-equal of that God, and they were practically mutually dependent upon one another. Out of this pantheism came a view of human nature which was easily translated into the doctrine of the sovereignty of man. Man was good, noble, and therefore perfectible. His imperfection was not the result of any fall of Adam into sin, nor the consequence of original sin in the race; it was simply due to the fact that he had not yet gone through the stages of development which were necessary for the achievement of that perfection which was his assured and rightful destiny. The optimism of the Transcendentalists in regard to man and his potentialities knew no limits for man, bearing the spark of deity within his soul, was capable of so conducting himself in his freedom that his spiritual nature would continue to evolve into something marvelously greater than could even be imagined in 1850. It was axiomatic for the Transcendentalists that if man partook of the divine nature, he must also share the divine character and its qualities. From these assumptions it was a very easy step to a belief in the complete sovereignty of man, and this view received its classic expression in their literature in the words of Emerson: "Let man stand erect, go alone, and possess the universe." This glorification of man was the central theme of Transcendentalism. Beneath its appeal to a new metaphysics lay this one supreme emphasis.

It was this glorification of the individual which explains their great antipathy for all institutions and organizations. This distrust of society is so often linked with the eccentricities of Thoreau, that it is often forgotten it was part and parcel of the whole movement. Reliance upon an organization of any kind was simply a confession of dependence. For the Transcendentalist all government should be self-government for no sovereign individual has the right to judge or govern another sovereign individual. They also decried the church as an institution which was guilty of trampling the freedom of man. As an institution it was not necessary for the religious development of man and, in the hands

of the clergy, it was actually guilty of impeding religious progress because of its slavish devotion to either the Scriptures or to
the dictates of right reason and natural law. This repugnance for
institutions was a natural product of the Transcendentalist belief
that instinct is good and should be obeyed rather than curbed
in accordance with the dictates of conventions and authority represented in such institutions as the church and the state. Thoreau
was simply carrying to an extreme one of the basic facets of their
philosophy. And yet, as paradoxical as it may seem, many of
the Transcendentalists, less consistent than Thoreau, looked to
the very institutions which they suspected of being inimical to
human freedom for the realization of their fondest dreams for the
reconstruction of every aspect of American society in the interests
of that freedom.

Transcendentalism was never a formally organized movement
in spite of the fact that a club was formed for the formulation
and advancement of this philosophy in 1836 by Frederic Hedge,
Emerson and George Ripley in Boston; it, in turn, undertook
to publish *The Dial* in this same year as a vehicle for its popu-
larization. However, this group was always an informal one, and
in its efforts to secure a wide hearing for its philosophical and
religious concepts it was rather ineffective. In spite of the fact
that Transcendentalism was a philosophy which spoke directly
to the emerging democracy of the common man and the frontier,
it never was able to have a wide appeal among those in whose
behalf it dared to speak. Though it decried the appeal to reason,
and renounced the intellectualism and coldness of Deism, it had
its appeal chiefly among the intellectuals of New England. Although they were able to enlist the cooperation of many others
outside of New England in their various reform projects, they
were never able to gain many converts to their system. Certain
facets of English Romanticism gained a wide following in the
South where Byron was widely read. But Transcendentalism, as
a religious fellowship, was almost totally unable to compete with

the rising tide of religious and political orthodoxy in that section of the country.

The Impact of Transcendentalism on American Theology

Transcendentalism was a revolt against all previous American theological systems, Calvinism, evangelical Arminianism and even Unitarianism. It was not only a revolt in the sense of a protest, but it was also a conscious effort to reform theology in terms of its own basic postulates. The ridicule which Oliver Wendell Holmes heaped upon Calvinism in his "One Hoss Shay" was paralleled by other equally critical attacks on the older Unitarianism, which had its roots in the Enlightenment of the eighteenth century. Theodore Parker believed it was his duty to reform the whole of Christianity and not just any one segment of it. But there can be no doubt that Parker, Holmes, and their fellow-laborers reserved for Calvinism their most bitter scorn and most severe attacks, as if they were aware that if this theology could be successfully demolished, the others would fall as a matter of course. In this assumption there was considerable validity. Transcendentalism and Calvinism stood at opposite poles in theological position and convictions, while these other schools stood somewhere between them, with evangelical Arminianism closer to Calvinism and the older Unitarianism closer to Transcendentalism than some of them were willing to admit.

Between Calvinism and Transcendentalism there was the widest possible divergence in regard to every article of religious faith. The latter provided a thoroughly humanistic answer to every basic orthodox doctrine, and no article of faith dear to the heart of evangelicals was immune to their criticism. These attacks on the Christian faith were not without their effects. Transcendentalism had a wide appeal among the intellectuals of New England and it gained a certain following in those areas of the country where the New England influences were most keenly felt. Thus, wherever Congregationalism had gained a foothold, particularly in the West, Transcendentalism was able to win a certain following. This influence is not to be measured solely in terms of those who accepted this more radical interpretation of the older Unitarianism. Indeed, if this had been the only direct result of the movement, its influence in our national history would have been largely confined to a certain group in New England and the literature of this era. This was not the case. Because the Transcendentalists spoke to the emerging democratic way of life with great appeal, they became a part of the Jacksonian era and played an important role in the rise of the common man, even though they, for the most part, were most uncommon men. Thus, their philosophy was important in the democratizing of American Christianity. It is at this point that we see the importance of the movement in the religious life of the nation rather than in the relatively small number of converts Transcendentalism was able to gain unto itself.

Even in those denominations which were historically evangelical and held strongly to a Trinitarian theology, there were strong influences at work for the creation of a "democratic theology," namely, a theology which would modify such Calvinistic doctrines as the sovereignty of God and the total depravity of the race, in favor of a theology which would emphasize the love of God at the expense of his justice and holiness, which would insist that man was not totally depraved and could, to some degree at least, cooperate with God in the achievement of his own salvation, and in the bringing about of the Kingdom of Heaven on earth. Hence there arose in Congregationalism what has become known as the "New England Theology" which was in essence a mediating position holding to much of the Evangelical position while yielding at other points, particularly in regard to the doctrines of the atonement, divine sovereignty, and justification, in the direction of Transcendentalist thought. Even the revivalist, Charles G. Finney, was not immune to the demands that the historic evangelical theology should be brought into harmony with the concepts of the democratic philosophy. Neither were the other large denominations able to avoid the impact of these secular intellectual forces. However, their influence was not so marked in those denominations which were already, in varying degrees, "democratic" in their theology, such as the Methodist and Disciples of Christ, for the Arminian theology which they embraced was already a step in this direction. On the other hand, it was much more important in Presbyterianism which had thus far been able to withstand the pressures from American society to rewrite its theology in terms of the American way of life. For this reason the resulting theological upheaval was all the greater and in 1837 the cleavage between those who were willing to make concessions and those who insisted that the Westminster standards should be kept inviolate brought about a rupture into Old and New School Presbyterianism. And, although the two churches were reunited in 1869, the causes of the disruption were never satisfactorily resolved and the division in the theology persists even until our own day.

One ultimate effect of Transcendentalism should be noted at this point, namely its relationship to Darwinism. Although Darwin's pronouncements had nothing to do with the emergence of this philosophy, there was a strong kinship between them as both philosophies had a common intellectual ancestry in the dialectical philosophy of Hegel. Transcendentalism was a form of evolutionary thought. This evolutionary attitude is clearly evident in Theodore Parker's concept of the transitory nature of Christianity in an evolving pattern of religious thought, and in the optimism of most of the Transcendentalists concerning the perfectibility of human nature and the inevitability of human progress through the instrumentality of reform movements of various kinds. This addiction to an evolutionary philosophy not only gave a great incentive to the leaders of the movement to become active participants in abolitionism, and other reform efforts of the day, but it also prepared the way for the acceptance of Darwinism in many of the denominations after 1870. In this sense Transcendentalism proved to be a living influence among leaders in American theology during the latter half of the nineteenth century long after the movement had ceased to exist, except as a memory. It was also a definite fore-runner of the Social Gospel Movement and, along with Darwinism, became one of the dominant influences in its formulation. The Transcendentalist optimism concerning the spiritual nature and destiny of man, reinforced by the optimism which Darwinism invited concerning man's physical and societal destiny, provided the philosophical substitute for the historic orthodoxy which the advocates of the Social Gospel found to be necessary for the popular appeal of their movement. Thus, ultimately, Transcendentalism inspired the liberalism or modernism which has dominated American theology during the first half of the twentieth century. In the emergence of modern liberalism the democratization of theology, which began in the age of Jackson, reached its dreary conclusion in the barrenness of evangelical vigor and scholarship which has characterized so much of contemporary theological activity.

The Political and Social Impact of Transcendentalism

Transcendentalism, more than any previous theological revolt against Calvinism in particular and evangelical thought in general, influenced American political and social development. Deism had provided the necessary theological foundations for the Jeffersonian democracy of 1776 and its radical nature had left a deep imprint on our early history as a nation. However, both in its theological effects, and its political and social impact, Jeffersonian democracy was a restrained radicalism and these restraints were the result of the fact that it was, to a great degree, advocated, and put into effect, by men who were disciplined characters. Even more important than this was the fact that Deism and early Unitarianism both held to an objective standard of theological and philosophical truth; private judgment was invited and even encouraged, but it was a private judgment which must look to the dictates of right reason and natural law if it was to have value and be worthy of respect. There was no place for either intellectual or social anarchy in Deist philosophy. Jeffersonian democracy was, by its nature, an incentive to political, social and economic reform, but these reforms must be in accord with the dictates of well-organized objective standards by which all human action was to be judged. A submission to natural law replaced the Puritan submission to a sovereign God.

Because Transcendentalism was a more radical departure from the last remnants of Calvinism and a Christian world and life view, its political and social influences were also more radical. Its glorification and deification of man, the common man, was a more logical expression of the secular democratic philosophy than were the restrained statements of a former era. It can be said that the Transcendentalists simply carried the basic assumptions of the Jeffersonian philosophy to their logical democratic conclusions, and there is much truth in such an assumption. But in Transcendentalism there was an inner pressure for radical reform in every segment of American life which was much greater than that found in Jefferson. The Revolutionary leadership had been primarily interested in bringing about a political democracy on the assumption that if this were obtained by a separation from England, an enlightened people would, in their own way, achieve the other blessings which must surely follow the creation of a democratic state. Curiously enough, many of the Transcendentalists proved to be very suspicious of the state, and Thoreau carried his dislike to the extreme of anarchism. Their suspicion of human institutions extended to the state itself. They tended to be much more a part of the Age of Jackson than they were of Jackson's administration; yet they were not consistent at this point and eventually, for the sake of their reform efforts, particularly for the success of their abolitionist crusade, some of them were willing to invoke the aid of the national government, and even to accept the idea of a centralized government, as a necessary corollary of their radical program.

Yet, in spite of their disgust for the state, it must not be concluded that the Transcendentalists avoided all contact with it, or were adverse to the further democratization of the American government. Such a conclusion would be quite misleading. It is true that they did not regard political democracy as an end in itself, but, at best, merely as a means toward an end, the end of a radical reform of every aspect of American life. That their philosophy logically and almost irresistibly drove them along the paths that led to such a reform was well recognized by the Transcendentalists themselves. Their great quest in life was individual freedom and to this cause they dedicated themselves. And, if they interpreted freedom in various and even curiously contradictory ways, this too was quite in conformity with their philosophy which placed a greater premium on the emotional striving for this priceless possession than it did on its logical definition as a national goal subject to constitutional restraints and limitations.

The close identification of Transcendentalism with the many reforms of the Jacksonian era was not accidental or peripheral, but the necessary expression of the essence of that philosophy. Its revolutionary character had to find an outlet in revolutionary activity. It must not be forgotten that Transcendentalism was a world and life view which characterized the New England of the nineteenth century just as much as Puritanism had been a characteristic in the seventeenth century. And as Puritanism spoke to every aspect of life in terms of presuppositions drawn from its biblical theism, so did this philosophy seek to speak to life two centuries later in the light of a new set of presuppositions drawn from pantheistic idealism and humanism. Emerson, Parker, Whitman, Thoreau, and their allies, left no institution unscathed, and very few social practices and customs escaped their criticism. For American life was to be rewritten once again in terms of the new metaphysics and the result would be social upheaval which would make the earlier American dream of a democratic utopia a veritable reality in the life of the people. Slavery, education, our legal systems, the problem of war and peace, the role of women in American society, marriage and the family, and the relation of the sexes were all to be reinterpreted in terms of this democratic philosophy, and no aspect of life could claim immunity from investigation. Such leaders of reform as Fannie Wright and Thomas Skidmore made free-thought, and even atheism the core of their philosophy. Skidmore went so far as to identify the cause of labor in this country with free thought. It is for this reason that the age of Jackson was an era of reform which would not be equalled or surpassed until the coming of Franklin Roosevelt and the New Deal. The difference between these two eras was this: the secular nature of the earlier reform movement was disguised to a great extent by the pantheistic idealism of the Transcendentalist philosophy, while the secularism of the New Deal was openly avowed as the political and economic expression of a philosophy which rested upon pragmatism and expediency for its motivation as well as its justification. A prominent contemporary historian showed great insight when he chose to write his *Age of Jackson* as a kind of introduction to his *Age of Roosevelt*: for the former era was, in a very real sense, a prelude to the latter, even though they were separated by a century. The problems which the New Deal faced were obviously quite different from those which the Transcendentalists attacked but many of the basic philosophical assumptions were the same for both programs. If pragmatism and the resort to expediency are more characteristic of the New Deal than they were of the earlier programs, it is simply due to the fact that the unstable idealism of the Transcendentalist philosophy had given way to the demands of the unvarnished humanism for practical solutions to practical problems. It must be remembered that this is the inner logic of the democratic philosophy and our national history from that time on, in part at least, is simply the account of its unfolding in our political development.

Emerson gave a classic expression to this mandate to reform society:

What is man born for, but to be a reformer, a Remaker of what man has made . . . . ? . . imitating that great Nature which embosoms us all, and which sleeps no moment on an old past, but every hour repairs herself, yielding us every morning a new day and with every pulsation a new life.[10]

In 1841 *The Dial* declared:

The triumph of reform is sounding through the world for a revolution of all human affairs . . . Already is the axe laid at the root of that spreading tree whose trunk is idolatry, whose branches are covetousness, war and slavery, whose blossom is concupiscence, whose fruit is hate. Planted by Beelzebub, it shall be rooted up. Reformers are metallic; they are sharpest steel; they pierce whatsoever of evil or abuse they touch.[11]

In his book *The Social Destiny of Man* Alfred Brisbane wrote:

Nature has implanted in man an instinct of social progress which, it is true, will lead him through a series of transformations, to the attainment of his destiny; but she has also reserved for his intelligence the noble prerogative of hastening this progress, and of anticipating results which, if left to the gradual movement of society, would require centuries to effect.[12]

These three citations, all representative of Transcendentalist thought, have a common theme, namely, that man, by his nature, is born to be a reformer, and that the motivating spirit for reform comes from the fact that he is a part of nature. Man's role is to hasten a process of progress which is inherent in nature but which would proceed at a much more leisurely pace if man were not to add his own intelligence to give it direction. Inherent in their thinking, although not openly expressed, is the dialectical conception of reality derived from Hegel.

They likewise agree that this progress is dictated by nature and subject to it. There is, in their thinking, no reference to a biblical

---

[10] "Man the Reformer," *The Complete Works of Ralph Waldo Emerson* I, p. 236, New York, 1892; Quoted in Curti, *Growth of American Thought,* p. 368.

[11] Merle Curti, *The Growth of American Thought,* New York, 1943, "The Dial," p. 368.

[12] Albert Brisbane, *The Social Destiny of Man,* Philadelphia, 1840, pp. 331-332. Quoted in Curti, *op. cit.,* p. 371.

conception of either justification or sanctification as the necessary foundations for any human progress. The progress to be
achieved is both secular and natural (in a pantheistic sense), for
man is a part of nature and as such, nature embosoms him in
its quest for improvement and a kind of self-realization. Brisbane does offer a goal for this process which he calls human destiny, but he does not define it. William Henry Channing tried to
supply this lack:

> We have full faith that the time is approaching, though it may yet
> be distant, when national greatness will be tested by virtue and
> wisdom, and not by numbers, wealth, or extent of possession;
> when the only policy tolerated will be rectitude; when the object
> of legislation will be not only the common weal, but the highest
> good of individuals; when those men will be raised to power who
> in their characters embody true greatness and thus prove their
> right to rule; when measures will be the result, not of artful ma-
> neuvering or party sway, but of the consenting judgments of an in-
> telligent and upright people; when castes will be broken down and
> reverence and courtesy act freely; when . . . the sway of fashion
> and the tyranny of public opinion will be banished; when all will
> seek to give the most favorable opportunities to each and will find
> his highest joy in blending his energies with the best design of all.[13]

Here the unalloyed optimism of the movement shines forth in
all its brilliance. Transcendentalism was optimistic, largely because it completely denied the biblical doctrine of sin and tended
to look on man as inherently good, spoiled only by his contact
with society and its institutions. We see no doubt of possible failure dampening their enthusiasm or their confidence in man's final
triumph over himself and his institutions. Evil is doomed, but the
Transcendentalists reached this conclusion because they did not
see evil in the biblical sense, but rather as a deficiency of proper
knowledge.

Under the inspiration of such a philosophy the Transcendental-

[13] William Henry Channing, *"Manifesto," the Western Messenger* VIII,
pp. 1-8, quoted in Miller, *op. cit.,* p. 430.

ists cheerfully and confidently attacked every social problem with the calm assurance that in time all would be well on the American social scene. No problem was too great or too complex that it would not yield to the magic formulas which Transcendentalism would provide and which they, and their allies, would apply through associations specifically formed for definite purposes and the resulting political action. They thus entered upon the crusade for world peace, the movement for labor reform, for women's rights, for prohibition, for prison reform, and for abolition with enthusiasm and determination. By means of the lyceum, their writings and their leadership in conventions and associations they made their influence felt in most of the reform movements of the day. In this way they affected the political life of the country. They not only provided an intellectual atmosphere for Jacksonian democracy but they gave it an effective and active leadership. The names of many Transcendentalist leaders like Parker, Emerson, and others, could be found in the literature of peace societies, and abolition groups. In this way they successfully bridged the gap between a rather abstruse philosophy on the one hand, and the democratic yearnings of the common man on the other. They did not center their efforts in winning the masses to Transcendentalism as such, but they entered the political and social contests of the day, giving them leadership and direction. They were quite successful in winning support from denominational and religious groups whose theologies, in varying degrees, had been democratized by contact with Transcendentalism. These reform efforts were not their monopoly and they were able to gain many allies for these various causes from evangelical churches whose theology had departed from Calvinism to a sufficient extent to allow them to hold out some hope for human effort and cooperation with God in achieving personal salvation and social progress. It was possible for those who held to a postmillennial theology to cooperate with the Transcendentalists in nearly all of the reform movements. Yet, it is to be noted that very few evangelicals are to be found in the vanguard of the abolitionist movement. There were some, but they tended to be associated with Charles G. Finney and the perfectionist groups holding to an Arminian theology.

The abolitionist movement was the main theater of interest and activity for the Transcendentalists. The peace movement was of great interest, and they were willing to engage in various projects for prison reforms, and even for changing what people should eat and wear. They were willing to lend their support for women's rights, but they never allowed any of these activities to divert their attention or energies from the one great passion by which they were possessed—the abolition of slavery. It is of more than passing importance that those who were the most radical in their theology were, for the most part, the most insistent that slavery should be abolished not only in the territories of the West, but also in the slave states of the South. Later on we shall have occasion to examine the implications of this fact in the southern reaction to the rise of the abolitionist movement and to the secession of the South from the Federal Union.

There can be no doubt that Transcendentalism achieved its greatest political and social prestige and effectiveness in the crusade against slavery. Perry Miller rightly points out that it was abolitionism which gave to Transcendentalism a respectability in the North which it might not otherwise have achieved. In this contest it eventually won a signal victory and left an imperishable impress on American political and social life, which endures even to the present day. But this was not a victory which was achieved on biblical principles. In this contest the abolitionists, for the most part, did not appeal to the Scriptures so much as they appealed to the democratic philosophy of the American Revolution, to Thomas Jefferson and to natural law. The main thrust of their attack on slavery was secular and humanistic rather than doctrinal. Thus the Transcendentalists and their abolitionist allies tended to become increasingly radical in their political and economic philosophy. This trend is quite apparent in their appeal to labor, and the evaluation of the issues existing between labor and capital at that time. The drift toward socialism is evident in the founding of the Brooke Farm Colony, and its capture by the follower of the French socialist philosopher, Fourier. The kinship between some of their views and the Marxian view of religion is quite apparent in Theodore Parker's *A Sermon on Merchants* (1846):

> Now the merchants in America occupy the place which was once held by the fighters and next by the nobles. . . . In virtue of its strength and position, this class is the controlling one in politics . . . your congress is its mirror. This class is the controlling one in the churches . . . . in the same way it buys up the clergymen . . . . the clergymen will do its work, putting them in comfortable places. The merchants build mainly the churches and endow theological schools; they furnish the material sinews of the church. Hence metropolitan churches are in general as much commercial as shops. . . . This class owns the machinery of society, in great measure, the ships, factories, shops, water privileges, houses and the like. This brings into their employment large masses of workingmen, with no capital but muscles and skill.[14]

In the first issue of *The Harbinger,* which in 1845 succeeded *The Dial,* which had given up in 1844, George Ripley wrote a declaration of policy which stands as the culmination of Transcendentalist thinking in this respect:

> The interests of social reform will be considered as paramount to all others. . . . We shall suffer no attachment to literature, no taste for abstract discussion, no love of purely intellectual theories to seduce us from our devotion to the cause of the oppressed, the down-trodden, the insulted and injured masses of our fellowmen . . . . *The Harbinger* will be devoted to the cause of radical, organic social reform as essential to the highest development of man's nature, to the production of those elevated and beautiful of character of which he is capable, and to the diffusion of happiness, excellence and universal harmony upon earth.[15]

---

[14] Theodore Parker, *Speeches, Addresses and Occasional Sermons,* Boston, 1852. Quoted in Miller, *op. cit.,* p. 450.
[15] Quoted in Miller, *op. cit.,* pp. 469-470.

This declaration makes it quite plain that Transcendentalism from then on was to be less theoretical and metaphysical and was going to become practical in the sense that it was embarking upon a policy of radical social reform, and that this was going to be accomplished by the means of governmental action. Transcendentalism was about to become identified with socialism and would now look to a strong central government to achieve the reforms to which it had devoted itself. In the field of labor reform this program met with only scant success; about all it had to show for its efforts was a presidential order limiting the working day to ten hours on government projects, but in industry as a whole, it had little influence.

It was in the area of the abolition of negro slavery that these reformers ultimately won their greatest victory. True enough, they secured victory only by an endorsement of war and the utilization of the powers of the central government in a manner quite repugnant to their basic principles. But they were, nevertheless, triumphant in a cause which surpassed all others in their thinking as to its importance. It was for this that they fought and struggled. Even though the victory was not obtained without the aid of other less radical groups and, even then, only in the throes of a civil conflict, they were the mainspring of the crusade for abolition. This, to a great extent, compensated them for their almost total failure in the peace campaign, for their very limited achievements in the area of labor, for their partial success in their movement for women's rights, and for the inconsequential results of other reform movements.

What then were the ultimate effects of the Transcendentalist philosophy and program on American political development? In the first place, they made social reform an integral part of the program of political parties. There had been acute differences in respect to the philosophy and conduct of American government before the advent of this movement, but they had not called forth active programs of political reform which became true after 1830. From then on various projects of political, social and economic reform became a part of nearly every platform of the political parties, and they constituted the basis of their appeals to the electorate. With the advent of Transcendentalism, reform was here to stay as a permanent feature of American political life.

Not only did reform become an enduring concept in party programs, but it also became an instrument for the increasing centralization of political power in the central government at the expense of the states. So far as this means of reform was concerned, reformers of various stripes and hues, all, either consciously or unconsciously, looked to Hamilton's broad construction of the Constitution as the method of interpretation to be preferred for the realization of their various programs. From then on, no major reform program looked to the strict construction of Jefferson for its justification. Strict construction, from then on, has become a weapon in the hands of conservatives (frequently conservatives in the minority) to defend constitutional government against the attacks of reformers.

In the second place, this Transcendentalist impulse for social and political change gave to the reform movements, until our own day, a radical bent. They tended to take the form of attacks on constitutional government in favor of popular democratic concepts, of attacks on property rights in favor of "human rights." All too frequently their only justification was based on the assumption that they represented what the people at large wanted and, just as frequently, little attention has been paid to the basic justice and rightness of such programs. Frequently these reform programs have been influenced by European political and social philosophies, thus reflecting the socialistic collectivism and communism of their European ancestry. Inevitably the Puritan world and life view has become almost extinct and practically without influence in determining national political, social and economic questions in the twentieth century.

In spite of their continuous emphasis upon human freedom, and their earlier distrust of government and other human institutions, the Transcendentalist reformers soon turned toward collectivism in their own day, and many of them became actively involved in the Brooke Farm Colony, and other collectivist experiments. (Emerson became disillusioned with this experiment and withdrew as one of its supporters.) This collectivist compulsion was inherent in the Hegelian and democratic character of their philosophy itself, and was neither accidental nor incidental. Not only the Transcendentalists of that era, but American reform leaders in general from the time of Jackson on, have been willing, and even glad, to have centralization of government and collectivism in society follow the democratization of government, on the assumption that big government is not a danger provided it is in the hands of enough people. Their trust in the benevolence of the people at large in contrast to their distrust of an aristocracy and its political leadership is a continuing characteristic of nearly all reform movements of the latter half of the nineteenth century and the first six decades of the present century. In turn, this stems from the basic theological and philosophical premises of all liberalism. It should be noted that modern political liberalism, with its economic and social overtones, stems from a theological liberalism which either seriously modifies, or totally rejects, Christian orthodoxy, Calvinistic and otherwise. There can be no reasonable doubt that the Transcendentalists were the first to bring about such an alliance between theological and social liberalism, and to make the former the necessary foundation for the latter. Neither can it be denied that from their day on, liberal reformers have increasingly looked to liberal theology, and the resultant philosophies, for support and justification for their programs. This is so much the case that there is scarcely a consistent program of reform from 1880 on in American history which was not colored and greatly influenced by liberal theology.

This does not mean that evangelicals failed to play a role in these attempts at reform, for many of them were very attractive, even if not truly biblical in character, and many of them seemed to be, on the surface at least, sufficiently biblical to justify an evangelical support. Many evangelicals supported (even if they did not lead) the abolitionist movement, many of them were very vocal in the support of the prohibition movement, and others have been found among those who were dedicated to the cause of world peace; some have even been able to justify their participation in socialistic programs on the basis of an evangelical commitment.

The fact that these major reform endeavors have been based upon humanistic and naturalist philosophies of life does not mean that they were all wrong in every aspect. Men may undertake biblically correct programs from very wrong, or unworthy, or insufficient motives. In the Providence of God the unregenerate carry out his will in society for the realization of his purposes even though they are consciously at war with the biblical message. The doctrine of common grace must never be forgotten as an integral factor in human affairs, making it possible for even sinful man to so conduct his civic and economic affairs that the church may operate and conduct its divine mandate, and that the individual Christian may faithfully carry out the will of God in his daily life. It makes it possible for the unregenerate to strive after what may be called "civic good" and to pursue those policies which seem to be conducive to human welfare. At the same time, it must always be kept in mind that common grace, in itself, is not redemptive and that the "good" which unregenerate man seeks to accomplish under it is not that good which is acceptable to a righteous and holy God.

Nevertheless the Transcendentalists and their radical allies relied upon a set of assumptions concerning God, man and the nature of evil which were, at best, sub-biblical and more frequently, quite contrary to the scriptural position on these matters. Their view of God was that of a Being who was entirely willing to accommodate himself to human aspirations for a better world, and to the perpetual quest for freedom. Their view of man made him divine to such an extent that the clear biblical delineation between God and man was nearly obliterated, or at least so blurred, as to make it difficult to maintain significant differences between them. Their doctrine of evil was equally foreign to the biblical view, and evil became a problem which could be curbed and even eliminated from the human scene by the use of the proper techniques in education and government. It was the minimizing of the biblical position which gave to the Transcendentalists their easy-going optimism concerning human destiny, and they bequeathed this optimism to the succeeding generations of reformers, to the abolitionists, to the radicals of the late eighteen sixties and early seventies, to the Social Darwinists, to the proponents of the Social Gospel and to the liberals of the twentieth century. In short, Transcendentalism bequeathed to all succeeding liberal reform movements its own serious distortion of the biblical message and its own vehement opposition to Calvinism as the embodiment of an orthodoxy of all life, and a definite view of the nature of freedom and society which constituted a sharp and definite rebuke to every aspect of the Transcendentalist dream for American life. This drastic cleavage between Calvinism and the reform movement has been a continuing feature of American history from that day until our own.

The Conservative Opposition and Reaction to Transcendentalism

From the foregoing it might well seem that Transcendentalism was the order of the day and had so successfully claimed the leadership in American thought that it was virtually without opposition and faced no serious challenge. To come to such a conclusion would be a serious error and quite far from the actual situation. Transcendentalism, and its allied radical reform movements, faced a formidable opposition, an opposition so strong that it often brought dismay to their leaders and caused some Transcendentalists to lose faith in their philosophy. This opposition was partly theological in character and partly pragmatic, arising from those who were not deeply committed to the evangelical theology from which a Christian world and life view emerged, but who were, nevertheless, zealous supporters of that biblical view of life. They liked the fruits of high doctrine, even if they were not greatly impressed by its roots. These opponents were greatly concerned with the rise of the democratic philosophy and the attending radicalism in political, social and economic thought. They were well aware of the danger which it posed to the Constitution as it had been written in 1787, and to the government which had developed under the benevolent influence of that document on American life.

There was still another source of opposition to Transcendentalism, and its radical influences, which saw the movement in its proper biblical perspective. In this group were those who saw that it was essentially a theological revolt against Calvinism in particular and evangelical thought in general. This theological opposition had some strength in Congregational circles, but it had its greatest influence in Presbyterianism; for here there was a growing distrust of the Plan of Union of 1801, by which the two denominations had sought to cooperate in the vast task of planting new churches in the growing West. Many Presbyterian leaders correctly saw in this plan a method whereby the lax New England theology (a moderating theology between Calvinism and Arminianism which was greatly influenced by Transcendentalism) was being brought into Presbyterian circles and thus was causing heretical departures from the theology of the Westminster Standards. The ensuing controversy reached such proportions that in 1837 there was a division in American Presbyterianism between the Old and New School groups. The Old School held strictly to the Westminster Confession of Faith, whereas the New School was willing to tolerate serious departures from Presbyterian orthodoxy and was, at the same time, much more friendly in its attitude toward the democratic reform movements of the day; and it was willing to allow to the church a much greater role in the political, social and economic life of the nation than had been allowed among those who held strictly to the Westminster Standards. The New School, with its more optimistic and less biblical view of man, and its more "democratic" theology, was much more likely to be found in support of the various democratic movements of the day than was the Old School.

Arminianism and its allied theologies, on the other hand, were particularly prone to the inroads of democratic liberalism because they were already democratized to a degree in their theology and they were less able to resist the appeal of the new liberalism. They had so modified the doctrine of the sovereignty of God that the idea of some sovereignty resident in man was not so distasteful to them, and their view of man allowed considerable optimism as to his natural ability in the civil areas of life, and as to his ability to cooperate with God. Thus the protest from these quarters was far less forceful and effective than that which came from the Old School Presbyterianism and the other Calvinistic groups.

The South was even more articulate in its opposition to democratic liberalism of all kinds. Here again we must distinguish between that opposition that was directed against abolitionism and the anti-slavery movement simply because they threatened a Southern institution, and the opposition which arose because of a very deep insight into the meaning of abolitionism as an expression of a basic radicalism which had far greater implications than a mere crusade against slavery as such. In the South, Old School Presbyterianism constituted a far greater majority of Presbyterianism than it did in the North, and it had much greater influence on southern thought than the Old School had in the North. As a result, there was in the South a far greater consciousness of the theological radicalism lurking behind the anti-slavery crusade, and also a much keener insight into the growing radicalism in northern thought in its many and varied implications for constitutional government in this country, and its effect on the American way of life.

Among many historians it has been customary and fashionable to find the causes of secession and the ensuing war in slavery as an economic institution, and in the southern insistence on state sovereignty and the rights of the states as their main weapon for the defense of slavery. There can be no doubt that these issues did play a part in bringing on war. But to reduce secession and the war to economic factors, and to overlook the intellectual and theological forces at work, is to seriously misread the records of the era from 1850 to 1860. The admission that economic factors were at work does not involve the denial that other, and equally important, forces were having a tremendous influence in the sequence of events which would ultimately lead to secession and to war. After 1830 there was a growing philosophical and theological cleavage between the North and the South. While the North was becoming increasingly subject to radical influences, the South was becoming increasingly conservative in its outlook. Some historians prefer to interpret this development as a defensive measure to protect slavery. Such a conclusion is superficial and in direct contradiction to some very important facts. While most of the denominations that were national in scope had their conservative elements in the South, it is not true that they were necessarily staunch defenders of state sovereignty, or even of slavery. Again we must turn to Presbyterianism in the South for an important illustration of the influence of theological position on political outlook. In the nullification controversy of 1828-1832, many of those who would soon be the leaders of Old School Presbyterianism in the South after the division of 1837, refused to support South Carolina and Calhoun because many of the leaders of this movement were very liberal in their theological outlook; Dr. Thomas Cooper, President of the University of South Carolina, noted Deist and Unitarian, was a vociferous supporter of nullification. Of even greater importance is the position which these men took on the slavery question. During the eighteen thirties, and even in the early forties, many of these leaders were not in favor of slavery and were seeking to find a way by which the institution could be brought to an end; and in such a way that it would demoralize neither the economic or social life of the South. They were not to be found in the vanguard of those who sought to defend slavery on biblical principles. This does not mean that they were abolitionists, or even anti-slavery in their attitudes, for they were well aware of the serious political and social problems involved in such an undertaking. But, it was also clear that their conservative theological orthodoxy was not a retreat for them by which they might more effectively defend the South's peculiar institution.

However, after 1840 these same leaders of Old School thought took a very strong stand against Abolitionism as a movement, not because it was opposed to slavery per se, but because of the philosophy and theology which it represented, and because they clearly saw that if this radicalism were to gain the supremacy in the national government, then there must certainly come in its wake a radical political and social program which would threaten the established order and constitutional government for the nation as a whole. J. H. Thornwell, Robert Dabney, B. M. Palmer and William Plumer were all of one mind in their own theological convictions, and in their discernment of the threat which the abolitionist movement held for the American people. Thornwell was one of the first to give voice to his fears and to seek to arouse the South to the danger which it faced in this radical political and social philosophy.

As early as 1850 Thornwell gave a graphic portrayal of the true nature of the Abolitionist movement in language which gives rise to the conclusion that he had some influence on Calhoun, in his *Address of March 4, 1850* on the Compromise then pending in Congress, and also in his *Disquisition on Government* which was published a short time after his death. Said Thornwell:

These are mighty questions which are shaking thrones to their centers—upheaving the masses like an earthquake, and rocking the solid pillars of this Union. The parties in this conflict are not merely abolitionists and slave-holders—they are atheists, socialists, communists, red republicans, Jacobins on the one side and the friends of order and regulated freedom on the other. In one word, the world is the battleground—Christianity and atheism the combatants, and the progress of humanity is at stake. One party seems to regard society with all its complicated interests, its divisions and subdivisions, as the machinery of man—which as it had been invented and arranged by his ingenuity and skill may be taken to pieces, reconstructed, or repaired as experience shall indicate defects or confusions in the original plan. The other party beholds it as the ordinance of God.[16]

This is an amazingly accurate description of the forces which were at work in American society before 1860, and it clearly indicates an insight into the nature of the intellectual conflict which was then raging, which makes it impossible to hold that either secession or the formation of the Southern Presbyterian Church can be regarded as nothing more than a defensive movement against northern attacks on slavery.

Thornwell was not alone in holding, or setting forth, such views. There were many others who came to his support and, at times, in even stronger language. During the war Thomas Smythe wrote in a similar fashion:

> Our enemies have a zeal of God, but it is not according to knowledge. Their faith is, therefore, fanaticism. They substitute opinion for truth, dogmatism for doctrine, philosophy (falsely so-called), for religion.[17]

Perhaps the most inclusive and weighty criticism of Abolitionism was given by B. M. Palmer in his famous *Thanksgiving Day Sermon* of 1860:

> The abolitionist spirit is undeniably atheistic. The demon spirit which erected its throne upon the guillotine in the days of Robespierre and Marat, which abolished the Sabbath, and worshipped reason in the person of an harlot, yet survives to work other horrors of which those of the French Revolution are but a type. Among a people so generally religious as the Americans a disguise must be worn, but it is the same old threadbare disguise of the advocacy of human rights. From a thousand Jacobin clubs here, and in France, the decree has gone forth which strikes at God by striking at all subordination and law . . . . Under the specious cry of reform it demands that every evil shall be corrected or society become a wreck—the sun must be stricken from the heavens if a spot is found upon his disc . . . . These self-

[16] *Collected Writings,* IV, pp. 405-406.
[17] *Southern Presbyterian Review,* April 1863, p. 478.

constituted reformers must quicken the activity of Jehovah and compel His abdication. It is time to reproduce the obsolete idea that Providence must govern man, but not that man should control Providence . . . . To the South is assigned the high position of defending before all nations the cause of all religion and of all truth. In this trust we are resisting the power which wars against constitutions and laws and compacts, against sabbaths and sanctuaries, against the family, the state, and the church, which blasphemously invades the prerogatives of God and rebukes the Most High for the errors of His administration.[18]

It is quite clear that these men who founded the Southern Presbyterian Church saw in abolitionism something far more significant than a mere protest against slavery as an institution. They saw it as a continuation of the French Revolution, motivated by the same philosophy and pursuing the same ends. They saw it primarily as a humanistic revolt against Christianity and the world and life view of the Scriptures. They saw in it the expression of a democratic philosophy which left no place for a sovereign God and accorded all prestige to a sovereign humanity. It is also noteworthy that Palmer insists that in secession and the ensuing war the role of the South was far more than that of defending slavery; rather was its role the defense of true religion. Such a claim may well be unfounded for the southern people as a whole and it may be doubted that they saw their role in this pure light. But, at the same time, this conception of the South was a powerful factor in the thinking of those sober minds who saw that the opposition to slavery was only a small part of the abolitionist program and philosophy, and that there was for the South something more noble and necessary to contend for than slavery as an institution. Thornwell, Dabney, and their contemporaries saw in abolitionism a threat to Calvinism, to the Constitution and to the proper ordering of society. They properly read abolitionism as a revolt against the biblical conception

[18] *The South, Her Peril and Duty, A Discourse Delivered at the First Presbyterian Church,* November 29, 1860, New Orleans.

of society and a revolt against the doctrine of divine sovereignty in human affairs. They saw in abolitionism all the inherent characteristics of a humanistic democracy in conflict with the Constitution.

In this evaluation of the secession movement they were at one with its leaders. It is a matter of great interest, and of even greater importance for a proper understanding of the secession movement, that its leaders never failed to make it clear that they had no quarrel with the Constitution of the United States. In 1866 Alexander Stephens wrote:

> Whatever may be said of the loyalty or disloyalty of any in the late most lamentable conflict of arms, I think I may venture safely to say, that there was, on the part of the great mass of people of the entire South, no disloyalty to the principles of the Constitution of the United States. To that system of representative government, of delegated and limited powers, that establishment in a new phase, on a continent, of all the essentials of England's Magna Carta, for the protection and security of life, liberty and property, with the additional recognition of a fundamental truth, that all political power resides in the people. To us it was simply a question as to where our allegiance was due in the maintenance of those principles, which authority was paramount in the last resort—State or Federal. To the maintenance of these principles of self-government my whole soul was ever enlisted and to this end my whole life has heretofore been devoted, and will continue to be so the rest of my days—God willing.[19]

In 1861 Jefferson Davis had argued in a similar vein before he left his seat in the Senate of the United States; and, as President of the Confederacy he constantly maintained that the Confederacy and the Constitution which it had adopted, and which was modelled on that of 1787 was the true successor to the Constitution which the North had perverted and undermined. It could well be said that the South seceded from the Federal Union

---

[19] "Address Before the General Assembly of the state of Georgia"; February 22, 1866, Milledgeville, Georgia, 1866, quoted in Ralph Gabriel, *The Course of American Democratic Thought,* New York, 1940, p. 116.

in order to save the Constitution, or at least to preserve it within a different political framework from that which had been created from 1787 to 1789 as the embodiment of the principles of the philosophy of government.

Theological Radicalism as a Factor in Reconstruction

The pre-war abolitionists became the leading architects of the Congressional policy of reconstruction as over against the Lincoln-Johnson plan of restoration for the South. It has not been so well-recognized that there was behind the radical program for the South a genuine religious and political radicalism which had in mind the reconstruction of the whole of national life. Too often reconstruction has been studied purely in terms of the radical program for punishing the South for its crime of secession, and rewarding the Negro for having been in slavery. There is a great deal of truth in this view of radical reconstruction, but it is by no means the whole story. When the abolitionists suddenly realized that by the passage of the thirteenth amendment their goal had been achieved, they were a group of reformers without a reform in view, crusaders without a city to rescue from the infidels, an army with no conflict in which to engage.

The more radical members of the Republican Party, now in control of the situation, were not and could not be content with such a frustrating situation. Neither would the very philosophy which had driven them on to this initial victory in the struggle for their version of human freedom, allow them to be content with the victory already accomplished. Thus, they could not be content with a mere restoration of the South if that restoration did no more than recognize the legal freedom of the former slaves. The radical element of the party was determined to carry out a reconstruction policy in the South as a prelude to the reconstruction they intended to bring about in the nation as a whole. The southern states were to be used as social science laboratories and were to be reconstructed according to the pattern delineated by the democratic philosophy as a kind of pilot study for reconstructing the whole nation in terms of a democratic pattern. Thaddeus Stevens, the leader of the radical Republicans in the House of Representatives, and a dominant figure in the Congressional program of reconstruction until his death, made this very clear in a remarkable address which he made in the House; in it he gives the clue to the thinking of the radicals in regard to the whole issue—remarkable for its clear statement of the basic philosophy which guided the radicals in their thinking and the basic details of a program which they hoped to bring to reality by means of reconstruction in the South:

> In my youth, in my manhood, in my old age, I had fondly dreamed that when any future fortunate circumstances should have broken up for awhile the foundations of our institutions, and released us from foundations the most tyrannical that ever man imposed in the name of freedom, that the intelligent, pure and just men of this Republic, true to their professions and conscience, would have so remodelled all our institutions as to have freed us from every vestige of human oppression, of inequality of rights, of the recognized degradation of the poor and the superior caste of the rich. In short, that no distinction should be tolerated in this puri-fied Republic but what arose from merit and conduct. This bright dream has vanished like the baseless fabric of our vision. I find that we shall be obliged to be content with patching up the worst portions of the ancient edifice, and, leaving it in many of its parts, to be swept away by tempests, the frosts and the storms of des-potism.[20]

His radicalism led Stevens to regard the writing and the adoption of the Constitution as the most terrible kind of tyranny ever imposed on mankind in the name of freedom. It is quite clear that in making such statements Stevens was not thinking pri-marily of slavery in the South, or simply of a reconstruction of the South. Rather had he hoped that the war would bring to the Republican Party the marvelous opportunity of rewriting the entire structure of the federal government. In this same address

[20] *Congressional Globe,* first session 39th Congress, p. 3148.

which he made in the House, Stevens went on to spell out exactly what he had in mind when he spoke of such a reconstruction of the entire American frame of government:

> There have been republics everywhere in the midst of despotism. You may call what you choose a republic. But what I am to speak to now is the Republic intended by the Declaration of Independence, and I deny that this government has ever been such a republic . . . . Now what was the Republic contemplated by the Declaration of Independence. "All men are created free and equal" and "all rightful government is based on the consent of the governed." Nothing short of that is the Republic intended by the Declaration . . . . Upon this Declaration alone stood the American Revolution. The people then had no actual grievance which justify the shedding of one drop of human blood.

> But they fought and bled for this sublime idea. In this sign they conquered. But when peace and security had come, and the several sovereignties attempted to form a more perfect union, they found themselves obstructed by a pernicious and unyielding institution in direct hostility to their avowed principles and they were obliged to trust to time to eradicate it . . . . They have left the scene of action . . . . If we fail to complete this superstructure in harmony with the foundation, we must be dwarfs in intellect or moral courage.[21]

In Thaddeus Stevens, and his fellow post-war radicals, the democratic philosophy of Transcendentalism was blended with that of the Revolutionary Era and they worked out a program for the reconstruction of both the South and the North which would faithfully follow its dictates. Radical ideals in theology have radical consequences in the political, social and economic life of that nation which falls victim to them. This is the inescapable conclusion from a study in the philosophical background of both the secession movement and the post-war attempt to reconstruct the South. But reconstruction in the South afforded to northern radicals another kind of an opportunity to put their

[21] *Ibid.*, p. 4778.

religious radicalism into direct operation. If the official program reflected the theological heresies of Transcendentalism, many of the private agencies which worked there were no less under such influences. In fact, many of the mission projects of northern churches were thinly disguised agencies for implementing Congressional action and for realizing a democratic type of society, rather than for preaching the Gospel of Jesus Christ. These southern home mission agencies all too frequently became pilot experiments for what, in a few years, would openly be called the Social Gospel.

However, after 1865 theological, social and political radicalism no longer found its inspiration directly in the Transcendentalist movement, for this philosophy had lost its impetus; theological liberalism, along with its political and social alliances, would look to new sources for its intellectual foundations. Transcendentalism was ill-equipped to appeal to the American mind in an age of railroads, big business, materialism, Marxianism and Darwinism. Theological liberals, and their allies in the social sciences, would now look to Darwinism and the theory of evolution for their views of God, man and sin, and American thought would be given that Darwinian context for which Transcendentalism had prepared the way.

4

Social Darwinism: Its Theological Background and Political Implications

Social Darwinism was the greatest single theological and philosophical movement in the second half of the nineteenth century, gaining an acceptance in intellectual circles in this country of much wider scope than that ever accorded to Transcendentalism, which had been largely confined to the educated classes and had its center in New England. Social Darwinism captured the thinking of the educated classes not only in New England, but over the North as a whole; it also penetrated the South to a much greater degree than was true of its predecessors. The influence of Social Darwinism was not confined to a relatively few leaders and their immediate followers, but it entered the schools, the colleges, the churches, business and government and gained an influence within the middle class.

This wide influence obtained by Social Darwinism can be explained in terms of several factors. In the first place, it was much more in harmony with the post-war spirit than was Transcendentalism, which was idealistic in tone. Social Darwinism, on the other hand, was essentially a materialistic philosophy and, as such, it seemingly had a message as well as an appeal to an age which was steeped in the mad quest for wealth. Thoreau, Channing and Emerson seemed strangely out of place in the age of Harriman and the Union Pacific, Rockefeller and the Standard Oil Company, Cornelius Vanderbilt and the New York Central Railroad, The Whiskey Ring and Tammany Hall, William Graham Sumner and Andrew Carnegie. Transcendentalism had little in common with the new America which had emerged from the tumult of a civil war, and this new America had little more than a passing interest in it.

In the second place, Social Darwinism fitted into the scientific temper of the times. It was an age which revered, if it did not actually worship, science and the scientific method. Darwinism was the newest pronouncement of the high priesthood of the microscope and the test tube which spoke with a positivistic infallibility which for many could neither be denied or ignored. The average American of the 1870's was far more prone to give heed to what a scientist would say not only in regard to his own chosen field, but on politics, social issues, and even theology itself. Social Darwinism was the attempt to apply the principles enunciated by Charles Darwin to the political, economic and social philosophy. Social Darwinism proposed to rewrite the entire field of the social sciences in terms of Darwinian theories.

As audacious as such an attempt might sound to the man of the twentieth century, it was quite in keeping with the outlook of that post-war era. Transcendentalism had, to a degree, prepared the way for the triumph of this new philosophy in that it was essentially an evolutionary philosophy, based on Hegelian, rather than Darwinian, conceptions. In this sense the triumph of Social Darwinism was simply a shift from an idealistic Hegelian form to a biological and materialistic interpretation.

In the third place, the triumph of abolitionism in the war had brought to radicalism, theologically and politically, a kind of vindication. The North had won and slavery had been abolished.

These facts could not be denied by either the most loyal Southerner or the most convinced conservative. In the defeat of the South with its theological, economic and social conservatism, conservatism seemed to have vanished to such an extent that it might even have been considered as part of the Lost Cause. There can be little doubt that the triumph of abolitionism in the war prepared the American mind for new forms of theological and social radicalism which would emerge shortly after its conclusion. The optimism which Social Darwinism brought coincided with that native optimism which victory had heightened to a new pitch. There was no limit on American progress; the future belonged to this country, and the abolition of slavery was only the first of many victories which in time would remake this land of the Puritans into a veritable Paradise of wealth and plenty, of power and might, far beyond anything that had ever been dreamed by those Puritan fathers who would have scarcely recognized the Boston of 1875, and who would have liked it even less. In the Massachusetts of the last half of the 1870's the doctrine of divine sovereignty had been replaced with the belief in natural determinism, and the infallibility of the Scriptures had given way to the inerrant pronouncements of scientists who constituted the new priesthood. Darwin and his cohorts restored science and its experimental method once again to the pinnacle which Newton had erected for it two centuries earlier.

Social Darwinism: Its Background

Although Charles Darwin in his *Origin of the Species* (1859), and his *Descent of Man* (1871), brought the theory of evolution to a new level of popularity, he was not the pioneer in the field of the theory of biological evolution. Rather did he advance on the speculations and actual scientific research of such scholars as Lamarck (1744-1829), Sir Charles Lyell (1797-1875), and his own grandfather, Erasmus Darwin. It was his role to give to it a scientific status which it had never possessed before, and to thus bring about a revolution in both scientific and social theory which had profound and far-reaching results in Europe and America in virtually every area of human knowledge. The theory of evolution penetrated the arts, philosophy and even theology; Darwinism became a formidable opponent of the established order in every branch of human learning. The theories advanced by Darwin were used in their day in the same way, and for the same general purpose, as Locke used the Newtonian pronouncements of his own era for the creation of a scientific foundation for society in all of its parts. It is important to notice that in each case it was natural law that was being interpreted and used; it is also important to notice that the Darwinian conception of natural law was quite different from that held by Newton. The natural law to which Newton held was fixed and unchangeable and the order which it set up in nature was of the same kind; in all of this it was close to the old Aristotelian metaphysics and logic. On the other hand, the conception of natural law set forth by Darwin was evolutionary in character and reflected the Hegelian logic.

The world and life view which emerged from Darwinism was different from that which Newton supplied for Locke and his followers, but it was quite as alien to the biblical position. Any political, social or economic philosophy which looks to natural law as its norm and frame of reference must lose its biblical character to the same degree to which it relies on a revelation in nature for the guidance of man in his various relationships rather than on the Scriptures.

At the same time there was a great difference between the position which Locke assumed in regard to Newton, and that which the Social Darwinists assumed in regard to Darwin. It was never the intention of either Newton or Locke to deny the biblical view of God or of creation; certainly it was farthest from their minds to deny that there was purpose and meaning in creation. Darwinism was a pointed denial of the biblical ideas of God and creation, and it was virtually an assertion that there was no purpose in life. Thus, in these respects, Darwinism was a step further away from the biblical position than was the Newtonian, even though the Newtonian may have contained within it certain ingredients which made further departures possible. It was, therefore, both logical and well nigh inevitable that Social Darwinism, the social expression of Darwinism, should also depart further from the biblical norm than the democratic outlook which emerged from Newton in the works of Jefferson and Locke. Certainly Locke had it in mind not only to sustain the Christian ethic, but to give that ethic a more enduring foundation in his appeal to natural law through his empirical epistemology. While a denial of purpose and ethical content might well have been the logical deduction from the use of his methods, such a possibility never entered Locke's thinking. But this is not the case with Darwinism. Not only was there an anti-Christian motivation in Darwin's own thinking on the subject, but this strong pressure toward philosophic determinism was as strong, if not stronger, among the Social Darwinists, most of whom were willing to rule the God of the Scriptures out of any place of dominion in the universe. Thus Social Darwinism in this country was founded on a conscious and sweeping repudiation of the biblical outlook and was, at the same time, a determined effort to replace that biblical foundation with one which was naturalistic in its totality.

For an age already conditioned for such a step by the naturalism of Theodore Parker and others, the positivism of Comte, Darwin's theory of organic evolution seemed to offer the most satisfactory basis for a thoroughly naturalistic interpretation of a universe in which man was the supreme and final triumph of the evolutionary process. In such a philosophy man was entirely free from any dependence on a sovereign God, since he was somehow now free to work out his own destiny through an increasing understanding of the working of the laws of nature in the evolutionary process, and how it might be used for his own benefit.

The philosophical belief in the inherent goodness of man and his capacity for self-improvement through the proper methods of education and government now received a new confirmation at the hands of science at a time when its infallibility was almost beyond question. On the other hand, orthodox theology in the eyes of many seemed to have received a death blow from which it would never recover, if it continued to insist on the biblical view of creation, and to deny the findings of Darwin and the other evolutionary scientists.

In the same manner the theory that man was continuing to develop both physically and morally seemed to leave little room for a doctrine of original sin which taught that man had fallen from an original sinless state of physical and moral perfection into the present debased condition. The evolutionists in psychology and philosophy would soon join hands with those in the biological sciences to laugh such a view of man out of court, certainly out of the world of scholarship. Sin, to the extent to which the word could now be used, was certainly changed in its meaning by those who accepted Darwin. At best, it represented only a lack of knowledge of human nature and the world in which man lived, and a lack of social and psychological adjustment to one's environment. Sin was no longer a "want of conformity unto, or transgression of, the law of God" but the result of ignorance in which man failed to live up to the highest and the most noble that was within him.

In such a frame of reference the biblical doctrine of salvation through the atoning work of Jesus Christ lost all meaning. It simply had no place in an evolutionary age. Modern man, with all the scientific knowledge at his command, no longer needs that kind of salvation, if indeed, man had ever needed it. Obviously, if man was not inherently sinful in the biblical sense, he did not need a biblical salvation. The doctrine of redemption was now redefined in terms of the evolutionary hypothesis. According to this conception the church was to help each individual work out for himself that salvation which nature had placed within his grasp and which he should direct toward socially desirable ends. Salvation was henceforth regarded as largely social in content and purpose, and only incidentally individual in nature. True enough, a major change of purpose and motivation was to take place in individual lives, but this was not an end in itself, but only a means toward an end—the perfecting of society here on earth. The unfolding of the individual was not primarily for receiving a future life in the biblical sense of the word. Indeed, a strict adherence to the evolutionary theory, and to Darwin's own pronouncements, prohibited any belief in a future life. In fact, in this scheme of things there was little or no promise of a union between the soul of the individual and the Over-Soul which Emerson taught. In Darwinism there was no room for a soul. Thus, the biblical doctrines of eternal life, and the reign of Jesus Christ in triumph were replaced by the vision of a society which would obtain its own millennial triumph, or eternal reign of righteousness (reinterpreted according to naturalistic ethics), in which state man would come to a kind of full self-realization of all that was potentially in him. The scriptural view of sanctification was replaced by the idea of progressive individual development, and there was no room at all for the doctrine of justification by faith. Faith in God was no longer a prerequisite for salvation; all that was necessary was a faith in man and in his capacity to progressively understand and utilize the laws of nature, as they were interpreted according to the evolutionary hypothesis, for his own purposes and perfection.

The Effect on Christian Thought

Even as Transcendentalism had prepared the way for the reception of the theory of organic evolution by American philosophy, so did it till the soil of American theology, and Darwinism met with a very cordial reception in many of the denominations. In the face of such a seemingly irresistible onslaught by scientific achievements and claims, many theologians yielded to what seemed to be the inevitable and they hastened to make their peace with this God of science by accepting the validity of the evolutionary hypothesis and tried to work out some kind of a compromise which would leave some acceptable theology out of the wreckage of their evangelical heritage. Darwinism made its greatest inroads among those churches which were strongest in the North; the Baptist, Congregational and Methodist churches there proved to be peculiarly susceptible to the pressures of scientific pronouncements. It was in these same churches that Transcendentalism had made its greatest inroads in the decades before the war. It was, therefore, not surprising that they should have welcomed the post-war evolutionary theories. They had already departed from the evangelical doctrines of the historic orthodoxy; but it must not be thought that orthodoxy departed overnight from these churches. Darwinism made its first inroads in the colleges which they supported, then in the seminaries which received the graduates from these schools, and some of these graduates ultimately became professors in the seminaries. Finally, these seminaries turned out young ministers who accepted to varying degrees the evolutionary thought to which they had been exposed in their theological training. By such a process the evolutionary theory made serious inroads into the Christian churches.

Darwinism did not enter all of them to the same degree and in some there was a vigorous resistance to it. In the North among the larger denominations the Presbyterian Church offered stout opposition to it, particularly at Princeton Theological Seminary, which school, fortified by the scholarship of the Hodges during the latter half of the nineteenth century, and in the early decades of the twentieth by such stalwarts of the faith as B. B. Warfield and J. Gresham Machen, continued to be a citadel of Old School Presbyterianism. There were other seminaries and church groups which also resisted the onslaught of the evolutionary philosophy. In the South before 1900 it made comparatively little headway.

In the North at large in the universities, as well as many of the theological seminaries, Darwinism made great headway and became the inspiration of an intellectual revolution which shook the very foundations of American life. Because Social Darwinism involved an almost complete rejection of historic orthodoxy in theology, it brought in its wake a rejection of those elements of orthodoxy which had lingered on in the political, social and economic thought of the country. It paved the way for the eventual triumph of pragmatism and materialism in the areas of political, social and economic thought, as a result of which the theistic foundations from the colonial and early national eras were openly rejected in favor of the naturalism inherent in Social Darwinism.

In consequence of the triumph of naturalism, the Christian ethic which had long been the guide of political, social and economic action, was openly shunted to one side, and declared to be no longer binding in an age which looked to science for its frame of reference, to assumptions which were derived from an evolutionary view of life. Questions as to what was right or wrong in these areas of action were no longer to be decided in terms of the biblical pattern, but according to what science decreed in the light of principles which were amoral at best, and more often immoral. The relativity inherent in the evolutionary view of life was transferred to the realm of ethics as they were applied to political, social and economic questions. Another necessary consequence of this revolution was a virtual negation of the historic Christian conception of liberty which, while not commanding the respect in the nineteenth century which it had once received, nevertheless, was still a living influence in American political thought. Even the Deists had not completely rejected the idea that liberty was a gift of God and was to be used accordingly. Neither had the radicals of the Jacksonian period completely driven this concept from American thought. But what these schools of thought had been neither able nor willing to do, the Social Darwinists consciously insisted upon. Accordingly, they re-defined the doctrine of human liberty and rights in terms which neither Calvinists nor Jeffersonian Democrats would have been able to recognize or, if they had, would have been willing to accept. The Social Darwinists, and their allies in the fields of psychology and philosophy, so re-defined nature, not only as to make man sub-human, but also in such a way as to make man incapable of possessing a soul and the necessary self-consciousness to be aware of his inherent rights, privileges and duties. In seeking to elevate man Social Darwinism virtually destroyed the very essence of human nature and actually degraded it.

This degradation of man centered in psychology, although it was also a part of the trend in philosophical thought and, in that day, the best example of its pernicious influence is seen in the work of William James, who, in his *Principles of Psychology* (1890), ushered in the Darwinian revolution, and, in so doing, has influenced this study from that time until our own day. His pragmatism was a thoroughgoing adaptation of Darwinian principles to the study of the human mind and personality, beginning with the assumption that truth is always relative, that "truth happens to an idea," that it can never be found, but is always in the process of being made, he went on to deny that the psyche was the soul of man, and to insist that it was only a biological process resulting from the evolutionary development of man. In so doing he contributed greatly to the separation of psychology from philosophy (and from theology), and sought to give it a new home in the natural sciences. He also insisted that his pragmatism was part and parcel of the democratic philosophy in that it accepted the dictum that every man was his own philosopher. The tacit assumption underlying all this was the belief that men were fully capable of directing their own spiritual destinies. James did not deny the God of Christianity, but he relegated him to a place of little or no importance in his psychology. The mind of man was no longer a part of the image of God in man, no longer a substance, but only an activity; by this he meant that the stream of consciousness simply reflects a series of states of mind, all of which are quite different.

The psychological theories of James gained an almost immediate popularity among scholars in all fields of learning in this country, and his influence was widespread; it was most notable, perhaps, in the field of education, but it also contributed to the acceptance of economic and social Darwinism in that it set forth a doctrine of man which was a necessary prerequisite for these other philosophical developments of William Graham Sumner and Lester Frank Ward.

William Graham Sumner and Social Darwinism

William Graham Sumner had been an Episcopalian rector in New Jersey, but resigned his pastorate to enter upon graduate work abroad. Upon his return he was called to serve on the faculty of Yale College in the field of political economy. In this chair he was able to wield a tremendous influence on the mind of American industrialists. As a graduate student he had become absolutely convinced of the correctness of Darwinism, not only as an explanation of the biological process, but also as the new frame of reference in the light of which political and economic thought must be formulated. His own social thought was based upon that aspect of Darwinism which is known as the "survival of the fittest," and Sumner believed that all of life is a struggle, and that liberty, likewise, is the result of a continual struggle by man against the forces of nature. Sumner insisted that all of life is governed by the struggle to survive. In 1879 in a public lecture he said:

> If we do not like the survival of the fittest, we have only one possible alternative, and that is the survival of the unfittest. The former is the law of civilization; the latter is the law of anti-civilization. We have our choice between the two, or we can go on, as in the past, vacillating between the two, but a third plan, the social desideratum—a plan for nourishing the unfittest and yet advancing civilization, no man will ever find.[1]

It is obvious that this could only have been uttered by one who had completely dismissed from his thinking the Christian view of man, and this was the case with Sumner. He denied that man was created by God in his own image and insisted that he is

[1] William Graham Sumner, *Essays*, edited by A. G. Keller and M. B. Davie, New Haven, 1934; cited in Richard Hofstadter, *Social Darwinism in American Thought*, Philadelphia, 1944, p. 43.

completely the product of blind natural (evolutionary) forces. That man has no real control over his own destiny, but is swept along by natural and cultural forces over which he has no control, and in the face of which, he is helpless. This was also true of the social order of which he is a part.

> The truth is that the social order is fixed by laws of nature precisely analogous to those of the physical order. The most that man can do is by his ignorance and conceit to mar the operation of the social laws.[2]

To Sumner, man is as helpless socially as he is physically for precisely the same reason—the laws of society are as immutably fixed as are those of the physical order. Thus, social planning, as the socialists envisioned it, was not only foolish but hopeless. Yet Sumner did leave a rather limited area in which man could try to do something about the inevitable. He believed that mankind is irrational, and therefore, most human activity is irrational. Mankind, according to Sumner, is governed by his mores, or folkways, and to prove this he wrote his famous *Folkways*.

Sumner likewise rejected the whole doctrine of natural rights so fundamental to the democratic philosophy. It would have been impossible for him to maintain a satisfactory doctrine of human rights in view of his total denial of the Christian view of man.

> Modern notions of equality are no doubt to be explained historically as revolts against medieval inequality and status. Natural rights, human rights, equal rights, equality of all men, are phases of a notion which began far back in the Middle Ages. . . . They were counter assertions against the existing system which assumed that the rights were obtained from sovereigns, from which it resulted, that perhaps, no two men had the same or equal rights. The case became different when, in the sixteenth century, the medieval system was gone, the fighting value of the doctrine of equality was exhausted, and it was turned into a dogma of absolute validity and universal application.[3]

---

[2] *The Challenge of the Facts, and Other Essays,* Yale Press, 1914, pp. 55-56.
[3] William Graham Sumner, *Earth Hunger and Other Essays,* New Haven, Yale University Press, 1913, pp. 87-88, quoted in Mosier, *op. cit.,* p. 279.

Thus the doctrine of human rights is a product of a particular era of history, of a particular struggle in which mankind happened to be engaged. At best it had a momentary usability and for this reason could be considered "true" for the moment. But these human rights were not permanent and did not arise from any fundamental characteristic of human nature which is unchangeable in its essence. They were accidental in the sense that if that particular struggle had not taken place in the manner in which it did, or, if it had not taken place at all, the doctrine of human rights could easily have never been put forth at all.

In the light of these more general aspects of his Social Darwinism, Sumner formulated a logically coherent economic and political theory which became a major force in American economic development in the decades after the close of the war, and a dominant factor in the political and economic thinking of the Republican Party in which his theories found a warm welcome. From this vantage point they played a major role in determining the attitudes and policy which the government would adopt toward emerging big business, and the trend towards trusts and monopolies which gained increasing momentum as the century drew to a close.

Basic to Sumner's whole position is his conception of the right as an ethical principle and he treated this point with great clarity.

> Nothing but might has ever made right, and if we include in might (as we ought) elections and the doctrines of the courts, nothing but might makes right now. . . . If a thing has been done and is established by force (that is no force can reverse it), it is right in the only sense we can know and rights will follow from it which are not vitiated at all by the forces in it. There would be no security at all for rights if this were not so.[4]

This is an amazing statement, constituting an open admission that might makes right and that right has no other source but might. In this statement Sumner goes beyond the previous quotation

[4] *Folkways,* p. 65 (Boston, 1906).

in assuming that right (and rights) are not only relative, but their whole existence is dependent upon the relationship which they bear to sheer force, and that without force they will scarcely exist at all. Right and rights belong only to those who are fit and who are thus able to survive in the struggle for existence.

"Rights can never be natural, or God-given or absolute in any sense."[5] The relationship between this conception of rights and that expressed by Machiavelli in the Renaissance is rather obvious, but it is most unlikely that Sumner drew these ideas directly from him. This position flows logically from Social Darwinism. From this basic premise, Sumner then drew the conclusion for economic and political practice. Particularly did he enunciate the justification for the emergence of business monopoly, and for the practices by which they emerged, and in so doing he set forth the role of government in this process.

> Combination and cooperation are so fundamentally necessary that even very low forms are found in symbiosis for mutual dependence and assistance. A combination can exist where each of its members would perish. Competition and combination are two forms of life association which alternate through the whole organic and superorganic domains. The neglect of this fact leads many to socialistic fallacies. Combination is the essence of organization, and organization is the great device for increased power for a number of unequal and dissimilar units brought into association for a common purpose.[6]

According to this theory then, industrial combinations are highly desirable, and monopoly is nothing less than the expression of the laws of nature in economic relations among humans. Monopoly is good in the only sense in which man can know the good. Those forming them had the might which made their actions right. Thus, it was not only foolish but positively harmful for Congress to attempt to legislate in an effort to prohibit the rise of such forms of business combination in this country. It was an

[5] *Ibid.*, p. 29.
[6] *Ibid.*, p. 17, 1940 edition.

attempt to prevent the inevitable as well as the good; and in so doing, Congress would only become an opponent of true human welfare. The only thing left for Congress to do was to gracefully accept the inevitable growth of monopoly and to realize that it was actually in the best interests of the people.

The tremendous difference between this and previous economic thought cannot be denied. It was a drastic innovation in economic theory and constituted a radical departure from both the biblical concept and that which was generally accepted in the formative days of the republic. One could argue that it was not too different from the laissez faire doctrines of Adam Smith which were part of the Revolutionary appeal to the Newtonian conception of natural law. This is true, but it is also true that Adam Smith did recognize the existence of a common good, objectively definable, and this common good was moral in content. His assumption that each man in seeking his own good was, at the same time, aiding that of his fellowman was erroneous and at times, in an industrial society, quite dangerous. But this weakness should not blind us to the fact that this earlier version of laissez faire did hold to an objective moral good which should be the guide for all economic activity. In Sumner's economic theory there is no common good and the moral requirement was totally lacking in his concept of proper economic behavior. Indeed, there was no room for any such requirement in his deterministic conception of economic life and his sub-biblical view of man.

In the second place, it must be pointed out that this theory of Sumner's was contrary to all previous American constitutional philosophy and political practice. The Constitution countenanced no such view of man or of his economic activity advocated in this theory. The Founding Fathers would never admit that the role of Congress in economic regulation was either dangerous or futile, and they would have been utterly bewildered by the assertion that it was actually contrary to the common welfare. They were agreed that it was the function of government to advance and aid commerce and industry. Even though Jefferson, and his allies, were in dissent from Hamilton in his views on commerce, they did not dissent for this reason, but because they were largely agrarian in their outlook and did not like the idea of the industrialization of the new nation.

It must, therefore, be concluded that Social Darwinism, as it was expressed by Sumner, was nothing less than a very sharp break with all existing interpretations of the Constitution and a definite repudiation of all previous federal economic policy.

Sumner himself was quite pessimistic concerning the future of society, and he had come to the conclusion that technology had made democracy virtually impossible in the contemporary world. His basic pessimism was well expressed in the following:

> The great stream of time and earthly things will sweep on in spite of us. It bears with it now all the errors and follies of the past, the wreckage of all the philosophies, the fragments of all the civilizations, the wisdom of all the abandoned ethical systems, the debris of all the institutions and the penalties of all the mistakes. It is only in imagination that we stand by and look at and criticize and plan to change it. Every one of us is a child of his age and cannot get out of it. It will swallow up both us and our experiments. It will absorb the efforts at change and take them into itself as new but trivial components and the great movement of tradition and work will go on unchallenged by our fads and schemes. The things which will change it are the great discoveries and inventions, the new reactions inside the social organism, and the changes in the earth itself on account of the changes in the cosmic forces. These causes will make of it just what, incidentally to them, it ought to be. The men will be carried along with it and be made by it. The utmost they can do by their cleverness will be to note and record their course as they are now carried along, which is what we do now, and is that which leads us to the vain fancy that we can make or guide the movement. That is why it is the greatest folly of which men can be capable to sit down with a slate and pencil to plan out a new social world.[7]

[7] A. G. Keller and Maurice Davie, editors, *Selected Essays of William Graham Sumner*, I, p. 301, Yale Press 1934.

Man could only submit to the nature of which he was a pawn. Pessimism was the only possible conclusion from such a philosophy of life. It was not difficult for Sumner to accept such a conclusion for he had long ago, according to his own testimony, surrendered his Christian faith. Sumner's only hope was that somehow human reason could achieve some few variations in the mores which govern the masses. But Sumner could only say for himself in 1910:

> I have lived through the best period of this country's history. The next generations are going to see war and social calamities. I am glad I do not have to live on into it.[8]

Ultimately, Social Darwinism made a mockery of the very freedom the theological and social liberals were so vociferously defending. To a man, they were charging that Calvinism was destructive of human freedom because of its reliance upon a sovereign God as the supreme sovereign in the affairs of man. Therefore Calvinism had to go and should be replaced by a philosophy of life more congenial to democracy and human liberty. But in the denial that man is a morally responsible being under God, Social Darwinism struck a lethal blow against freedom of any kind, for the sovereignty of God who made man both responsible, and therefore free, was shoved aside in favor of the sovereignty of impersonal natural forces cooperating in human affairs without any foresight or purpose.

Yet, in spite of its unconstitutional character, in spite of its break with previous American political practice and in spite of its denial of the fundamental concepts of freedom, Social Darwinism had a tremendous appeal to many segments of American life, particularly to the emerging business leadership and their allies in the commercial, political and professional life of the nation. Its emphasis upon individualism and its seeming relationship to the actualities of frontier America proved to be a powerful magnet for many, but its basic strength lay in the fact

[8] A. G. Keller, *Reminiscences of William Graham Sumner*, 1933, p. 109. Quoted in Gabriel, *op. cit.*, p. 250.

that it provided a ready-made, and seemingly incontrovertible, justification for the monopolies which were appearing in many segments of the business and commercial life of the nation. It seemed to provide a scientific rationale for the economic actualities of the day. Leading industrialists were not slow to see that they could now claim in their behalf a scientific theory of seemingly impeccable character. The fact that Social Darwinism did lend support to their deeds in the realm of finance and business promotion, needs to be remembered by those who, looking at that era, in the light of a different economic philosophy, come to see these actions in a very different category. There can be no doubt that the growth of monopoly, and many of the methods used to achieve its growth, were the result of, and in thorough agreement with, the concepts of Social Darwinism; and, those who carried out these policies did not feel that they were guilty of anti-social behavior, and they were far from feeling that they were engaged in criminal activity. This does not mean that some of them did not engage in that kind of activity and that they were not aware of it, but it does mean that many of the financial activities of that day were so much a part of the prevailing economic philosophy that they were regarded as legitimate, if not entirely ethical. A case in point was an attempt to merge the Northern Pacific, the Great Northern and Chicago, Burlington and Quincy Railroads into a single operating unit by means of the formation of the Northern Security Company. In 1904, in the famous Northern Securities Company case, the Supreme Court declared that this merger was a violation of the Sherman Act of 1890.

However, by 1950 or so a dramatic change of thought had taken place so that Congress began to assume a very different attitude toward such railroad mergers and began to regard them as desirable. In fact the prevailing opinion in many circles during the 1950's was much like that of those who had favored the formation of the Northern Security Company in 1902, namely, that such a development was good for the country.

Andrew Carnegie set forth the prevailing ideas of the last

twenty-five years of the nineteenth century concerning the meaning of free enterprise and the role of the government in the regulation of the business community in an often quoted article which appeared in the *North American Review* in 1889.

After reviewing the great changes which had taken place during the nineteenth century in the production of goods, a change which had brought such a bounty of improved goods that "the poor enjoy what the rich could not afford" and "what were the luxuries have become the necessities of life." Carnegie went on to say:

> The price which society pays for the law of competition, like the price it pays for cheap comforts and luxuries, is also great; but the advantages of this law are also greater still, for it is to this law that we owe our wonderful material developments, which bring improved conditions in its train. But whether the law be benign or not, we must say of it, as we say of the change of the conditions of men to which we have referred: It is here; we cannot evade it; no substitutes for it have been found, and while the law may sometimes be hard for the individual, it is best for the race, because it insures the survival of the fittest in every department. We accept and welcome, therefore, as conditions to which we may accommodate ourselves, great inequality of environment, the concentration of business, industrial and commercial, in the hands of a few, and the law of competition between these as being not only beneficial, but essential for the future progress of the race. . . .
>
> Objections to the foundations upon which society is based are not in order, because the condition of the race is better with these than it has been with any others which have been tried.[9]

John D. Rockefeller also defended Social Darwinism as a guide to business conduct.

> The growth of a large business is merely the survival of the fittest. . . . The American Beauty Rose can be produced in the splendor

[9] *North American Review,* Vol. CXLVIII, 1889, pp. 253-255.

and fragrance which brings cheer to its beholder only by sacrificing the early buds which grow up around it.[10]

It is quite clear that in this economic philosophy held by Carnegie and others, the doctrine of free enterprise as it was found in Puritanism has undergone a radical change. No longer was it moored in the biblical ethic, but looked to a naturalistic interpretation of natural law. Thus Carnegie, and others, argued that the results of the natural law could not be changed. There was nothing that society could do about its influence in the economic life and furthermore, there was nothing that the American people should desire to do about it. Its justification lay in the pragmatic argument that it worked—it worked by producing a higher standard of material life than the American people had ever enjoyed before. The laboring man now lived better than kings had at one time. The fact that individuals might suffer unduly under such a conception of free enterprise should not alarm society as a whole, for it was a necessary consequence of the survival of the fittest in the economic struggle for existence.

The great weakness in such arguments lay in one area, a weakness inherent in the scientific method of which the theory was a product, namely, its pragmatic character. According to Carnegie, the final test of this philosophy of free enterprise, cast in a Darwinian form, was the fact that it had raised the standard of living for many people, even though its effects were quite hard on some. It was at this point that its vulnerability became very apparent. Deprived of any real defense by the appeal to the Bible and to the moral law revealed in it, Social Darwinism could only stake its claim on the assumption that it brought more benefits than harm to society. For a country which was becoming increasingly democratic, and in which the laboring man was beginning to acquire an increasingly powerful voice, this proved to be a weak defense, for many laboring men, as well as many farmers, took a rather dim view of the law of the survival of the

[10] Quoted in Commager, *The American Mind,* Yale University Press, New Haven, 1950, p. 209.

fittest when it was applied to economic affairs. If a majority of these groups should decide that its effects were not beneficial to the best interests of the nation, then the pragmatic defense which Carnegie, Rockefeller and others had used would fall of its own weight. In an era when the biblical ethic was falling into disrepute under the impact of scientific attacks, and the only ultimate authority was the voice of the majority, then utility would become the final arbiter of what was right and true, a poor substitute, to be sure, for the biblical authority, but one which would have its way in an era which had, to a great extent, deprived itself of its biblical frame of reference, and which had replaced it with man himself.

Lester Frank Ward (1841-1913): Social Darwinism and the Welfare State

In this dilemma which the discontented elements in American life faced with the triumph of Sumner and his form of Social Darwinism, Lester Frank Ward supplied an answer, an answer which he found in the very same Darwinism which Spencer and Sumner had used. By relying on other aspects of the Darwinian thesis he set Darwin in opposition to the Social Darwinism of Sumner and the industrial leaders of the nation.[11] Ward relied, as did Sumner, on the theory of organic evolution for his social and economic theories, but he chose other aspects of Darwin's position to support it. He was repulsed by the concept of the survival of the fittest and its lack of ethical content, its contempt

[11] Many authors prefer to restrict the term "Social Darwinism" to the economic thought found in Sumner, but there is no real reason or necessity for restricting it to Sumner. The economic and social philosophy which Ward developed was as much a part of Darwin, and came from his position as logically as that which found its inspiration in the "survival of the fittest" doctrine. It would almost seem that there has been a silent conspiracy to shield Ward from that reproach which has come to be associated with Social Darwinism in an effort to confer on his position a respectability which it hardly deserves, for it contained all of the essential elements of Sumner's interpretation of Darwin and was just as dangerous, if not more so, to the American constitutional tradition. Ward wrote *Dynamic Sociology and Pure Sociology*.

for democracy and its emphasis upon an industrial aristocracy for economic advancement.

In a determined effort to free social and economic thought from the determinism which was inherent in the use which Herbert Spencer and Sumner had made of Darwin, Ward introduced modifications which he professed to find in Darwin, and in a very real sense, he set up Darwin against the Social Darwinism of the day. Ward admitted that in all lower forms of life environment was the determining factor in the evolutionary process, but that with man the case was quite different, for here the mind of man could, and should, exercise a determining influence on environment. Ward was one of the first to see that the use which Spencer and Sumner were making of Darwin's theories was essentially negative and, that from this negative approach, they had been able to find new strength for the old doctrine of laissez faire in the relationship between government and business. In his *Dynamic Sociology,* and subsequent works, Ward sought to prove that sociology was a positive subject and that man was able to control the process of evolution toward goals which he would choose, and for the realization of which, he would plan a social program. Through his mind man can determine the goals which he wishes to achieve in society. He wrote:

> In this great struggle (for survival) brute force played a diminishing part, and mind an increasing one. Low cunning and animal sagacity, though very prominent, were more and more surplanted by more refined and subtle manifestations of the same psychic principle. This advance was greatly accelerated by the growth of institutions and the establishment of codes of conduct requisite to life in collectivity. The rude animal methods were intolerable and by natural selection, if not otherwise, society discarded them.[12]

Relying entirely on Darwinian principles, as Spencer and Sumner had done, Ward nevertheless came to new and quite different conclusions, conclusions which were much more in line with the

[12] Lester F. Ward, *The Psychic Factors of Civilization* (Boston, 1893), pp. 156-157.

optimism of the American Revolution and Transcendentalism, and which were certainly more attractive to the native optimism which imbued the American of his own day. By applying the dynamic principles of sociology to the problems of American life Ward was convinced that the American people could utilize the forces of evolution for the realization of a new and better life. Man could naturally plan for a better tomorrow by what Ward conceived to be the very simple method of deciding what characteristics the next, and succeeding, generations should possess and then, by simply using the proper methods, to make them a part of the contemporary generation. According to the concept of acquired characteristics, the characteristics that one generation consciously acquired for its own betterment would be transmitted to those which should follow it. Ward called his social philosophy "Meliorism," by which he meant a program for society which reflected a scientific optimism. It was a program of the scientific betterment of the human situation, for Ward insisted that science was the only means by which mankind ever has been, or ever can be, improved, for science utilizes the materials furnished by nature for this purpose. It was really a process by which the forces of evolution would be guided toward the realization of human happiness which, for Ward, was man's chief end in life. Science was to be utilized by society for this purpose. In his writings he lavished upon science, and the scientific method, a kind of praise which virtually deified it.

> Science is the great iconoclast. Our civilization depends wholly upon the discovery and application of a few profound scientific and philosophical principles, thought out by a few great minds who hold the shallow babble of priests in utter contempt and have no time to dabble in theology.[13]

For Ward, science was the salvation of society and sociology was the queen of the sciences. All the evils present in society he attributed to the existence of the competitive system and he

[13] *Iconoclast*, August 1870.

pleaded for its replacement by a system which he called collective achievement. In this insistence on group action for the achievement of human happiness he differed quite radically from Sumner who insisted that human happiness was the product of individual initiative and achievement.

In the actual realm of politics Ward called for the establishment of a sociocracy in place of our government under the Constitution. It was an ideal state, resembling at some points, that set forth by Plato. In his scheme, legislation would not be the product of an elected assembly but the result of legislative experiments carried on by sociologists. Under their trained leadership the sociocracy would be the vehicle by which the different problems to be solved such as poverty, disease, and ignorance, would yield to the magic touch of the new statesmanship. The earth was to be transformed into a kind of Eden where even labor would become pleasant.

But how was all this to be accomplished? Where were the sociocrats to be trained and how would ignorance be banished from the American scene? Ward had an answer—education—for, in his eyes, it was the great panacea. The purpose of education was to enable man to achieve the conquest of nature, which, in turn, would lead to that happiness which is the goal of every human being. In 1893 he wrote:

> Give society education strictly held within assigned limits, and all things else will be added. Even the philosophy required to coordinate existing knowledge would be certain to come in time.[14]

In 1866 in an address, "The Importance of Intellectual Culture" Ward was even more clear in his devotion to education.

> The great panacea for all our doubts and dangers is the thorough and universal education of all the mental powers. With a lofty and polished intellect, the moral and religious natures will shape themselves right. Show me a man with an intellect, refined, lofty,

[14] *Solution of the Great Problem,* quoted in Samuel Chugerman, *Lester Frank Ward,* Duke University Press, Durham, N.C., 1939, p. 465.

and enobled by service in the vast field of science, art and letters, and I will show you one of exceptional moral character and a profound respecter of the sublime and imperishable truths of Him who spoke as never man spoke. Show me an intelligent people and I will show you a moral and religious people.[15]

The importance of Ward's work does not lie solely in the fact that he is considered to be the father of American sociology and that he gave a permanent direction to sociological philosophy in this country. If his influence were largely confined to sociology it would be interesting and would lay claim to some importance, but he still would not have much to say to American political and constitutional historians. Rather it is more accurate to say that in giving this direction to sociological endeavor in this country Ward, in turn, gave to sociology an importance which may not ever have been achieved otherwise. For, in Ward's interpretation of Darwin, sociology was to replace political science and statesmen, the Constitution and the government which had grown up under it in this country. While Sumner had a much greater contemporary impact on the political and business development of this country during their life times, Ward has had the greater influence on American political and constitutional development in the twentieth century.

In his open advocacy of social achievement through the government he laid the foundations for the welfare state philosophy, the New Deal and the other programs which followed it. Because of the very excesses of business in its adolescent era, Ward captured the fancy of many thinking people who were greatly concerned with the trend of economic and social events in the latter decades of the nineteenth and early twentieth centuries, and who looked on competition, sanctified by a laissez faire philosophy, as the cause of the many problems which were emerging. For them Ward offered a solution to the rampant competition which they saw as the great destroyer; this remedy was the collectivist state bringing forth collective achievement—the realization of

[15] Chugerman *op. cit.,* p. 538.

human happiness for human beings who could not realize it by their own individual actions.

It should be noted that this collectivist state offered by Ward was actually nothing more than a thinly disguised totalitarian regime. Not that he intended it to be such, but his position in regard to the individual finding his happiness in the collectivist state was little more than the Hegelian dictum that the individual is nothing outside of the state and that in the state he comes to himself, and from it he derives his rights. Ward replaced the Darwinism of Sumner, which upheld individual action, with a Darwinism that was closely akin to Marx and Nietzsche. For Ward, a sociocratic state was the all in all.

In claiming education as the great ally for the realization of the sociocratic state Ward was really borrowing from Marx the insight that education, properly controlled, would become the very effective means of producing a collectivist state, for, public education was, and is, a form of collectivism. In advocating this policy Ward became the spokesman for Dewey, and the hosts of progressive educators, who joined his ranks in looking upon public education in this country as the great weapon for "the democratizing of the United States," by which they actually meant the socializing, communizing and collectivizing of this country. The collective achievement of Ward was partially fulfilled in the New Deal of Franklin Roosevelt, the ensuing Fair Deal of the Truman era, and the Kennedy administration became the heir to this philosophy of government. The social security programs, medical aid, federal aid to education, and similar projects, all reflect the Social Darwinism of Frank Lester Ward.

It is for this reason that Ward's theological and philosophical outlook become matters of paramount importance for the proper evaluation of social and political philosophy. Although he differed from Sumner in his interpretation of Darwin, he was no less a Darwinian and, no less consistently than Sumner, did he seek to apply Darwinism to the social, economic and political issues of the day.

Ward was more avowedly hostile to evangelical Christianity than was Sumner and he openly broke with Christian orthodoxy at every essential point. Indeed, his attitude toward Christianity was one of active hatred and contempt at times, rather than an intellectual disdain. He was equally opposed to all metaphysical theories and was very close to Marx in his materialism. Materialism permeates every aspect of his system. Man is a product of natural forces and at the same time he is the result of the evolutionary process. All forms of life beneath man are determined by natural law. Man, standing at the apex of the evolutionary scale, has a mind and by its powers he can transform his environment in accordance with his knowledge of nature and its laws. In spite of the fact that Ward repeatedly spoke of the spiritual nature of man, he denied that man has a soul in the biblical sense of the word and he meant by "spiritual qualities" his intellectual capabilities or mind. Man was not created in the image of God and Ward denied the entire biblical account of creation. He believed that science made no provision for such a supernatural origin of man or of the world in which he lives. Ward was probably not a formal atheist, but his philosophy made no allowance for the supernatural or for any activities which the Scriptures ascribe to God in his providential government of nature.

Ward's rejection of the supernatural came out very clearly in his explanation of the rise and functions of human institutions and in his ethical and moral philosophy. He declared that the family in its origin was simply an institution "for the more complete subjugation and enslavement of women and children. . . . The primitive family was an unnatural and autocratic excrescence upon society."[16] He also declared that marriage, like the family is a "whited sepulchre." Thus he easily came to the conclusion that sexual satisfaction is a social necessity and morality is only the product of the rational faculty.[17] Religion for him was simply a mode of enforcing racial purity and safety and it in turn made the church a necessity.

[16] *Pure Sociology*, New York, 1903, p. 353.
[17] *Op. cit.*, p. 389.

Thus the origin of all human institutions was given a naturalistic or humanistic explanation. They all fulfill a purpose imposed on them by the race; the idea that the family, the state, religion and the church were ultimately divine in their origin and were given to man for his own good and for the stabilization of a sinful society was totally abhorrent to Ward. The very clear implication of his writings is that such institutions as the family, marriage, and the church will no longer be necessary or desirable nor will they even be allowed in a state which is under sociocratic control.

The break with orthodox Christianity and the resulting relativism and positivism of his social theory is vividly brought to the fore in his ethical outlook. In his declaration that morality and religion were devices by which mankind has been lulled into a passive acceptance of the status quo Ward came perilously close to Marxian dogma. He completely rejected the biblical view of the ethical and moral life of man and replaced it with one that was naturalistic and hedonistic in its tone. Accordingly he denied the fundamental biblical distinction between good and evil and denied that man was evil.

> The fundamental assumption of the old ethic is that there is something essentially evil in human nature. Its whole purpose is to destroy this evil element. No other science is wholly destructive. . . . But all true science is essentially constructive. Where, then, is the fundamental fallacy which must lurk somewhere in the current of moral philosophy? It lies in the very assumption of evil propensities. They underlie the social world and belong to the nature of man. They never would have been planted there if they had not been necessary to his development. They are evils only insofar as they conflict with individual or social interests. . . .

> This knowledge of the psychic and social forces constitutes the basis of the new ethics. But it seems folly to call it ethics. The real science to which all these ethical considerations belong is "social science"—a true constructive science.[18]

[18] *Glimpses*, V, pp. 275-276.

By such reasoning Ward was able to come to the conclusion that ethics should always be aware of the fact that the purpose of human life is the satisfaction of the desires or happiness. It is not to be found in either our duty to God or to our fellow men. On this point Ward was as clear as he was insistent.

> The world labors under a brave and serious error. It has generally been supposed that our duties to our fellow men and to our Maker are vitally more important than the mere acquisition of knowledge. . . . So usually we devote ourselves to more moral than intellectual culture. This position, however sound it may seem, is as false in logic as it is pernicious in effect. . . . Moral culture leads to abstract sophistries and invalidity. Religious culture, to the exclusion of intellectual training, degenerates into morbid asceticism or bigoted fanaticism. Neither serves to accelerate in the smallest degree the onward march of civilization.[19]

In short, Ward taught an ethical hedonism. The aim of life is happiness. Pleasure means life and pain means death. That is ethical which is useful in the sense that it helps to achieve happiness and to avoid pain and death. Pain and pleasure, therefore, are the only real basis for moral judgment. The revealed will of God and his moral law play no part in the formation of ethical judgments in the sociocratic state. They cannot for they are part of a morality which the true understanding of science will banish from the mind of man. Only dynamic sociology can give the necessary moral insights for the truly educated man.

Even as Ward banished the Christian view of God, man and the ethical life, so did he banish from society the rule of law. Law, as an expression of that which is just and right, had no place in his system. Along with the biblical revelation of the law of God, Ward also rejected the earlier doctrine of natural law as a fixed body of commands and prohibitions. Using the Darwinian interpretation of the law of nature, he not only overturned the Newtonian concept of nature, but along with this he

---

[19] From the unpublished address "The Importance of Intellectual Culture," 1866, quoted in Chugerman, pp. 537-538.

destroyed the foundations of Deism and the American Revolution. For Ward, law, at best, could only be the result of an ever-changing human insight into the workings of nature explained in terms of the Darwinian thesis.

Thus, for the followers of Ward, as for those of Sumner, the political philosophy of the Constitution, along with its actual provisions for the government of the American people, was the product of a social and legal philosophy which could not stand the test of sociocratic scrutiny. The Constitution, for Ward and his group, had no place in a state given over to sociological concepts of government. The United States should no longer be a government of law, but of men, and the law could no longer be regarded as a supreme and fixed instrument of justice, but always subject to change and relative in its meaning and scope. Thus the Constitution should be interpreted according to sociological, rather than legal, principles and the decisions of the Supreme Court should reflect current sociological opinion derived from Darwinian sources, rather than the ancient legal principles coming from either the biblical or Newtonian principles.

Positivism and the Law

Although the Supreme Court remained relatively undisturbed by the theories of Ward and Sumner to a much greater degree than did Congress or the executive branch of the government, the effects of Darwinism and Positivism began to be felt in American jurisprudence and legal thought before the turn of the century, and after 1900 these alien philosophies made startling headway in both our legal theory and practice. Neither did the Supreme Court remain unaffected or totally immune to this kind of constitutional interpretation. As early as 1873 in his dissenting opinion in the *Slaughter House Cases,* Justice Field had voiced an awareness of the dangers of sociological jurisprudence and the inevitable legal relativism involved in it. Field denied the idea that human rights were relative and were the creatures of the state; he held that they were inalienable since they were bestowed by God on man. Field was becoming increasingly disturbed and concerned with the growing radicalism of the Republican majority as he had a very clear insight into the danger of rule by a majority—that it could easily become capricious and very injurious to human rights under the guise of democratic action. The court rejected his arguments, but in 1883 he reiterated his position, and in 1895 in his opinion which declared the income tax provisions of the Wilson-Gorman Tariff Act to be unconstitutional, Field declared:

> If the provisions of the Constitution can be set aside by an act of Congress, where is the course of usurpation to end? The present assault upon capital is but the beginning. It will be but the stepping stone to others, larger and more sweeping, till our political contests will become a war against the rich, a war growing constantly in intensity and bitterness.[20]

In this opinion Field accepted the arguments of ex-Justice Campbell of the Supreme Court who argued for the plaintiffs in this case.

It seems quite clear that Field adopted the use of substantive due process as the best method of defending property rights against the usurpations of a democratic majority which would trample the rights of men in property under foot in their anger against what they considered to be intolerable wrongs committed against them. It cannot be denied that substantive due process was an ideal weapon by which property could, and should, be defended in principle against the unwise and illegal actions of a majority which looked to lawless means to obtain redress. It is also true that after 1885 his views on substantive due process became those of the court, and in several important decisions of this period affecting private property, his views prevailed. But even substantive due process had no defense against the rise of sociological jurisprudence if this theory of the law should gain

---

[20] *Pollock v. Farmer's Loan and Trust Co.* 157 U. S. 607, 1894.

the ear of the court and become the determining factor in its interpretations of the law.

The fears of Justices Field and Miller were not, to say the least, without foundation, although they did not live to see the ultimate triumph of relativism and positivism in our legal theory and practice. Only gradually did the older American concept, that law was rooted and grounded in the very nature of things as an expression of the will of God, give way to the conclusion that law should meet the needs of man rather than conform to the will of God. The former concept resulted in the view that law is not really made, but only discovered, that it is the function of God to give law *(jus dare)*, and it is the function of human government to proclaim and to apply to particular cases the known will of God in statutory legislation.

The exponents of the democratic philosophy from Jefferson on had rejected this view of law and government because of its undemocratic character. It implicitly denied the sovereignty of the people and the idea that the voice of the people is the voice of God. It was for this reason that such eminent American lawyers as Kent and Story had been strongly in favor of incorporating English common law principles into the American legal system while Jefferson had opposed such action even to the point of excluding the study of Blackstone from the curriculum at the newly founded University of Virginia. The philosophy and principles of English common law were directly opposite to those which the exponents of the democratic philosophy felt to be necessary for the new nation, for it looked back to an era when the principles of right and wrong were regarded as being part of the immutable law of God, whether that law be revealed in the Scriptures, or in the unchangeable laws of nature, as discerned by right reason. Conformity to these laws and principles was the duty of a reasonable man.

In 1902 the new jurisprudence, based on philosophical pragmatism, reached the Supreme Court in the appointment of Oliver Wendell Holmes, Jr. as an associate justice by Theodore Roosevelt. He was the recognized leader of the movement to apply the pragmatic methods used in the social sciences to the law. He had clearly set forth this thesis in his *Common Law* (1881), in which he said:

> The life of the law has not been logic; it has been experience. The felt necessities of the time, the prevalent moral and political theories, intuitions of public policy avowed or unconscious, even the prejudices which the judges share with their fellow men, have a good deal more to do with the syllogism in determining the rules by which men should be governed. . . .

> The law embodies the story of a nation's development through many centuries, and that in order to know what it is, we must know what it has been, and what it tends to become. Much that was taken for granted has been laboriously fought for in past times; the substance of the law at any time corresponds fairly well with what was regarded as convenient by those marking or interpreting it, but the form and the machinery and the degree to which it is able to work out desired results, depends much upon its past.[21]

Holmes wrote in 1897: "It is revolting to have no better reason for a rule of law than that it was laid down in the time of Henry IV" (Commager, *American Mind*). And so he insisted that the law must adapt itself to a changing social environment. Law ceases to represent eternal moral principles and comes to be merely an expression of popular sentiment at a given time. The first victory for sociological jurisprudence in the Supreme Court came in 1908 in Muller vs. Oregon, a case dealing with an Oregon statute providing for a shorter working day for women. Brandeis adopted this philosophy and Roscoe Pound and Felix Frankfurter gave it a new strength and wider support.

Although the progress of sociological jurisprudence was slow and uneven, it gained strength in the twentieth century, and after 1940 achieved an ascendency in the thinking of the Supreme

[21] *The Common Law*, Boston, 1881, pp. 1-2.

Court and in many law schools. It also had an equally important and deteriorating influence in criminology, bringing with it the conviction on the part of many criminologists that criminals should be dealt with in terms of the causes of their actions, rather than in terms of the crime. Crime, all too often, ceased to be regarded as such and came to be viewed as merely a type of anti-social conduct. It thus becomes the function of the court to rehabilitate the criminal and to help him to forsake the anti-social behavior of which he is guilty, rather than to punish him according to the dictates of justice for the wrong he has committed. The well-intentioned efforts to find out why criminals commit crimes has become, in too many cases, an instrument for the sacrificing of justice for sociological considerations and the explanations for criminal action have, all too often, become the means of shielding the criminal from the punishment which he deserves. Sociologists have been preferred to lawyers, and sociological theories to the historic concepts of jurisprudence in many American criminal courts. Crimes are explained away in terms of environmental pressures, and criminals are excused because they have yielded to the effects of their environment on their behavior. The accused persons are turned over to psychologists, psychiatrists, and social workers for their rehabilitation, a practice not wrong in itself under certain conditions, but too often this kind of treatment lends itself to a kind of rehabilitation which pays little or no attention to the problem of guilt involved in the crime, but simply seeks to bring back the accused one into a better pattern of social adjustment. The sense of guilt is frequently erased as the prisoner is made to feel that he was a victim of environmental factors and his responsibility to society consists in refinding his place in it.

Criminologists trained in this philosophy are too often the source and inspiration of these movements which seek to do away with capital punishment on the grounds that it does not deter crime, and makes no provision for the rehabilitation of the prisoners. Both of these charges have an element of truth in them, but they stem from an improper conception of the reason for the death penalty in certain types of cases. The advocates of the abolition of the death penalty fail to realize that there are certain kinds of crimes so offensive in the sight of God, and so dangerous to the well-being of society, that those who are guilty of them do not deserve a program of rehabilitation, and that the interests of justice, divine and human, are only served when capital punishment is the only method of properly dealing with them.

It should be observed that those who advocate the abolition of the death penalty have already departed from biblical standards and no longer see sin in its biblical perspective. Either consciously or unconsciously, they look upon sin primarily as an offense against society rather than a violation against the will of God. Thus, society has the final say as to how it should be dealt with; sin is no longer an offense against the commands of a righteous and holy God, but merely a lack of the proper social adjustment. It thus becomes the role of psychology, or psychiatry, to restore the criminal so that he may once again take his place in society.

The Further Invasion of Darwinism and Pragmatism in American Society

The acceptance of Darwinism not only reshaped American constitutional and political thought in the narrower sense of the word, but it also wrought a veritable revolution in every aspect of American thought and practice. It brought into focus a new world and life view by which every aspect of intellectual interest was to be reshaped according to the principles of Darwinian thought. Thus, there came into being an evolutionary concept of economics, an evolutionary concept of education, an evolutionary concept of human history and all these, in turn, were the result of the fact that a whole new evolutionary concept of man replaced the biblical doctrine; even the democratic philosophy of the Jeffersonian and Jacksonian eras was rewritten to give place to this evolutionary conception of human nature. It was this new conception which furnished the mainspring for the new philosophies of history, education, economics, and literature. Man, rather than God, was now the center of reference, and neither theism or Deism had much to say to the Darwinian mind. John Fiske tried to salvage something of theism in his theistic evolution, but his effort was futile and rather pathetic. The self-conscious Darwinist left no more place for the biblical view of Providence in the affairs of man than the Darwinian biologist left for it in the process of creation. The God of the Scriptures was being banished from the affairs of men in much the same way as he had already been banished from any control over the laws of nature. Evolution, the process of progressive change, was now the deity controlling human life, as well as the universe, of which man was but an infinitesimal part.

American philosophy immediately reflected the changing intellectual environment with the appearance of pragmatism and empiricism in the works of William James, Charles Pierce and John Dewey. William James popularized the term "Pragmatism," but John Dewey carried it to its logical conclusions. The philosophy itself seems to have had its origins in the informal discussions which were being held at Harvard University by a group consisting of John Fiske, Oliver Wendell Holmes, Jr., William James and others about 1870. In 1876 James blazed new trails in the study of psychology when he established the first psychological laboratory in this country, and in 1890 he published his *Principles of Psychology,* in which he applied Darwinian naturalism to the study of the mind. The radical trend of this thinking is clearly seen in his insistence that the mind is not a substance, but only an activity.

John Dewey applied the pragmatism expounded by James to the whole field of education; his educational philosophy was simply an application of his basic thought which he called Instrumentalism. By this term he meant that ideas become true if they are of use, if they can be used in society. Dewey said that knowledge is always a matter of the use which is made of experience and natural events. The origin of knowledge is in the senses, but Dewey went further than a mere empiricism; the mere experience does not constitute knowledge, but the use which the individual makes of this knowledge gained through experience. Dewey took the Darwinian theory to its logical conclusions and regarded all of life as an experiment itself. For Dewey there was no such thing as objective, absolute truth, but only a warranted assertibility, by which he meant something that could be taken to be true because it had worked in human experience and therefor had an instrumental worth, or value.

Dewey left almost no room for the supernatural in his philosophy, and little more for metaphysics in the traditional meaning of the term. He, like William James, operated within a framework supplied by Darwin's evolutionary naturalism. Dewey was convinced that supernaturalism had no place at all in his system, and, in this, he was quite correct, for he saw that there is no common ground between Christian theism on the one hand and evolutionary naturalism on the other.

Dewey's importance as a philosopher does not lie only in his rejection of the traditional methods and concepts of philosophy, but in his attempt to give his radical empiricism, or instrumentalism, a social value in spite of its highly individualistic character. His instrumental approach to truth, or unwarranted assertibility, was highly subjective and logically destroyed the possibility of any public apprehension of what the individual conceived to be true. But Dewey was tremendously impressed with the possibility, which he thought he saw in his system, for a planned progress in society through the use of the experimental method. Thus, Dewey was a philosopher of democracy and, in a certain sense, he was an apostle of democracy, and education was the institution through which he would work to remake society in the light of Instrumentalism.

Dewey's greatest importance in a theological interpretation of American history is to be found in the revolution which he brought about in the philosophy, principles, purposes and methods of education. He applied his Instrumentalism to education in a remarkably consistent and thorough manner and, in so doing, he re-wrote American educational practice in the light of his evolutionary philosophy, largely derived from Darwin. By 1895 Dewey was putting his educational theories to the test in his famous experimental school at the University of Chicago, but the final victory in this revolution in education did not come until after 1920 when Dewey flooded the American public schools with his disciples, and local school boards and local school systems became saturated with a philosophy which more often than not they little understood, until it was almost too late to undo the damage which had been done in the intellectual and spiritual development of several generations of students in the name of education.

It is, of course, too much to say that a "Darwinizing" of American society would not have come without the pragmatism of James and the instrumentalism of Dewey, for Darwinism had an appeal all of its own. But there can be no doubt that the introduction of the theory of evolution into the philosophy and practice of American education gave to Darwin a far wider reach, and a far greater hearing, than he would have gained without such a powerful ally located in such a strategic position. For the revolution in education became a powerful means for the furthering of the intellectual revolution which Darwin made possible.

It was the purpose of Dewey to bring education to the aid of society so that it would have those experiences which would contribute to its material progress and its further democratization, which for Dewey and his colleagues meant, a collectivization of industry and commerce in the hands of the central government. Dewey without accepting all that Ward had in mind, obviously agreed with Ward that the hope of society lay in education and that education was the pathway to a socially desirable collectivism.

Thus Dewey democratized education so that it might give to

the youth of the country those democratic experiences in the learning processes which, in turn, would eventually produce that type of leadership which would welcome this collectivism, and to be so trained as to help bring about its realization in America.

For this purpose the "child centered" curriculum was advocated to replace the traditional subjects which dealt with objective truth and factual data in the sciences, mathematics, history, language, and other related fields. The historic liberal arts training in the high school was replaced by a new curriculum which ostensibly was designed for the training of better citizens, but was actually a tool for producing a generation bereft of theological, moral, and even intellectual convictions. The essential anti-intellectualism of Dewey's instrumentalism was translated into actual educational practice and truth as such was no longer the concern of the teacher for his students. Rather was the purpose of the curriculum to produce correct attitudes, which correctness was largely dependent on the contribution which they would make for the further "democratization" of American society.

Inevitably the older insistence that students master mathematics, the sciences, history, English grammar and composition, and foreign languages for their own sake and intrinsic importance was replaced by the belief that these were the subjects which were not important for their own sake, but were the most instrumentally useful for the training of good citizens for a democracy; this belief gained currency in educational circles to an alarming degree.

As alarming as this trend was, an even greater menace was the underlying philosophy which guided this new educational development. Dewey's conviction that there was no truth, but only a "warranted assertibility" had many dangerous implications which were not always apparent to some of his faithful and enthusiastic devotees who took progressive education theory and practice to every corner of the nation. This educational philosophy was, as Dewey himself conceded, anti-Christian. It struck at the very heart of biblical principles. The psychology on which it was based denied that man had a soul but taught that he was just an animal, but higher in intelligence than other animals. It never seemed to occur to Dewey that his denial of God and truth logically led to a denial of the men who were to be taught. In spite of the fondness of the progressives for proclaiming that they were interested in the child, and that the curriculum must be child-centered, it was at this very point that one of the most basic weaknesses of the whole program became most apparent. Their philosophy denied that children were personalities and were, therefore, worthy of being taught. Dewey not only had no truth to teach, but no one to teach it to except animals of a fairly high intelligence, who were to be taught by other animals of the same general level of intellectual ability. The psychology of the Progressives made a shambles of the entire program because it denied that there were persons to be taught.

In the light of these facts, it is no wonder that progressive education made a mockery of the very practice of teaching. The democratic philosophy which they followed as a kind of gospel demanded that democracy be practiced in the classroom if the educational program were to contribute to the further democratization of society. Thus, the teacher no longer taught his classes in subject matter, or even insisted upon a minimal amount of discipline as necessary for learning to take place. The class rooms became democratically managed, which usually meant that the teacher was to abdicate his place of authority and allow the students to set up a democratic regime for the management of the class. In the progressive schools discipline broke down; in some places a virtual anarchy resulted.

Beneath these obvious dangers lay two greater ones for the future of constitutional government in this country. The strong antipathy which these Progressives had for the teaching of history, as such, and their equal insistence that it must be studied as a kind of current events situation, that only those facts which had some relationship to the dominant purpose of furthering the democratic society be presented, brought disastrous consequences upon the students. They lost almost all contact with the history of the nation, except as certain selected events and movements were used to illustrate contemporary events and issues, and actually knew so little about their national past that the present lost most of its meaning for them. Several generations of students were graduated as young citizens who knew little or nothing of the real issues and movements in American history, and even less of the Constitution, its philosophy, provisions and implications for their own day. There was in Dewey's philosophy of education a devouring anti-intellectualism which, if not checked, would ultimately destroy the entire system.

Of even greater danger than this anti-intellectualism was the flagrant and almost complete denial of the Christian faith which underlay the whole movement. Not only were the doctrines of God and man set aside in favor of evolutionary concepts, but there was no room for such Christian truths as sin, redemption, eternal life, the necessity for living one's life for the glory of God and eternal damnation for those who rejected the offer of salvation in Jesus Christ. An essential materialism characterized this philosophy which made it, in many cases, an easy stepping stone to a complete acceptance of Marxian communism. Dewey held in common with Marx several basic doctrines which both had received from John Locke. It was not accidental that many communists came from the ranks of Progressive philosophers, teachers and students. Communism was the logical, if not the inevitable, destiny of those who consciously adopted Dewey's system of thought in its entirety.

Thus education became increasingly the greatest danger which constitutional government had to cope with in this country. In spite of the fact that advocates of public education loudly proclaimed its virtues in the teaching of patriotism of the best kind, it was not only failing to accomplish this purpose, but was actually introducing into the intellectual life of the nation a philosophy of government which was destructive of all the values which the Founding Fathers of 1787 had sought to write into the frame of government which they were providing for the new republic.

The Bible has been estimated to have furnished seventy-five per cent, or more, of the total curriculum of the colonial schools, but this preponderance began to decline in the Jacksonian era, and the process of eliminating biblical material from the curriculum accelerated after 1870, and in the twentieth century scarcely five per cent of the curriculum can claim to have any particularly biblical significance or relationship. The democratic philosophy of education, as well as of the state, could not tolerate this biblical foundation for education; and, since 1940 the aid of the Supreme Court has been enlisted in a battle against any Christian material in the educational program of the nation. The issue at this point transcends such controversies as those which rage over whether the Bible shall be read, and prayers be a part of the daily school program. As important as these acts of worship undoubtedly are, they are not the central issue. The heart of the controversy lies in whether our educational program shall be theistic in nature, at best neutral, and at worst, directly hostile to the Christian faith.[22]

The demand that education be freed from any sectarian control and indoctrination has merely been a convenient wedge for the advocates of democracy to lead a campaign for the paganization of the school systems of America. The changes which have taken place in education are not merely a subtraction of a former definitely Christian philosophy; they are an addition of elements which can only bring about the destruction of the American system of government.

Pragmatism and the New Trends in Historiography

Far more than the previous revolts in American scholarship against orthodox Christianity, Darwinism worked itself into every aspect and every area of the American intellectual scene to an astonishing degree, and the writing of history no less than social, economic and political theory reflected the advances registered by

[22] Actually no school system can be neutral in regard to the truths of Scripture for the simple reason that no man can be neutral in regard to the truth of God revealed in Jesus Christ.

the evolutionary interpretation of life by American scholarship. Coming as it did at a time when historical scholarship in this country was coming into a new era of importance and was achieving for itself a firm place in the curricula of the graduate schools which were being formed under the impetus of the model offered by the German universities and Johns Hopkins Graduate School, their American counterpart, Darwinism was in a strategic position to become the philosophical basis for the professional historians being trained by these institutions. Historiography was now to become "scientific," and by scientific the new historians meant adjusting their concepts of history to the evolutionary outlook of Darwin. In accomplishing this purpose it also abandoned the romantic outlook which had characterized the earlier historians, such as George Bancroft, and adopted a naturalistic realism offered by the Darwinians. Nearly all the historians of the romantic era had looked to a moral frame of reference in their interpretation of men and events; Bancroft had seen in history the evidence of a divine government in the affairs of men and his enthusiasm for democracy was tinctured with these other two ideals.

However, in the new history which emerged in the last two decades of the nineteenth century, and which became dominant in the twentieth century, this democratic idealism was no longer the dominant role in the interpretation of history. The Darwinian postulate replaced the democratic theories of the Age of Jackson, particularly the idea that adaptation to environment is the key to historical development. By using this aspect of Darwinism the historians were able to bring about a synthesis between two seemingly incompatible concepts, democracy and determinism. Not all historians were able to retain in their thinking this romantic faith in American democracy for they saw that in the new determinism, furnished by Darwin, there was no place for democracy or even human freedom in any form.

Brooks Adams yielded to the pessimistic thrust of his Darwinian position and wrote:

As the universe which at once creates and destroys life is a complex of infinitely varying forces, history can never repeat itself. It is vain, therefore, to look in the future for some paraphrases of the past. Yet, if society be, as I assume it to be, an organism operating on mechanical principles, we may perhaps, by pondering upon history, learn enough of those principles to enable us to view more intelligently than we otherwise should, the social phenomena about us. What we call civilization is, I suspect, only in proportion to its perfection a more or less thorough social centralization while centralization very clearly is an effect of applied science. Civilization is, accordingly, nearly synonymous with centralization and is caused by mechanical discoveries which are the application of scientific knowledge . . . and we perceive on a little consideration that from the first great and fundamental discovery of how to kindle fire, every advance in applied science has accelerated the social movement until the discovery of steam and electricity in the eighteenth and nineteenth centuries quickened the movement as the movement has never been quickened before.[23]

For Adams, history was governed by impersonal forces: "If men move in a given direction, they do so in obedience to an impulse as automatic as the impulse of gravitation."[24]

Likewise, Henry Adams was forced to forsake his earlier romantic ideas of democracy in history in the face of the almost inescapable conclusions of his deterministic frame of reference. Appointed to teach medieval history at Harvard University under Charles Eliot, he shared the common purpose of his contemporary historians of trying to make history a social science. In pursuing this aim, Adams felt compelled to surrender the study and teaching of the Middle Ages, and accordingly chose the early national period of the United States as his field of effort, turning out in 1891 the first volume of his justly famous *History of the United States in the Jefferson and Madison Administrations,* but

[23] Quoted in Henry Steele Commager, *The American Mind,* p. 288. Yale Press, New Haven, 1950.
[24] *Idem.*

even here he could not find the satisfaction for which he was seeking. He was betrayed by the success of his endeavor; history as a social science failed to yield the meaning which he felt it must contain to make its study worthwhile. He came to the conclusion that there is a force and nothing more in this world, that "man is a part of nature's deterministic scheme, a pawn in a cosmic chess game."

> No one is likely to suggest a theory that man's convenience has been insulted by nature at any time or that nature had consulted the convenience of any of her creations. . . . In every age man has bitterly and justly complained that Nature hurried and hustled him for inertia almost invariably ending in tragedy.[25]

The theories of history held by Brooks and Henry Adams were significantly different from those which the Founding Fathers held and it is quite certain that their determinism made mockery of the whole concept of constitutional government and human liberty. Needless to say it stood at great odds with the whole biblical perspective of man as a moral agent and of the historical process in which man played an important role. The denial of Christian theism in the ranks of historians logically led to the abandonment of the serious study of history as a quest for meaning.

But these pessimists who turned in despair from the optimism of the democratic philosophy to a meaningless determinism as the key to history were a lonesome minority in American historiography in the period from 1890 to 1940. The dominant note was one of optimism, an optimism derived from the very Darwinian determinism which had driven some to despair. These optimistic historians interpreted American history in terms of the forces of environment, forces which man could and had controlled and which he would continue to control. The historians of the new era reduced these forces to two, namely economic influences and the frontier. The leader, if not the originator, of the new group was

[25] Henry Adams, *The Education of Henry Adams,* Boston, 1918, pp. 496-497.

Frederic Jackson Turner whose *The Significance of the Frontier in American History* proved to be an epochal work, bringing into almost instant popularity a thorough-going environmental interpretation of American history, the dominant factor in which Turner found to be the frontier. He said:

> American democracy is fundamentally the outcome of the experience of the American people in dealing with the West. . . . Western democracy through the whole of its earlier period tended to be the production of a society of which the most distinctive fact was the freedom of the individual to rise under conditions of mobility and whose ambition was the freedom and well-being of the masses. American democracy was born of no theoretical dreams. . . . It was not carried in the Mayflower to Plymouth. It came out of the American forest, and it gained new strength each time it touched a new frontier. Not the Constitution but the free land, and abundance of natural resources opened to fit the people, made the democratic type of society in America for three centuries.[26]

The pragmatic nature of this approach to our national past is quite obvious. Our environment has produced our democracy, our freedom and our free institutions. Each advance of the frontier westward was actually another successful response to the challenge of the environment and could mean the continued enrichment of the democratic process.

Another group, almost as numerous, claimed to find the key to American history in terms of economic developments and this school sought to rewrite the colonial era, the coming of the Revolution, the writing of the Constitution, the conflict between Jefferson and Hamilton, the coming of Jackson, the slavery struggle and secession strictly in terms of the economic issues involved. The dean of this group was Charles A. Beard who was a contradictory character. He rejected every view of history which impinged on human freedom (including Calvinism and all other

[26] Frederic Jackson Turner, *Frontier in American History,* pp. 266-293. Quoted in Commager, *op. cit.,* p. 296.

forms of evangelical Christianity), yet he became the means for the widespread adoption of the view that history is economically determined. His inaugural statement of this view is found in his *An Economic Interpretation of the Constitution* (1913), and his *Economic Origins of Jeffersonian Democracy*. The approaches of both Turner and Beard found their way into the graduate schools, the colleges and high schools of the nation and thousands, perhaps even millions, of students, were unconsciously molded into a pattern of thought concerning our national origins which was not only quite misleading, but ultimately very dangerous to the stability of the government under the Constitution. An increasing number of members of Congress, state and federal judges, and state and federal administrative officers were trained under professors who taught history in the light of these philosophies. At a time when the teaching of history in schools and colleges was coming of age, economic determinism was gaining the ascendency in historical scholarship to a degree which the public failed to recognize. As a result, thousands of students received a view of the American past which ruled out not only all divine participation and control in the affairs of man, but which also denied any moral aspects to human action in the past. God and morality were banished from the American scene by these historians who fondly imagined that they were preserving the dignity and freedom of man by interpreting human history in terms of an economic determinism which could only make a mockery of the very democracy they were seeking to preserve.

Revolutionary concepts and the accompanying pragmatism also played a dominant role in the emerging study of economics. The study of economics was just beginning to be recognized as a discipline, independent from political science and sociology, at the time when Social Darwinism was invading American thought. Historians were seeking to make the study and teaching of history a distinct social science. American economists were very anxious to assert the value of the study of economics in the academic life of the nation on the one hand, and to give evidence of their independence from the Manchester School of Economics on the other. A group of young economists met in 1885 at Saratoga Springs, New York, to found the American Economics Association; among them were Richard T. Ely, Simon Patten, Washington Gladden and Edwin Seligman. In their statement of principles they declared:

> We regard the state as an agency whose positive assistance is one of the indispensable conditions of human progress.

> We believe that political economy is still in an early stage of development . . . and we look not so much to speculation as to historical and statistical study of actual conditions of economic life for the satisfactory accomplishment of that study.

> We hold that the conflict of labor and capital has brought into prominence a vast number of social problems whose solution requires the united efforts, each in its own sphere, of the church, the state and of science.[27]

This group openly avowed its rejection of the laissez faire theory of economic policy as "unsafe in politics and unsound in morals" and "suggesting an inadequate explanation of the relations between the state and the citizens." Actually the basic principles of this group were: the belief that the study of economics should be inductive and pragmatic and that the state should have an increasing role in the economic life of the nation. Their emphasis on ethics as a guide was more apparent than real. Their avowal that there must be an appreciation of ethical as well as scientific considerations was quite misleading, for Ely said that the ethical school of economists (by which he meant his group as against the Manchester School), had it as their aim to direct the economic and social growth of mankind, but these ethical considerations were to be found in the laws of human progress, which laws were pragmatically obtained and were not to be found in the Scriptures. It is obvious that there was a division of purpose in the thinking

[27] *American Economic Review,* Sup. March, 1936, p. 144. Quoted in Ralph Gabriel, *The Course of American Democratic Thought,* pp. 298-299.

of this group. While there were some who placed their faith in free enterprise, others placed a greater faith in the intervention of the state in economic affairs, and were in their thinking headed in the direction of the contemporary theory and practice of the welfare state. On the whole, it can be safely said that this group was inclined to pay little heed to the biblical concept of government and to scriptural mandates concerning the use of wealth.

Social Darwinism: An Evaluation

Social Darwinism was the inspiration for the greatest intellectual revolution that was to take place in the intellectual history of this country. It achieved a degree of penetration in the major areas of American cultural activity and a following that neither Transcendentalism or Deism had been able to gain previously, or that subsequent movements would achieve in the twentieth century. Its triumph was due to three factors: its intimate relationship to the latest developments in scientific thought, its pragmatic character which brought it close to the American temper, and its alliance with progressivism in American education. But it would be a mistake to locate its importance simply in terms of its penetration into the intellectual life of the nation. Rather does its influence lie in the fact that it brought into focus a new and totally different world and life view. Darwinism was not simply a new development in philosophical and theological thought; it was a revolution which not only banished Christian theism and all of its implications from political, social and economic theory, but it sought to rewrite the whole ideological structure in terms of Darwinian naturalism and the scientific method with their corollary of pragmatism. Darwinism was not only incompatible with Christian orthodoxy in the narrower or theological sense, but it was diametrically opposed at every point to that world and life view which is inherent in biblical orthodoxy. Darwinism set aside the Christian view of the state, of economic activity and social relationships in favor of a philosophy which looked to the theory of organic evolution for its sanctions and norms. The very foundations of our intellectual inheritance from the past, colonial and early national, were threatened by an inundation of a philosophy with which it had nothing in common.

Neither did its mechanistic conception of man and his political, social and economic life look well when set alongside of the philosophy of the era of the Revolution. The freedom which Jefferson had envisioned in 1776 was in as great jeopardy as that which the Puritans had in mind. The democracy of the Declaration of 1776 could not long survive in a world which was mechanistically determined and in which human liberty and human values were interpreted according to the dictates of an evolutionary process which laid the emphasis on change rather than on their fixed character. As the result all values could only become relative, and, therefore, no longer trustworthy or authoritative guides to political, social and economic action.

The theological conflict between Darwinism and orthodoxy in the area of theology gave birth to a more extensive and intense conflict on a far-flung battlefield for the minds of men. If orthodoxy should lose this battle, there would be no defense against the utter collapse of that civilization and culture which looked to that orthodoxy for their very life blood. If Darwinism and Pragmatism should win, then every aspect of American life would be subject to a revolution which would ultimately overthrow constitutions, government, free enterprise and that social structure with its emphasis on the family, the church, the school and the state itself as agents for the realization of the will of God for human society, sanctioned by him, endowed by him with certain powers and responsibilities and ultimately responsible to him for the manner in which they conducted the discharge of these responsibilities.

This was the philosophical and theological issue which confronted the United States as it greeted the dawn of the twentieth century with an optimism concerning the culture of the nation which many Americans find very difficult to understand as they contemplate the history of its first six decades.

5

The Social Gospel and Its Political
Effects in American Life

It is fitting at this point in the discussion to recall the basic thesis of this study; namely that political, economic and social actions are the expression of the dominant philosophy of a given era in American history and that this dominant philosophy is ultimately the product of a theological climate. When Calvinism was dominant the political, economic and social life of the people reflected this fact; when Deism gained the ascendency, this change was made manifest in the Revolutionary era. When Deism gave way to Transcendentalism, corresponding changes took place in the political, economic and social currents. The effects of Social Darwinism were equally profound. The impact of the Social Gospel on American life was probably of even greater importance simply because this movement avoided the outright determinism of Sumner, the iconoclasm of Ward and the paganism of the rising socialist movement with its strong ties with Marxian materialism. Because this Social Gospel movement claimed to be Christian in outlook, and appealed to the Bible, it acquired in the eyes of many people a respectability which the more obvious departures from orthodoxy, as evidenced in Sumner and Ward, could not achieve. The misuse and misinterpretation of the historic Christian message involved in the Social Gospel was not obvious to many Christians and they did not seem to see the vital shift in emphasis which was a necessary consequence of this movement.

The Social Gospel was not simply the result of a sudden urge on the part of religious leaders to produce a new message for the church because they were tired of the old, old story of personal redemption. That this was true of some of those in the vanguard of the Social Gospel movement cannot be doubted, but it would be highly inaccurate and grossly unfair to much of its leadership to reduce the movement to such simplified causes. There was much more to it than this. The honest evangelical must take into account these other factors in his evaluation of the movement which has left such an imprint not only on the church of America, but on the whole social, economic and political fabric of the nation.

It would not be misleading to say that the greater majority of these ministers and intellectual leaders who espoused the new gospel did so because they were convinced that the old Gospel of redemption of the Reformers, was no longer applicable to the problems of their day, that its message was no longer an adequate statement of the needs of man, nor a completely satisfactory answer to those needs. They were likewise convinced that the discoveries of Darwin, and others, had rendered it virtually impossible for honest scholarship to hold to the inspiration of the Scriptures, the doctrine of creation and the fall as these truths had been presented by the church. It was their conviction that unless the message of the church were to be made intellectually tenable and respectable, the church could not long survive in a scientific age in which the test tube and the microscope had gained a kind of sacramental character, and the laboratory itself had become a kind of temple in which man delighted to worship a God which science would bring to him infallibly.

These scientific pronouncements which had issued forth from Darwin and his fellow scientists had given a new respectability to the age-old urge of man to refashion the biblical account of the fall of man, and to make him something much more than a sinner worthy of, and condemned to eternal death by a righteous and sovereign God. The very awe in which scientific pronouncements were held by a large segment of the public gave those intellectuals a new courage and a new boldness in their open renunciation of the evangelical message. The temptation constantly confronts man to make such a decision and it was reenforced by the scientific formulas of the age. However, the appearance of the Social Gospel cannot be reduced to this basis. There was much more to it.

The second major factor was the fact of the industrial revolution and the many social problems which it brought to the nation. These issues assumed a new and a vital importance after 1865, and they could not be ignored. The industrial revolution had come to this country during the second dispute with England which culminated in the War of 1812. But our industrial growth, while important and notable in the intervening decades, was not so sudden and so dynamic in character as to bring the pressing problems which would appear soon after 1865. There had been a very impressive industrial and commercial expansion in the North and, to a certain extent in the South between 1850 and 1860, but the coming of the war in 1861 intensified this development in the North in an unexpected manner. The war placed a heavy demand upon the railroads, industry and agriculture for the first time in American history, and big business was firmly established in the economic pattern as a result. This is not to say that combinations and the "trusts" would not have eventually come to this nation, but there can be no doubt that the war not only accelerated their arrival in an unusual manner, but also gave them a peculiar character. Big business not only grew up with almost no federal regulation to guide and control it, but its development was, to a great extent, the result of governmental pressure. The federal government was dependent upon manufacturers, the railroads and industry in general for the successful prosecution of the war to a degree unprecedented in American history; and this very dependence precluded any great amount of government regulation of business growth and practices both during the war and in those years which immediately followed the coming of peace. A rather "chummy" relationship had developed between the party in power and industrial leadership which made any effective regulation and business practices well nigh impossible. Thus, with the connivance of government and perhaps its active inspiration, big business developed an attitude of irresponsibility toward its thousands of employees and the public in general, which was not conducive to a sound economy or social structure.

It is possible to make too much of this trend and to emphasize this aspect of our history beyond all proportion as some extremely liberal scholars have done, so distorting the picture in favor of socialism; but, it is also possible to ignore those economic and social developments of the period after 1865, and in the early years of the twentieth century, and bring about a falsification of another sort. It cannot be denied that the railroads played fast and loose with the public interest, charging rates and indulging in practices which were against the public welfare. It cannot be denied that monopolies and trusts appeared in almost every segment of American industry; that a financial monopoly developed in New York which controlled the economy to a much greater extent than was desirable or healthy. Neither can it be denied that slum conditions infested the large cities, that unhealthy working conditions and long working days brought only drabness and dreariness to the lives of hundreds of thousands of workers who spent their days in factories which were dangerous and unhealthy, working for very low wages which barely made it possible for them to purchase the necessities of life. There is abundant evidence of all of this, and also that there was a growing social unrest among the working classes and the farmers; this unrest was united with communist overtones in the depression of 1873, and with a dangerous radicalism during the Populist Movement of the 1890's. Many observers were fully aware of the fact that all was not well on the American economic and social scene and they were searching for remedies adequate for the occasion. All of this must be said as an explanation for the rise of the Social Gospel and for a proper understanding of its background and import for theology and for the political development of the nation since 1865. It can and should be said in behalf of the advocates of the Social Gospel that they were very much aware of these developments and felt that the church must play a role in their solution. They were also convinced that the Gospel as it had been preached did not speak with sufficient clarity or authority to their own day. They were likewise of the opinion that evangelicals, on the whole, were not really interested in the problems or their solution.

They were obviously in serious error in their assumption that the historic Christian message was neither relevant or adequate for the issues of an industrial era and they were on even more dangerous ground when they felt that the biblical message should be brought into harmony with the scientific temper of the times in order to be intellectually attractive. They were correct, to a degree, in their assumption that evangelicals did not share their burning passion for the correction of the problems of an emerging industrial social order. However, they too often failed to understand why they were unable to enlist the sympathetic interest of the evangelical church in their program of social reform. For this apparent insensitivity to these evils on the part of the evangelicals there were at least two causes. In the first place, the very swiftness of the transition from an agricultural to an industrial urban culture was such that many Americans of all political and theological persuasions did not comprehend the nature of the change taking place before their very eyes and did not catch up in their thinking with the situation as it actually existed. This "social lag" was by no means confined to evangelicals, but was rather common among all groups. There was also a second factor which brought a hesitancy on the part of many Christians as to what their duty was at such a time. They had grave doubts about the whole program of the Social Gospel, both as to the theology which guided it, and the program which its advocates were pursuing. Evangelicals who had a great awareness of their own personal responsibility to society were in great doubt about the course which many liberals were urging on the church as a corporate body and they were alienated by the heresy and obvious deviations from the historic orthodoxy which characterized the Social Gospel movement.

This is not an issue which is easily settled, for conservatives still look, with deep suspicion, on social and economic programs which liberals in the church seek to urge on the denominations as part of the Christian message, entertaining well-founded doubts that the Scriptures would support the programs which the liberals advocate. They have a deep conviction that often times the social expression of Christianity which liberal groups so consistently uphold are not really the social expression of the Gospel at all, but the expression of a spurious gospel which denies the great truths of the Scriptures.

The Social Gospel as it developed in American Christianity was not, therefore, simply an expression of the world and life view inherent in Christianity as Puritanism was in the colonial period. It was a new world and life view having its inspiration and foundations in the radical departure from that orthodox Christianity which was Puritanism. The Social Gospel was not the Gospel, thus the political program it sponsored for the nation was not derived from the Scriptures, but from a new theology, partly biblical, to be sure, but to a greater extent, a religious adaptation of Darwinism mixed with not a little Pelagianism and humanism. The Social Gospel, in its essence, represented at many points a complete negation of the basic truths of orthodox Christianity and, at many other points, such a synthesis of Christian and non-Christian elements that the original Gospel could only be dimly perceived beneath the layers of human philosophy. Evangelicals had good and sufficient reasons to be distrustful of the leadership of the movement and the reforms which they were advocating. Their uneasiness over the increasing radical nature of the movement certainly justified their reluctance to become a part of it and reenforced their doubts as to the soundness of the entire program. Evangelicals were really convinced that both the diagnosis of the leaders of this movement, and the remedies they proposed, were the product of a very superficial attitude toward the problem of sin, and an equally optimistic and superficial trust in the ability of government programs to deal with the basic issues of the human personality.

The Theological Roots of the Social Gospel

The preceding discussion of the emergence of social problems in American life is not intended to support the thesis that they were the principal cause of the emergence of that movement which is now known as the Social Gospel for, at best, they were an occasion which could be suitably used for giving voice to old heresies in new dress. They were a convenient excuse, or justification, for new attacks on orthodoxy in the name of progress and humanity; there is little doubt that the underlying theological liberalism would have come even if there had been no great social and economic pressure for a new ideology of human society. The roots of the Social Gospel were theological in nature; it was essentially a new revolt against Calvinism and the evangelical position. Its roots can ultimately be traced back to those developments which took place in European theology as a result of the rise of Hegelian Idealism, to the theologies of Ritschl and Schleiermacher in Germany which attempted to refashion Christian thought according to the prevailing philosophical currents and the attacks of German Higher Criticism on the inspiration and authority of the Scriptures. The more immediate background for the new theology is to be found in Transcendentalism, the

New England theology and the writings of Nathaniel Taylor and Horace Bushnell, and the Oberlin theology popularized by Charles G. Finney. It also had something in common with the New School theology of Presbyterianism. To be sure, it was a more open avowal of liberal principles and a further departure from evangelical truth, but the inspiration for this liberalism was the latent Pelagian tendencies in the theologies which were making themselves felt in the North before 1860. These theologies not only seriously modified the doctrine of total depravity, but they presented a plan of redemption which was, in varying degrees, synergistic. This synergism, giving to man some merit and some ability to accomplish his own eternal salvation, almost inevitably led to a view that man also has both the power and the mandate to make a heaven out of this earth and to transform it into a kind of Garden of Eden. Thus Finney, and many other leaders of that era, were easily persuaded that part of the task of evangelism was a direct attack on the social evils of the day, not only from the point of view that Christians should forsake them, but that they could, with the aid of the government, banish many of them from American society. It was, therefore, not only not difficult, but natural that the leaders of these theological movements should be swept into the currents of Jacksonian reform movements, that they should embrace the cause of abolition, world peace, the movement for equality for women, and the many other crusades which called for their loyalty. Because of their optimistic and sub-biblical view of human nature, they failed to take the problem of sin as seriously as the Bible presents it. Thus, they redefined evangelism as a means of promoting Christian action in the social and economic areas of life and they were guilty of identifying support of such causes as evidence of regeneration and sanctification. Regeneration was all too often regarded as little more than a willingness to join in a crusade for the realization of the Kingdom of God on earth—for the banishment of slavery, for the triumph of world peace, or for the introduction of some kind of socialism into American society. This theological and social ferment of the Age of Jackson was also an important part of the heritage of the Social Gospel movement.

This Movement had another root which was lacking in the earlier liberalism—Darwinian evolution. The optimism of the Transcendentalists, and their reforming allies in the evangelical churches, had been a hope, a powerful stimulus to action, but, nevertheless a hope, lacking any firm scientific foundation in an age which was coming to regard scientific respectability and validity as an absolute requirement. The Social Gospel looked to Darwin quite as much as it looked to Schleiermacher or the New England theology and it gave it more credence than it accorded to the historic Gospel.

On the other hand, it is also necessary to point out that the Social Gospel as a movement did not accept the frank skepticism of Lester Frank Ward and his school of thought and it was likewise repulsed by the approach of William Graham Sumner to social issues. However much it looked to Darwinian principles for support, it could not accept the naturalism inherent in the prevailing interpretations of his theories as they were being applied to the American social scene. The Social Gospel was, as the name very clearly implies, an attempt to socialize the Gospel, to give it a sociological frame of reference and purpose, and to make it a decisive force in the shaping of the new America of the twentieth century. In order to do this, the historic Gospel had to be brought into a harmonious relationship with evolution in such a way that it was both scientifically respectable and oriented toward the Bible. The advocates of the Social Gospel were firmly convinced of the truth of the evolutionary theory of Darwin and they also believed that this theory held out to mankind a marvelous future, much like that offered by a postmillennial interpretation of the Scriptures. Thus, a frame of reference adequate for the America of the twentieth century, with all its promises of material greatness and cultural advancement, was a synthesis of the best aspects of Christianity (its ethical teachings and an acknowledgment that behind the wonders of science lay the God of the Bible) and the Darwinian account of the ascent of man. The solution of the problem was found in the theory of theistic evolution which was put forward at an early date in an effort to save something of evangelical Christianity from the doom which Darwinism threatened to bring upon it.

The theory as it had been advanced by Darwin, as Charles Hodge and others clearly saw, left no room for the God of Christianity, no room for miracles, and eventually deprived man of all the glory which the biblical doctrine of creation gave to him, even as a fallen creature. The Darwinian thesis stripped life of all purpose and placed man under the control of thoroughly impersonal forces. The only real philosophy of life which could logically be drawn from the writings of Darwin was an unabashed determinism which denied any real meaning to human existence and which made a mockery of the process of evolution itself. But the theory of evolution had too much of a hold and appeal to the modern mind to be lightly dropped simply because it logically led to a pessimism quite opposite to the optimism of the evolutionists. The belief that man was evolving from lower to higher forms of organic and cultural existence seemed to give him an independence from the doctrine of total depravity that no other theory had ever been able to offer, and so Darwinism could not be cast aside as a dominant factor in any world and life view suitable for the twentieth century mind, but neither must its most unfortunate aspects be allowed to so define man as to render him something unworthy of and incapable of enjoying the process guaranteed to him by evolution. Philosophical and biological determinism must be modified in the interests of human personality and freedom. Sumner had been willing to make no such an allowance and the concessions of Ward and his followers were more apparent than real. The solution to this dilemma was found in theistic evolution, a position popularized by John Fiske, but accepted by many in the churches who were unwilling to surrender every vestige of their Christian heritage to the demands of science. Theistic evolution then became a meeting place between science and Christianity; it was a position for those of an eclectic turn of mind enabling them to pick as much of these two currents of thought as their tastes might dictate. Primarily theistic evolution was a device to insure the role of God in human affairs and, at the same time, to insure that mankind had it within his own power to bring about his own progress. John Fiske was one of the first to advance the cause of theistic evolution in his *Outlines of Cosmic Philosophy* (1874). It was a rather feeble effort to maintain the sovereignty of God and the role of man in his own development. Accepting evolution as the true and only key to the meaning of reality, Fiske insisted that man can only know that which is caused, and that which is relative. His epistemology led him to the conclusion that man can never know the absolute which is the Uncaused and the Infinite. Although he was greatly influenced by Herbert Spencer, he did not deny the existence, but admitted the possibility of a Supernatural Power. His position described a cosmic theism, but it led him to the conclusion that there is no basic incompatibility between science and religion. He felt that science leads man to God and he set forth this position in his *Through Nature to God*. It is obvious that Fiske stood at the far left of those who held for the possibility of theistic evolution, but his pronouncements were not satisfactory to many in the church who felt that God and the Scriptures should be given a much more definite role than that which Fiske had been willing to accord to them. To satisfy the minds and the consciences of many scholars and theologians who came from a profoundly Christian background, more honor had to be accorded to the Bible as a revelation from God and more security had to be granted to cherished Christian beliefs. The nebulous position of Fiske was most unsatisfactory, but it did point out a path which could be used for formulating a theory of evolution which would seemingly allow Christian orthodoxy to survive in its main outlines. Asa Gray, Professor at Harvard, had prepared the way for such a development in an article which appeared in the *Atlantic Monthly* magazine in which he held that natural selection was not incompatible with either a natural theology or the belief in the doctrine of design in nature. The fact that Asa Gray championed Darwinism was a powerful influence in bringing most American scientists to an acceptance of the theory. But Gray did not allow his belief, newly found, in evolution to upset his devotion to the historic creeds of the church; Frederick Wright, a professor at Oberlin College, went so far as to say that Darwinism was the Calvinistic interpretation of nature. These first generation scientists were, to a great extent, theistic in their interpretation of evolution and they found themselves in general agreement with a growing number of theologians who followed Dr. James McCosh of Princeton into an acceptance of a view of evolution which seemingly allowed the major portion of the content of Christian orthodoxy to remain unshaken. But it remained for Henry Ward Beecher, Lyman Abbott and Henry Drummond to popularize this theistic version of Darwin.[1] In a sermon which Beecher preached on May 31, 1885 he said:

While evolution is certain to oblige theology to reconstruct its system, it will take nothing away from the grounds of true religion. . . . Evolution will multiply the motives and facilities of righteousness, which was and is the design of the whole Bible. It will not dull the executive doctrines of religion, that is, the forms of them by which an active and reviving ministry arouses men's consciences, by which they inspire faith, repentance, reformation, spiritual communion with God. Not only will those great truths be unharmed, by which men work zealously for the reformation of their fellowmen, but they will be developed to a breadth and certainty not possible in their present philosophical (by which he meant theological) condition. At present the sword of the spirit is in the sheath of a false theology. Evolution, applied

[1] It should be noted that not all scientists in that day or succeeding years yielded to the attractions of the evolutionary theory and an even more impressive number of ministers and theologians refused to accept it in any form whatsoever. One of the most acute and penetrating criticisms of the Darwinian thesis was offered by the brilliant and orthodox Princeton theologian, Charles Hodge in his *What is Evolution,* a book which should be read by, every Christian concerned with the problems offered by Darwinism.

to religion, will influence only as the hidden temples are restored, by removing the sands which have drifted in from the arid deserts of scholastic and medieval theologies. It will change theology, but only to bring out the simple temple of God in clearer and more beautiful lines and proportions.[2]

In spite of his protestations to the contrary, it is quite obvious from this sermon, that his belief in evolution had already drastically changed Beecher's whole outlook on Christianity which, for him, was little more than a system whereby one group of men with a clearer insight could reform the lives of their fellowmen. In this sermon there is a conspicuous lack of emphasis on human sin, and the redemptive work of Jesus Christ. When Beecher drove theology from the Christian Church he would replace it with a moral system which he fondly believed would not in any way be harmed or weakened by the new insights given by the theory of evolution. Whether he realized it or not, the very theory which he was proclaiming was already doing its deadly work on the historic faith he was seeking to defend.

A more forceful and somewhat more evangelical presentation of the case for theistic evolution was given by Henry Drummond when he lectured at Chautauqua. In these lectures, and in his *Natural Law in the Spiritual World,* Drummond sought to harmonize evolution and Christianity by making the point that they both had the same author and the same purpose for man. He also maintained that natural law as it was interpreted by Darwin, had its perfect analogy in the laws governing spiritual development. There is no need to question Drummond's own spiritual devotion to Jesus Christ, or his evangelical piety, but there is a serious question concerning his understanding of Darwin's interpretation of natural law. The well-intentioned efforts of Beecher, Drummond and Lyman Abbott all foundered on their effort to understand the basic implications of the evolutionary hypothesis and its ultimate irreconcilability with historic

[2] Henry Ward Beecher, *Evolution and Religion*, New York, 1893, *passim,* pp. 49-54.

Christianity. Although the theistic evolutionists were fighting a losing battle on the theological battle line, their efforts toward finding a synthesis between the Gospel and Darwin had profound effects in both the life of the evangelical churches and in the political, social and economic life of the American people. Theirs was a losing battle in the sense that such a harmony between these two opposing systems was an impossibility, but notwithstanding the inevitability of defeat at this point, the theistic evolutionists won another battle in that they succeeded in capturing the minds of the leadership in most of the major denominations for a modified Darwinism, hence for the Social Gospel. Although there is no way to take an accurate poll of the leading ministers and seminary and college professors of the various churches of the era between 1870 and 1900 as to the exact number of them accepting theistic evolution in some form, there can be no question of the fact that this theory not only gained a theological respectability in most of the denominations of the North, but that it also became the focal point of their interpretation of the Gospel and human society in this country. It seems quite clear that it made the greatest headway in those denominations whose Arminian theology had already seriously modified the biblical doctrine of sin and human depravity, and which had already asserted the natural ability of man to cooperate with God in his personal redemption and that of society as well. Its success was hardly less in those churches whose denominational structure offered little or no defense against such heresies. Thus, the Methodist Church in the North and the Congregational and Northern Baptist Churches experienced the greatest inroads of theistic evolution. This is not to say that the Presbyterian Church USA, or the Episcopal Church, or even those denominations in the South, were entirely free from the blighting effects of this false ideology; the increasing number of heresy trials before the general assemblies of the Northern Presbyterian Church testify to the fact that it had not escaped unscathed. But the fact remains that the theory of evolution made the greatest inroads in those churches in which the doctrinal and governmental structures were the least able to cope with it. The presence of postmillennialism also was another factor of great influence, for this eschatology was itself a product of a pre-Darwinian optimism concerning the future of man in this world.[3] It was not too difficult to blend this particular eschatology with Darwinism for they had a natural affinity for each other. After all, the Social Gospel needed some pretense of a biblical eschatology to affirm its Christian affiliations. Darwinism, with its blind and meaningless determinism was quite unsatisfactory for their purposes and the very optimism of the movement demanded a view of society and its progress which could not be found in the theory of evolution itself, but in a philosophy or theology which allowed meaningful interpretation of the historical process and gave it a goal. For this reason postmillennialism filled a void which was inherent in Darwinism.

Washington Gladden (1836-1918), along with Graham Taylor and George Herron, was an early leader of the Social Gospel Movement, but the name which is indissolubly associated with it above all others is that of Walter Rauschenbusch (1816-1918), whose three books, *Christianity and the Social Crisis* (1907), *Christianizing the Social Order* (1912), and *A Theology for the Social Gospel* (1917), provided the inspiration and goals for the whole movement. In these he analyzed the problems facing America, the role of the church in their solution and the kind of theology the church needed for the fulfillment of its social task. At first glance it might seem from these titles that Rauschenbusch first promoted the social application of Christianity and then, later in his career, set forth a theology to suit his purpose. This would be quite misleading for his theological presuppositions appear in all of his writings and the last-named book is simply a formal statement of that theology with which he first started in his quest for the social application of Christian principles to

[3] The close kinship existing between theistic evolution and the Social Gospel on the one hand, and postmillennial thought on the other is a major factor in the later popularity of premillennial thought in the ranks of the Fundamentalists.

the ills of society. Actually, very early in his career he had come into contact with German higher criticism and theological developments which lay at the very heart of his own position. He began with a conception of Christianity which was quite different from that of the historic evangelical position and when he used the term "Christianizing" the social order, he was not thinking in terms of orthodoxy but rather in terms of a gospel which reflected the principles of German philosophy and Darwinism.[4] He could not possibly have arrived at most of his conclusions if his initial thinking had been based on the historic Christian faith. Thus his remedy consists of a series of demands which he had no right to make on the orthodox Gospel and which his own version of Christianity and the church could not possibly fulfill. But neither Rauschenbusch nor his followers were aware of the paradox involved in their position and the ultimate frustration which must be the lot of its advocates. Only in the closing months of his life in 1918 did Rauschenbusch seem to be aware of this dilemma which his theology imposed upon him. It was an inescapable dilemma which would reveal its terrifying weakness in that the very evil in human nature which he sought to minimize as a determining factor in the social milieu was too great for his theology to cope with. In short, he had no answer for the predicament which he saw in this country. But, on the other hand, his optimism, also engendered by his theory of human nature, blinded him to the paradox which stalked his efforts at elaborating a social gospel.

Thus, the Social Gospel in the hands of Rauschenbusch and his successors was both the result of drastic modifications in historic orthodoxy and the cause of further departures from the true faith. Indeed, it could not be otherwise. The very nature of the revised

---

[4] On the other hand, it is also true that Rauschenbusch did not go as far as many of his later disciples in repudiating theology and neither was he as devoid of theology as many of his evangelical critics maintained. Neither can it be denied that the Christianity of Rauschenbusch is quite different from that of the evangelical churches. Rauschenbusch was not a socialist at all points, nevertheless the logical thrust of his position was toward a complete socialism.

message demanded these drastic changes. Rauschenbusch centered his message around the Kingdom of God, but in doing this he did not mean the Kingdom as that concept was set forth in the Scriptures and as it had been consistently treated by theology. He not only separated it from the church, and all eschatological context, but from theology as well, at least from theology as it had developed in the Roman Catholic and Protestant Churches, for he insisted that the Kingdom of God is the Social Gospel. He also insisted that theology itself must be rewritten so as to give a central place to it and revise all other doctrines so that they would be organically related to this one determining idea. All evangelical doctrines, with their emphasis upon the future life and individual salvation, were to be revised in terms of the idea of the Kingdom of God with its emphasis upon this life and the social salvation of the masses. This, in turn, involved a complete reappraisal of the doctrine of God as it is set forth in the Scriptures. Rauschenbusch argued in his *Theology for the Social Gospel* that the concept of God held by any social group is a social product. Therefore, the Christian idea of God has undergone tremendous changes in the long and varied history of the church. He further argues that in the time of the Reformation despotic government was still in full swing and this fact had an unfortunate effect on the thinking of the Reformers concerning the nature of God. Because of this Calvin and Luther were not in sympathy with democracy and their view of God was not democratic. To Rauschenbusch, this was a very serious lack in their theology—the God of the Reformers was not democratic:

> The old idea that God dwells on high and is distant from our human life was the natural basis for autocratic and arbitrary ideas about Him. On the other hand the religious belief that He is immanent in humanity is the natural basis for the democratic ideas about Him.[5]

It is quite obvious that the god of the Social Gospel is not the God of the Scriptures, the Holy One of Israel, the sovereign

[5] *A Rauschenbusch Reader*, p. 122, edited by Benson Landis, New York, 1957.

creator and governor of the universe and man. He is some sort of an immanent being who depends on the democratic philosophy for his own esteem and worship by men. For his own best interests the god of the Social Gospel must cooperate with men in the attainment of their own ideals.

> A God who strives within our striving, who kindles his flame in our intellect, sends the impact of his energy to make our will restless for righteousness, floods our subconscious mind with dreams and longing, and always urges the race on toward a higher combination of freedom and solidarity—that would be a God with whom democratic and religious men could hold converse as their chief fellow worker, the source of their energies, the ground of their hopes.[6]

But such a God could not be worthy of our worship or of our confidence for either this life or that which is to come. This god is little more than a fellow democrat.

This redefinition of the doctrine of God by Rauschenbusch brings in its wake the necessary changes of the other Christian doctrines. Salvation becomes social in character rather than individual, concerned with the conditions of human life in this world, and not too much concerned wtih the problem of where men will spend eternity.

Rauschenbusch did not completely deny the doctrine of sin; he simply denied the biblical teaching in regard to total depravity and he did not hold that sin is a violation of the law of God which leads to eternal punishment. On the other hand, he recognized that man is prone to a type of evil and that society is the victim of many evils which cannot be traced directly to environment or to other causes which would release man from his own personal guilt in these social evils. But, to him, sin is not an offense which requires the substitutionary atonement of the Son of God for the pardon and the restoration of the sinner. He did not banish the Cross of Christ as having no significance, but saw in it a symbol of the fact that "God has always suffered with and

[6] *Ibid.*, pp. 122-123.

for mankind and that the cross is a permanent law of God's nature." God may suffer with man, but this suffering involves no reconciliation between them, no forgiveness of sin, no newness of life. Such doctrines as regeneration, justification, sanctification, adoption and the resurrection from the dead have no place in his theology; what theology he had was more concerned with life in this world and of transforming this world into the Kingdom of God.

Looking on the church primarily as a fellowship for worship, Rauschenbusch defined the Kingdom of God as a fellowship of righteousness, and he looked upon the Kingdom ideal as the test and corrective of the church. The Kingdom of God, for him, was that means by which the moral and ethical teachings of Christ were brought into effective application on society. As a doctrine it was absolutely necessary in order to establish that organic union between religion and morality. Basically, its purpose is to bring about an industrial and social as well as a political democracy. Socialism would be the ultimate expression of the Kingdom of God in an industrial era and Rauschenbusch did not shrink from this conclusion, although he did not share all of the Socialist aims or methods. He was quite willing to invest government with the necessary powers to speed the Kingdom of God on its way and, needless to say, he took a strong stand that the church should speak on all political, social and economic issues in order that it might be more closely identified with the Kingdom of God. In fact, this was the divinely assigned purpose of the church, for this is what Christ himself had come to preach.

The Social Gospel would be a most interesting phenomenon and worthy of study if it had been nothing more than the idea of a few scholars and men in the pulpits, but without much tangible influence in the church at large, or on American life. But its influence and message were not confined to seminary cloisters and to a few pulpits. Rather was it a dominant influence not only in Protestantism, but in the Progressivism of Theodore Roosevelt, Woodrow Wilson and American liberalism in general in the early

decades of the twentieth century. It gained a tremendous following in most of the major denominations of the North and was
preached from scores of pulpits. It was the gospel which many
people in and out of government heard all over the land. It was
the gospel which many political leaders of the day claimed as
their own and on which many members of Congress, and other
agencies of the state and federal government, were nurtured.
It gained the ascendency in denominational circles and brought
a new era to Protestantism in its political and social activities.
It was the mainspring behind the formation of the Federal Council of Churches in 1908, for this organization was brought into
being to be the voice of the Social Gospel not only among the
denominations but in national affairs as well. The organized voice
of the Protestant Churches when they spoke to the nation would
be that of the Social Gospel; and, through the Federal Council,
this new Gospel would increasingly take precedence over that
once delivered to the saints. Many Protestants were, as a result,
unwittingly brought into the support of a political, social and
economic liberalism and radicalism which was too frequently
strangely at variance with their Christian doctrine and they were,
on more than one occasion, represented as supporting a world
and life view which denied their Christian faith and the foundations of the nation at the same time. The Protestant Churches
were frequently being claimed as being in support of socialism,
pacifism, and other causes which were the product of philosophies
which struck at the very heart of the evangelical position.

By the same token, in the name of progress, Protestants were
being used to advance programs which were not only unconstitutional in character but represented a type of liberalism which
was actually socialism, or even communism, in its basic philosophy. Its support was sought for political programs which called
for the centralization of power in the hands of the central government to such a degree that a totalitarianism would surely
emerge from the ruins of the Constitution and the government
it brought forth. In the same way, Christians were urged to sup-

port social and economic "reformers" who were, more often than not, definitely contrary in their thinking to biblical standards and who looked forward to the creation of a society which would be definitely hostile to the evangelical Gospel and which would eventually destroy human rights and the whole cultural legacy which we have inherited from Colonial America and its Puritanism. In short, the liberalism preached by many, if not most, of the advocates of the Social Gospel threatened with destruction the Christian world and life view which this country had received at its founding and offered, in its place, a new world and life view which was humanistic and naturalistic in its essence. And all of this was done in the name of democracy.

Even before Rauschenbusch had finished formulating his own position, the Methodist Episcopal Church, North, brought forth in 1908 its own version of the Social Gospel in its Social Creed. This action is of major importance for it was the first time that an evangelical church gave sanction to a creed which looked to liberal and democratic sources rather than to the Scriptures for its authority; this denomination was the first to admit officially that the historic Gospel was not entirely adequate for the age of the twentieth century, that it needed reenforcement from extrabiblical sources. That the Methodist Church should have been in the vanguard of those who sought to give the Social Gospel a dominant role in its life, need not seem surprising, for the theological deterioration, and the move away from Wesleyan theology, had long been in process; the enthronement of the Social Gospel was the theological consequence of their growing theological laxity. Indeed, there were elements in the Wesleyan theology which formed convenient bridgeheads for the transition to the new emphasis. The democratic tone of Wesley's Arminianism was, in itself, a springboard to the more humanistic democracy of Rauschenbusch, and the social interests of Wesley formed a convenient link between the social application of the Gospel in Wesleyan thought and the Social Gospel of the twentieth century. This "Social Creed" did not openly reject any great evangelical doctrine and its affirmations were, in general, not radical in their tone and were certainly in accord with evangelical convictions as to how Christians should conduct their economic activities.

The significance of this "Creed" lies in the fact that the Methodist Church was willing to become associated with an economic and social program per se and that as an ecclesiastical body, it felt it should take a stand on economic, social and political issues. This church was willing to become a partner in the cause of democracy and in a program which eventually would bring tremendous powers over every segment of individual lives into the hands of the federal government. The importance of this pronouncement lies in the fact that it began a trend which would eventually bring not only the Methodist Church, but other churches, to the place where the evangelical Gospel would be almost lost in their desire to become allies of the great cause of democracy and social justice. Quite soon the conservative pronouncements on social and economic issues would be replaced by those which often had the endorsement of the radical socialist and communist groups; and prominent churchmen would be able to say twelve years or so later that they found in Russian communism the most significant application of the social teachings of Christ in the modern era.

In this same year, 1908, the trend toward social pronouncements by the churches received another impetus with the formation of the Federal Council of Churches and its "Social Creed of the Churches." Already the inherent trend in the new emphasis was being brought to light. Although based on the Methodist Creed of the same year, the pronouncement of the Federal Council went further in the direction of governmental controls and the assumption that sin can be dealt with successfully by political manipulation was more apparent. Underlying both of the pronouncements was the assumption that man is inherently good and capable of transforming his world into a kind of paradise, provided that he gives democratic government enough power to cope with his own tendency toward evil. This willingness to enlarge the power of government was not openly stated at this time, but it was implicit in the philosophy which prompted it; and the history of the larger denominations from that time on in their individual pronouncements and collectively in the Federal Council is convincing evidence of their reliance on government to usher in a millennial existence for man.

The kinship of the "Social Creed of the Churches" with radicalism was affirmed at a later date by Harry F. Ward, Secretary of the Methodist Federation for Social Action, when he wrote:

> It is a revealing exercise to put in parallel columns the social creed of the churches; the earlier programs of organized labor; the populists and the socialists; the later platforms of the progressive party and the statement of ideals adopted by members of the national conference of social work. . . . When those who wrote the Social Creed, under the impulse of a long religious tradition, mentioned some of the things that labor and farm leaders and also the socialists had been striving for and when later the social workers and the progressives repeated in substance the main things that all the rest had said, it did not mean that any were borrowing language or ideas from the others. It meant that a common movement in American life was coming to expression, that organized religion should take both direction from it and put it into an older sanction and power is an instance of how God is revealed in human life.[7]

Among other things, this statement is a very candid confession that the social creeds of 1908 did not have their origin in the Scriptures, or in a Christian world and life view, but were rather the products of contemporary social and political thought which was in turn prompted by contemporary conditions facing this country. Professor Ward was quite correct when he said that it would be quite revealing to place the statements of these various groups in parallel columns. It would reveal that there was little difference, if any, between the church in its thinking, and American society and that the church had abandoned the Scrip-

---

[7] *Christian Century*, April 19, 1928, pp. 502-503.

tures for the opinions of sociologists and economists. Instead of speaking to the world the church was allowing the world to dictate its message and what it believed.

These social creeds were actually not creeds at all in the ordinary sense of the word. They were not statements of what Christians actually believed as great facts of social life enduring for all time and eternity. Rather were the affirmations of these creeds a series of statements of an economic, social and political nature, a kind of current platform of expectations, of goals which the churches hoped would be true in the sense that their attainment would be in keeping with the social conscience of the day. But that prophetic note upon which Rauschenbusch was insisting as a very necessary ingredient for his Social Gospel at that very time was being evaporated by the forces of secularism to which the liberal forces were yielding. The theological liberalism of the movement made it very difficult to retain the righteousness of those prophets whose writings were being brought into disrepute by higher criticism.

Another very significant aspect of this development, but which did not receive too much attention at that time, was the growing willingness of the evangelical churches to assign to government a role and accompanying powers for which there was no scriptural support. The identification of the Kingdom of God with something other than the Church of Jesus Christ was a serious confusion which had important ramifications which were not always too clearly perceived at that time. The departure from New Testament standards for the church and the willingness to allow it to become an agency in the quest for social justice brought in its wake a concept of government and its role in society, which was a radical denial of the biblical view and which gave to government a vast scope of power for which there was not only no biblical warrant, but which constituted a rather flagrant transgression of those limits which the Scriptures set on political activity. It was at this point that theological liberalism, in alliance with the advocates of the Social Gospel, prepared the way for a centralization of power in the hands of government constituting a severe threat to human freedom and to the liberty of the evangelical church. The fact that this hostility, which is necessarily inherent in any government which tends toward absolutism, democratic or otherwise, has not become dominant in the relations between church and state in this country should not blind us to the intrinsic threat which centralization always poses for the free expression of evangelical convictions and the Gospel message.

Previous mention has already been made of the great popularity and vast penetration of the theory of evolution into almost every segment of American life. The same was true of the Social Gospel. In fact, the two movements were remarkably parallel in many respects. This new version of the message of redemption found its way into many leading seminaries and into a much greater number of pulpits. It gained a sponsor of high repute in the *Outlook,* under the editorship of Lyman Abbott and Theodore Roosevelt. This magazine was a voice for liberal Christianity in the early years of the present century and had an influence much like that which the *Christian Century* later achieved. The Social Gospel movement gained the ear of a large segment of Protestantism through the use of pulpit and press and it began to shape the political, economic and social thought of the American people to a much greater degree than is generally recognized by historians who have been prone to trace the success of the Progressive Movement to the secular writers of the era. Ralph Gabriel is quite correct in stating that the Progressive Movement was essentially humanistic in its character, but he apparently did not see that this secularism was actually nurtured by the religious liberalism of the day which itself had become largely humanistic under the guise of applying the Gospel to social issues.

This seemingly strange alliance between the Social Gospel on the one hand, and the radicals in religion and politics on the other, did not raise the apprehension among the followers of Rauschenbusch which might have been expected. They were willing to engage in cooperative efforts and to support the same crusades with them and even to form political parties with them, as in 1912 when Theodore Roosevelt appealed to all liberal groups for their support. The divorce which Rauschenbush pushed between the church and the Kingdom of God, and his identification of the latter with a Christianized social order allowed him, and his followers, to include any and all social reformers as followers of Jesus Christ. Rauschenbusch went so far as to include by claim, Robert Owen, the noted free-thinker and socialist, as a follower and apostle of Jesus Christ.

The Election of 1912

This presidential campaign was of special significance for several reasons, not the least of which was the high quality of the nominees put forward by each of the three major parties. It was also important because it gave to the voters a more meaningful selection of issues than almost any campaign since 1860. Roosevelt, Taft and Wilson, and their respective platforms, gave to this presidential contest a character that was distinctive in the annals of American political history. Not only were vital differences in political philosophy discernible during the campaign, but the more fundamental theological questions also made their appearance in a most unusual manner. In particular the *Outlook,* edited by Lyman Abbott and Theodore Roosevelt, and speaking in behalf of the Progressive Party, boldly asserted the philosophical and theological assumptions of the Progressive credo in a manner most unusual in such debates. This magazine, in drawing the issues between Roosevelt and Wilson very sharply, was very frank to point out the consistency in Wilson's political and theological orthodoxy as against the consistent liberalism in the Progressive platform.

> The Democratic Party appeals to those who are dissatisfied with present conditions and desire to return to the conditions of a previous age. They look to the past for their ideal; they wish to return to the simplicity of the fathers. They are men who in their theology go back for their beliefs to the creeds of the sixteenth

century, or even to those of the fourth, and regard all new doctrines as heresies.

In politics men of this temperament desire to make the principles and policies of the fathers of 1787 the standard for their children of 1912. They are Progressive in that they desire to get away from the present; but they desire to do so by going back to the past. He (the Wilsonian Progressive) wishes the understanding of the Constitution of 1787 to bind the nation in 1912; tradition, not practical efficiency, to determine its meaning. Such is the temperament which seems to us to characterize Governor's Wilson's speech of acceptance. It is not extreme for he is not an extreme man. But it regards the social evils of our times as due to a departure from the spirit and principles of our forefathers. It proposes no definite remedy except such as are involved in a return to those principles and that spirit.[8]

The Progressive indictment against Wilson and the Democratic Party was theological and philosophical. They wanted to allow the theology of the Reformation and of the Council of Nicea to determine the theology of their own era and they also wanted the Constitution, as it had been interpreted by the Founding Fathers of 1787, to bind the nation in 1912. While this editorial does not openly link the Constitution with the theology of the Reformation, it recognizes that those who accept it are those who will insist upon the unchanging nature of the Constitution as a guide to political conduct in the twentieth, as well as in the eighteenth century. This description of the temperament of the Democratic Party in 1912 was quite valid, but as an indictment was very wide of the mark.

Abbott went on in this same editorial to give an appraisal of the philosophical and theological position of the Progressive Party.

We look forward, not backward, to the Golden Age. We believe in a new theology, a new science, a new sociology, a new politics. We believe that in every day walks a better tomorrow; the world

[8] *Outlook*, September 21, 1912, pp. 101-102.

is steadily growing better, though with lapses, failures and retro-gressions. We believe . . . that the twentieth century is as com-petent to make its theological creed as was the sixteenth or the fourth; that the counsels of men of this decade are better able to decide the destiny of America than the voices from the graves of men of a century ago; that the traditions of the past are useful as guides but poor governors; that the Constitution is to be con-sidered as an instrument to promote growth, not as an impedi-ment to prevent it. We believe that progress lies not in going back to the past, but in going forward to the future; that the age of regulated combination is better than the age of unscrupulous competition; that fraternalism is better than the individualism; a self-governed democracy of self-governed individuals. . . .

This party will repel the men of contented mind who are satisfied with the world as it is. It will repel the man who thinks this is a degenerate age, and the cure for its evils is a return to neglected ideals and neglected duties. But it will attract men who have faith in themselves, in their fellows and in the future; who think that the present discontent is but the shadow cast by a splendid aspira-tion. . . . It is the party of life and courage. It appeals to the eager and the adventurous, and to those, whatever their years, who are eternally young.[9]

This is one of the frankest statements for the Progressive Move-ment to be found in its literature; it is a candid confession that it was a new philosophy of government for which new concepts of theology, political science and sociology were necessary. These concepts were to be found in the Social Gospel and Darwinism rather than in the political philosophy which brought forth the Constitution and the theology of the Reformation. The theology of evangelical Christianity was no more adequate for the needs of the twentieth century than was the historic understanding of the Constitution. Both had been weighed in the balances and found wanting.

The Progressives were searching for a new view of man, of his

[9] *Op. cit.*, p. 103.

social and economic relationships and of the world in which he lived. All of the orthodox theology of the past and those social, economic and political philosophies which had stemmed from it, must be changed in order to meet the needs of a democratic era. Here is the tacit assumption that political liberalism could not long survive in an intellectual climate characterized by adherence to Christian orthodoxy. Thus the Progressives insisted that each age had the right to rewrite its traditional theology and political philosophy in keeping with its own needs and aspirations. No age should feel bound by the formulas of the past, no matter how well they might have served previous generations. Progressives were really calling for a new theology which centered in man rather than in the God of the Scriptures.

The attitude of many liberals and progressives was well summarized by Arthur C. McGiffert when he wrote: that democracy "demands a God with whom men may cooperate not one to whom they must submit."[10]

In the Progressive outlook on life in general there was no place for such biblical doctrines as total depravity, salvation by grace alone accomplished through the atoning work of Jesus Christ and the doctrine of divine sovereignty in human affairs, for they placed great emphasis on human sovereignty and cooperation with God (probably on terms settled by man), redemption through education and governmental action and a humanly achieved millennium in which a completely democratic society would be the apex of the evolutionary process in human experience.

The proud insistence that Progressivism must be free from traditional interpretations in theology and political thought was not completely sincere and accurate. Nor was the assertion that each age should write its own political thought and theology well-founded. The Progressives were not free from the past and did not intend to be; they merely substituted one segment of the past for another. They were quite willing to allow eighteenth

---

[10] "Democracy and Religion" in *Religious Education*, 1919, Vol. XIV, p. 161. Quoted in Wilbur Smith, *Therefore Stand*, Boston, 1945, p. 40.

century Deism and Jeffersonian political concepts, nineteenth century Transcendentalism and Darwinism to dictate to twentieth
century minds. It was a question of whether biblical standards
should determine twentieth century thought or whether human
scientific achievements should become the authoritative standard.

In the rise of Progressivism in this country the Social Gospel
came into its own. The party platform clearly reveals its liberal
background in political circles for many of its provisions were obviously inspired by the Methodist Social Creed of 1908 and the
statements issued by the Federal Council of Churches in this same
year. This declaration of Progressive principles called for the
enlargement of the powers conferred upon the federal government in order that it might be able to protect the people against
what its framers called the "tyranny of special privilege." It endorsed such measures as the direct primary, the initiative and
the referendum and recall; Roosevelt added the recall of judicial
decisions as well. It also promised an easier method of amending
the Constitution than that provided by the Founding Fathers in
order that the document would more accurately reflect the popular opinion of the day. It called for a federal commission to
supervise corporations, a Department of Labor, and a graduated
inheritance tax. In essence, this platform of the Progressive
Party called for a new paternalism although its framers called
the program the "New Nationalism." True to the democratic
philosophy which it represented, it called for the democratization of the whole political structure while, at the same time, it
willingly conceded to this democratized government much greater
power than was contemplated by that Convention of 1787 which
wrote the Constitution. It was at this point that its kinship with
social pronouncements of the church became most marked.
As the churches showed an increasing willingness to place a
greater trust in, and give a greater role to, the federal government
in the achievement of the better life for the American people,
so were the people themselves, speaking through their political
parties, showing the same confidence in government itself to ac-

complish objectives and to assume responsibilities which were totally alien to the biblical, and to the traditional American, concept of the role of government in human affairs.

The Social Gospel: Its Later History

The defeat of Roosevelt and the Progressive Party in 1912 was not in itself a defeat of the cause which they represented, nor of the Social Gospel by which they had been largely inspired. The triumph of Woodrow Wilson and conservative reform meant that some aspects of the Progressive agenda would yet be enacted into law and, although the coming of war would bring Wilson's program to a grinding halt, in one sense, the very exigencies of war would accentuate the trend toward centralization of power in the hands of the federal government and make necessary, for the time being at least, a tax program which would help to accomplish the redistribution of income which was so dear to the Progressive heart.

Much has been written about the "rise and fall" of the Social Gospel and there is a running debate between scholars on this issue; both sides have some strength in their argument. It cannot be denied that as a formal movement springing from Gladden, Rauschenbusch and its other early leaders, the movement lost much of its steam and influence as a result of World War I and the loss of spiritual values among so many people in the years that followed the conflict. The war also brought an end to the Progressive Party as it had been developed under LaFollette, Roosevelt and others in the decade before 1914. Even as the spirit of social and economic protest continued however, without a political home, so did the Social Gospel live on in somewhat unorganized form. It drew its inspiration from the liberal theology of the day, more popularly known as "modernism" and looked to the *Outlook,* and after 1920 more especially to the *Christian Century* for its articulate literary support.

It is for this reason that it is somewhat inaccurate and misleading to speak of the death of the Social Gospel. The Federal

Council of Churches, founded in 1908, in part at least, for the special purpose of making this Social Gospel felt in every aspect of American life, continued to speak in its behalf on almost every conceivable issue which came before the American people. In a manner reminiscent of the Transcendentalist Movement of nearly a century earlier, the Federal Council entered into one crusade after another, war and peace, prohibition, labor issues, racial equality, socialism, the New Deal, birth control, the ecumenical movement and the union of denominations, and kindred matters. Liberal leaders did not enter, after 1919, into all of these contests at the same time, nor with the same degree of zeal. One issue at a time usually engaged their attention predominantly and claimed their greatest zeal. The passion of the Federal Council for peace was severely strained by the rise of Hitler and the subsequent aggressions on the helpless countries surrounding Germany. The *Christian Century,* and other liberal denominational journals, entered into most of these crusades with zeal and fervor, if not always with understanding, and it will be the task of succeeding chapters to evaluate the theological influences on American history after 1920.

In the same sense that liberal theology is generally preoccupied with social and mundane questions relating to what is fondly believed must eventually result in the establishment of the Kingdom of God on earth, the Social Gospel certainly lived on. Liberal theology lived on and became more liberal until the line dividing it from sheer humanism became exceedingly blurred and little Christian theology or expectation was left. This drift toward liberalism became increasingly pronounced not only in those churches which at an early date succumbed to its enticements, but it was making itself felt in those denominations which had been citadels of orthodoxy during the nineteenth century. Thus, as a continuing expression of the social concern of many churches, the Social Gospel continued to exert a tremendous influence in national affairs.

The Social Gospel: An Evaluation

What were the effects of the Social Gospel on the church and on the nation? What has been the permanent influence of this movement and to what extent has it been successful in the achievement of the aims and purposes which its early advocates laid out for it? These are very pertinent questions and the answer, in part, depends on the short range effects as against the continuing results of this movement. Some of the goals have been obtained, such as the abolition of child labor and, for about fourteen years, the nation had prohibition through the eighteenth amendment and the Volstead Act. On the other hand, other goals are as far short of realization now as they were fifty years ago. Certainly war, crime and poverty are as much a part of the national picture today as they were at that time, even though some laws which the Progressives advocated for their abolition have been passed. In the sense that the Social Gospel was intended to remake American society, the movement has fallen far short of its announced goals. This is not to say that it has not had certain very definite effects on our national life, and not all of them were foreseen or intended.

In the first place, it should be noted that in redefining salvation largely in social rather than individualistic terms, the Social Gospel helped to bring about a great loss of evangelistic zeal in those churches which had once been noted for their fidelity to the preaching of the message of personal redemption. Once the belief that men were eternally lost if they were not Christian was removed from the vocabulary and the consciousness of Christian people, their zeal for preaching the Gospel receded accordingly. And in most cases this lessened enthusiasm for evangelism was not replaced by an equal fervor for the preaching of the social message for it lacked the magnetic power to bring conviction upon those who heard it in the same way in which the historic Gospel brought conviction of sin and eternal condemnation. It is true that some preachers were very zealous in their proclamation of the social message of redemption, but by and large, their message failed to evoke the kind of response which attends the faithful exposition of the Scriptures.

The impact of the Social Gospel was also felt in other ways which struck vital blows at the historic Gospel and the biblical view of the power and role of the state, and which, in turn, had a tremendous influence on the development of American politics in the twentieth century. The greatest weakness of the Social Gospel and yet, at the same time, the source of much of its political strength, was its identification of the Kingdom of God with the cause of American democracy. The confusion of the biblical teachings on this subject with American democracy was a further refinement of the Puritan American Dream previously discussed, just as the Social Gospel itself was a further refinement of the historic Gospel of Puritanism. Even as the latter movement replaced the Calvinism of Puritanism with a kind of Pelagianism, so did it change the political constitutionalism of the Puritans into the democratic philosophy, in part derived from Jeffersonian and Transcendental strands of thought and, in part, a reflection of the democratization of Christianity inherent in the theology of Rauschenbusch and Gladden. The democratization of theology could only lead to a further democratization of political thought and practice, especially since this process gave to the democratic way of life a biblical foundation and status which was quite foreign to its real character. Identification of the Kingdom of God with the triumph of democracy went a long way to sanctify democracy in the minds of the American people who felt that to be an American was the equivalent of holding citizenship in the Kingdom of God.

However, this democratization of theology in the life of the church had very serious consequences for both the church and the state. It allowed the advocates of the Social Gospel to encourage the church to venture into political, social and economic paths which it should never have followed and to become embroiled in issues and controversies which were outside of its domain. In a very real sense the church, under the impact of the Social Gospel, ceased to be the church to a great extent and became a kind of social organization at the beck and call of the reformers and crusaders of every hue and stripe who led it into many blind alleys. In becoming the ally of programs of social reform the church strayed far from its biblical commission and performed services and espoused causes which it was not commissioned to undertake and, in so doing, it lost its zeal and its message. In losing sight of its true purpose it was set adrift on the seas of uncertainty and doubt, finding that it could not possibly succeed in the tasks assigned to it by men. It is for this reason that many voices have arisen to charge that the church has failed in its mission and that it has little to say to modern society. There is a sense in which these charges are true for the church has, and must, ever fail in carrying out duties which men assign to it for it must neglect the Great Commission given to it by her Lord. The church only fails man when it fails her Lord. It is not, and cannot be, democratic in its philosophy or practice and, least of all, can it fit into a democratic society. To do so is to bring death to that very society to which it accommodates itself; to do so is to condemn to eternal death those who fail to hear the true Gospel because of the failure of the church to proclaim it.

This humanization of the Kingdom of God which was an inescapable consequence of the democratization of the church had a very serious effect upon American political development after 1920, setting in motion a trend still much in evidence which can only result in the creation of a political absolutism if the present trend in government is not reversed. When the Christian Church deserts the biblical role assigned to it and turns its back on the theology by which it is nurtured and strengthened for its task among men, and assumes functions contrary to its divine charter, it confers an invitation on government to do likewise. This was particularly true in the case of the Social Gospel which identified the Kingdom of God with the democratic state in this country. It will be remembered that the Puritan theology assigned to government a role which was truly biblical and therefore not despotic, but constitutional. The political philosophy of the Social Gospel, with its very frank democratic leanings, actually called for a state which would have no frame of reference except that democratic philosophy and the will of the majority as that will might be expressed at the polls, or by a decision of Congress on specific issues. The idea that law is supreme depended upon the more fundamental conviction that the Scriptures are the infallible rule of faith and practice, and the former cannot long survive in a theological climate which denies the latter proposition. Thus, the reliance of the Social Gospel on a liberal theology which denied the biblical view of the state brought with it a new political philosophy which allowed the state to take on many functions, and to invade areas of life of the private citizen heretofore regarded as outside its domain. The only check on the expansion of political power was now the will of the people. If the majority should agree on the necessity of such vastly enlarged powers for the central government that an absolutism of some kind must result, there was no effective method of warding off such a catastrophe short of a revolution in which a new majority might voice its opposition to such encroachments upon personal liberty.

Finally, then, the liberal theology which underlay the political liberalism of this movement became a negation of the very freedom which it claimed to protect. Because it denied the only view of God and truth which sustains freedom, democracy in theology and in the state it became freedom's most dangerous enemy. The old Augustinian and Puritan insistence that true freedom arises from a complete subjection to the will of a sovereign God was almost completely lost by a generation which preferred to seek its freedom in the democratic philosophy which emphasized the sovereignty of man rather than that of God. This is the ultimate tragedy of contemporary liberalism, theological and political, so far as the affairs of this life are concerned. Because it forsook the only possible source of true freedom the Social Gospel itself was the real failure. It might continually agitate causes and even influence Congressional action at various points; it might even see some of its most cherished ideas enacted into law, but there was one thing it could not do—remake the human race and bring in the Kingdom of God. The strictures which Rauschenbusch and his followers brought against evangelical Christianity were grossly unfair because the church did not fail in its divinely assigned task; it only failed to fulfill certain roles which were foreign to its mission, while the Social Gospel failed in its accepted role. The failure is not merely a negative inability to attain its objectives. Its basic failure lies in the fact that instead of the millennium and the freedom which it sought, it so alienates man from God that it invites the very despotism which it seeks to avoid.

6

Theological Liberalism after 1920 and Its Political Consequences

In this country theological liberalism, or "modernism" as it is more popularly known, continued to become more liberal and to spread its influence over most of the larger evangelical denominations until some of them came to a position in which liberals dominated denominational policies to such an extent that the evangelical forces had little to say concerning the message which the church would officially proclaim. This process was made possible because the forces of liberalism were able to gain a commanding position in the liberal arts colleges and seminaries run by most of the major denominations. It was in these institutions of higher learning and ministerial training that liberalism, in all of its forms, made the first and the most complete inroads. The popularity of Darwinism in academic circles was a perplexing problem to college faculties who wished to remain abreast of current scientific thought in an age which worshiped science; there was, indeed, a very real need that the colleges related to the church must remain intellectually alert and aware of current development in all fields of human endeavor. It became increasingly difficult for these colleges to maintain a degree of intellectual respectability if they denied the findings of science in such an important field as biology and its related areas of study. To understand the theory of evolution in all of its implications for science, and to be able to comprehend it in terms of the Scriptures, called for a degree of scholarship which faculties of these colleges did not always possess and they tended to yield to the popular ideas as to what comprehended intellectual status and to find areas of agreement between the Christian faith and the theory of evolution.

Likewise, the seminary faculties faced a similar problem in the dogmatic assertions of higher criticism and the students of comparative religion and anthropology. As a matter of fact, the problem was somewhat more acute for the seminary faculties, in that they not only had to face the problems offered by the evolutionists, but those brought by all forms of biblical criticism, and they too yielded to the demands of the day.

Even in view of this assault of liberalism on the educational institutions of the church, the progress of modernism was uneven and was not obtained without great struggles. It gained greater strength in those churches which were Arminian in their theology, or which had no creeds of any consequence to guide their theological development. It made relatively little headway in some of the churches and met with great opposition in others. Although heresy made itself felt in the Presbyterian Church USA in the closing years of the nineteenth century, this church, with the help of a group of stalwarts for the faith at Princeton Seminary, continued its testimony for the historic faith until well into the twentieth century; it was not until the appearance of the Auburn Affirmation in 1923, and the ensuing reconstruction of Princeton Seminary at the close of this decade, that liberals could be said to have officially taken over this once great church. It met with even greater resistance in the Southern Presbyterian Church, and in some branches of the Lutheran Church in this country. The conquest of Princeton Seminary by the forces of liberalism was a strategic victory, and of great consequence for the evangelical church in the nation, for this school had given forth a scholarly defense of the Gospel for over a century and the Princeton "theology" was a vital force in the life, not only of Presbyterianism, but of evangelical Christianity wherever it was found. The Hodges, Alexander, Warfield, Machen and others had given forth a mighty testimony for the faith that was felt and honored all over the country and the loss of Princeton Seminary was an event the importance of which cannot be denied in the history of theology in this country.

Even before this change had taken place at Princeton the theologies of the evangelical churches in this country were all showing the ravages of the inroads of German higher criticism and philosophy. These intellectual currents from Europe fed and strengthened the native grown liberalism which had emerged from nineteenth century American philosophical and scientific developments. As we have seen, it had been developed before 1914, and after 1890 the Presbyterian Church USA was increasingly troubled by heresy as it was developed at Union Seminary in New York. After 1918 forces of unbelief made significant gains in practically all of the major denominations until in some of them the evangelical testimony was all but hushed by the strident voice of a liberalism which was sweeping all before it, capturing the major posts in many churches, as well as control of the colleges and seminaries. The downfall of the old Princeton theology in 1929 was not so much the beginning of a liberal denomination as it was the final proof that such a situation was now a reality in a church which had once been the very center of an evangelical zeal of scholarly orthodoxy which had been the life blood of the evangelical forces in this country.

The extent of the modernist penetration into American religious and theological life can be rather easily realized from a study of the leading books which were appearing and of the religious journals of the day. Although J. Gresham Machen, and

other evangelical scholars, made important contributions to the
world of theology which could not be ignored, there can be no
doubt that their offerings were considerably outnumbered and,
in terms of quantity, overwhelmed by those from liberals. The
inroads of liberalism are very apparent in the great denominational journals after 1920, and in such publications as the *Christian Century,* which very accurately mirrored the trends in liberal
opinion. There were exceptions, of course, like *The Presbyterian,*[1]
The Watchman Examiner, and those of some of the smaller and
more evangelical bodies, but, on the whole, the trend in religious
publications, both denominational and independent, were definitely toward a liberalism which at times was almost indistinguishable from humanism and socialism.

A series running in the *Christian Century* at that time was indicative of what was taking place in American theology. The
general title of the series of articles was "What Salvation Can
the Church Offer Today," and the articles were contributed by
leading figures of American Protestantism such as Edward Scribner Ames, Rufus Jones, and William P. Merrill. Most of these
writers insisted that the church must concentrate its message on
the social problems and offer a social salvation. They were not
disposed to rule out entirely the message of personal salvation, although they agreed that it must be done in less spectacular ways
than formerly; Rufus Jones admitted that modern man had virtually lost the sense of any need of personal salvation because his
sense of sin was blurred.[2]

William Pierson Merrill echoed this kind of thought in a similar article. After pleading for a message of salvation for the world
of the twentieth century he said:

> That means that we shall take the social or the common outwork-
> ing of the Christian faith and set it in the center, where once the
> rescue and final bliss of the individual stood. . . . It means that

---

[1] In 1930 Dr. Samuel G. Craig was ousted as editor because of his
editorial support of Westminster Seminary and criticism of the "changes in
control (of Princeton Seminary) which guaranteed that its attitude and
influence would hereafter be Modernistic." *Time,* Jan. 27, 1930, p. 64.

[2] *Christian Century,* February 9, 1928, p. 171.

as we honestly believe, so must we frankly avow that the most essential, the final and the real meaning of being "saved" is not the possession of a mystic experience, or a title-deed to a mansion in the skies. These are great possessions, they come most surely and fully to the Christian; indeed the Christian alone is sure of them; but the richest and deepest meaning of Christian salvation is fellowship with Christ in His mission, and the man who, whatever he believes about the doctrine of the church, and whatever he expects when life is over, gives his life for Christ's sake to the organized enterprise of making the world over on Christ's plan, is a saved man and a Christian, in the best and truest sense.[3]

Statements of this kind could be multiplied many times over, but to do so would serve no good purpose and would be foreign to the basic purpose of this study. It is quite obvious that theological liberalism was considered to be a necessary prelude to the social task of the church of remaking society. Liberalism would not entirely do away with the older concept of individual or personal redemption, but it would be reinterpreted in the light of the Social Gospel. It must be earned and could not be considered as a gift of imputed grace. If the individual was to be saved he must join in the great social enterprise and thus be worthy of his individual redemption; this redemption would not be in terms of the historic theology which placed that redemption in the atoning work of Christ alone. For the liberal there was no such thing as amazing grace, but rather an amazing cooperation between God and man.

Inevitably the historic doctrines of evangelical Christianity in general, and of Calvinism in particular, were denied and ridiculed as the residue of an outworn theology which could have no place in modern thought and no attraction for the mind of the twentieth century. With increasing boldness leading ministers in many of the larger, and even of the smaller denominations, openly denied the great evangelical truths and, in many cases, refused to preach from the Scriptures, preferring to give book reviews, philosophical addresses and moral and ethical homilies in their place.

[3] *Christian Century*, July 12, 1928, pp. 877-879.

Perhaps the most dramatic event in this liberal march to victory was the appearance of the Auburn Affirmation in the Presbyterian Church USA in 1924. This document, signed by 1,274 ministers of that church, was put forward as a protest against certain actions of the General Assembly of 1923, and the action of the General Assembly of 1910, which declared that there were five necessary doctrines to which all ministerial candidates must give their assent for ordination in that church. In its narrow construction the Auburn Affirmation was a complaint against the action of an assembly in amending the Westminster Confession of Faith, but in its broader scope it was a protest against the historic interpretation of the Scriptures required of Presbyterian ministers. The signers of the Affirmation claimed that they did not deny the facts or doctrines which the previous assembly had declared to be necessary, but that they were not to be bound by the interpretation of the doctrines as it had been set forth by that assembly. The five doctrines, or interpretations, in question concerned the divine inspiration and infallibility of the Scriptures, the Virgin Birth of Jesus Christ, the substitutionary atonement of Christ upon the Cross, the literal resurrection of Christ from the dead on the third day and the miracles which He wrought while on earth. After affirming their acceptance of the facts involved in the fundamental doctrines the signers went on to say:

> But we are united in believing that these are not the only theories allowed by the Scriptures and our Standards as explanations of these facts and doctrines of our religion, and that all who hold to these facts and doctrines, whatever theories they may employ to explain them, are worthy of all confidence and fellowship.[4]

Although some of those who signed this document may have actually intended to convey nothing more than the idea that there were other possible theories concerning the interpretation of the doctrines in question, it was well known at the time, and has since

[4] Maurice Armstrong and Lefferts Loetscher, *The Presbyterian Enterprise*, The Westminster Press, Philadelphia, 1955, pp. 284-288.

been overwhelmingly proved, that the great majority of them actually denied both the facts and their interpretations. It is, of course, also true that those who were simply asserting that other interpretations were possible, were violating their ordination vows, for the Westminster Confession couples the doctrines and their interpretation in such a way that the acceptance of the fact is the acceptance of the interpretation which the Scriptures give to its own doctrinal system.

Attempts were made to minimize the importance of such an affirmation and protest, and to point out that the more than twelve hundred ministers who signed were a minority of the ministers serving the Presbyterian Church USA. In a sense this is true, but the fact that such a large number of ministers in that church would and could sign such a document was strong evidence that something was seriously wrong with the denomination which allowed such an action. The document was heretical and no attempt to gloss over its errors could hope to conceal its pernicious character.

The question arises: why was this affirmation put forward at such a time? Had scholarship brought forward such startling new evidence as to the untrustworthiness of the Scriptures, or of serious errors in their historic interpretation that the old orthodoxy must be surrendered for a greater freedom of doctrine as the signers maintained? Were the signers completely candid when they wrote:

> We do not desire to go beyond the teachings of evangelical Christianity. But we maintain that it is our constitutional right and our Christian duty within these limits to exercise liberty of thought and teaching, that we may more effectively preach the Gospel of Jesus Christ, the Saviour of the world. Finally, we deplore the evidence of division in our beloved church in the face of a world so desperately in need of a united testimony to the Gospel of Christ. We earnestly desire fellowship with all who like us are disciples of Jesus Christ. We hope that these to whom the Affirmation comes will believe that it is not the declaration of a theo-

logical party, but rather a sincere appeal, based on the Scriptures and our Standards, for the preservation of the unity and freedom of our church, for which we most earnestly plead and pray.[5]

This study is not concerned with all the connotations of this Affirmation, but it is important to note that this statement is quite misleading from several points of view. A study of the full context of this Affirmation and the atmosphere out of which it grew reveals the fact that most of those who signed it were quite convinced that the historic Gospel and Presbyterianism had lost their hold on the American mind and were not suited to the intellectual climate of the twentieth century. Therefore, they must be changed and brought up to date; the high view of Christ and his Virgin Birth, the emphasis upon his miracles during his life on earth, his atoning death and resurrection must be replaced by an ethical interpretation of the Gospel of Redemption that would make the message of the church relevant to an age of ethical and moral confusion. The problem of sin must be dealt with in psychological terms and redemption must be social rather than individual. Evidence for this deeper motivation of the Affirmation is found in the names of those who signed it and it is quite revealing to trace their activities both before and after 1924. The greater majority of them were more interested in preaching the Social Gospel than they were in proclaiming the message of redemption; the names of all but a few are found in the ranks of the most radical groups in Protestant circles.[6]

The Auburn Affirmation is perhaps the most striking and important manifestation of the growing liberalism within circles that had once been evangelical in theology and preaching. In this same decade another manifestation evolved in the Northern Baptist Convention; the situation was so acute that three new seminaries were formed to provide evangelically-trained ministers: one in Chicago, one in Philadelphia, and one in the Pacific

---

[5] *Ibid,* p. 288.

[6] It is true, and we gladly concede, that some of the signers later realized what they had done and repudiated their previous stand.

Northwest. There were sporadic and isolated outbursts of opposition in the Methodist Episcopal Church, North and some other denominations, the most notable of which was the founding of Westminster Seminary in Philadelphia by a group of Presbyterians who were greatly dissatisfied with the trends in theological education in the Presbyterian Church USA. For other evangelicals who did not share the Calvinism of these groups, independent fundamental churches provided the answer along with the appearance of newly created colleges and seminaries.[7]

In all the major denominations, more particularly in the North than in the South, the story was the same. The denial of the inspiration and infallibility of the Scriptures proved to be tantamount to a rejection of their doctrinal authority; one by one, the great evangelical doctrines of the past were reinterpreted in such a way as to be scarcely recognizable in much of the denominational literature and pronouncements, as well as in the sermons. Official Christianity in all too many denominational circles seemed to be little more than an ethical system, a somewhat more refined and less violent kind of socialism, or native communism, rather than a system of truth and life based upon the Scriptures. At the same time Christianity was losing its biblical heritage, it was failing to gain that prestige among the intellectuals of a scientific age which so many writers in the *Christian Century* were predicting for it, if it would only abandon its pre-Darwinian outlook on life and join hands in the great adventure of the evolutionary process.

To the extent that liberalism came to dominate the churches, to that same extent those churches seemed to become appendages of the League of Nations, the World Court, the labor movement, the Socialist Party, and at times, even of the Communist Party. They

[7] Although the fundamentalist revolt is an important factor in the history of the American church and theology, it is not pertinent to the main thread of this study. Because it was largely dispensational in its theology it had relatively little effect on American political development, except as a kind of protest against economic, political and social liberalism. But it had no positive theological solution of its own to offer.

seldom acted as a church, spoke as churches speak, or seemed like churches. Too often they assumed the role of institutions simply organized for the purpose of aiding any and all reform movements inspired by the democratic philosophy. This was particularly true of the Federal Council of Churches and those journals dedicated to the advancement of its policies, such as the *Christian Century*. The evangelical voices were muted and the humanism and scientific naturalism of the theological and secular liberalism of the nineteen-twenties and early thirties proved to be an inadequate basis for a world and life view which could speak with authority to the problems of the day. But this was not the end of the matter. The very ineffectiveness of this liberalism and its obvious failure to bring about the America which it desired, even less the achievement of the world of its dreams, led to a sense of frustration among the liberals themselves. The first and almost immediate effect of the growing awareness of the futility of the Great Crusade on the part of some was a willingness to accept other patterns of social and economic reform as acceptable expressions of their own position. Those who followed this tortuous path were able to claim communism as the expression of the social concerns of Christianity. The voice of authority inherent in this movement, coupled with the success which it had achieved in overthrowing the old regime in Russia and its often repeated boasts that it would bring about a democratic order in that country, offered to liberals the very certainty for which they were seeking and which their own theology could not provide. Liberal leaders like Harry F. Ward even went so far as to say that Russia was putting into effect a practical Christianity which was the hope of the world.[8]

This resort to communism was not entirely a new development in American liberal circles. Rather was it the intensification of a movement which had begun before World War I and which gained both prominence and a certain respectability after 1920. As early as 1908 a group of liberal ministers, representing twenty-four denominations, had joined in a socialist movement

[8] Harry F. Ward, *In Place of Profit*, New York, 1933, pp. 96-97.

and, in so doing, they affirmed that socialism and industrial democracy were actually the social teachings of the Scriptures in
practice in the modern world. The plain implication was inescapable: if Christ had been alive in their day he would have been a
socialist.[9]

For the great majority of liberals, however much they might
sympathize with the aspirations of the revolutionary leadership of
Russia in their publicly announced aims for a democratic Russia,
this identification of Christianity with communism was unacceptable and they struggled to bring about reforms in this country and
to cling to some remnants of a Christian theism. They clung to the
belief that it was quite possible to Christianize American democracy in such a way that it would be the vehicle for the realization
of the Kingdom of God. And, even if they accepted a somewhat
more secularized version of this dream than that which had motivated Rauschenbusch, they still were able to come to terms with a
philosophy of life that was completely secular in its outlook and
program. On the other hand, these liberals who emerged as leaders after 1918 were somewhat more inclined to rely on direct
political action for the realization of their dream and less on
the conversion of individuals as the best means of bringing about
the Utopia. Theological liberals threw themselves into the cause
of reform with enthusiasm and devotion and frequently found a
common ground with secularists and unbelievers in their support
of such causes as the League of Nations, world peace, disarmament, social and political equality, greater governmental control
over the economic life of the nation, and similar projects.

The fact that the liberals in many of these projects found a
common cause and ground with secularism presents a great difficulty in determining the direct and immediate effect of their liberal theology on political, social and economic events of this era.
This is contrary to a situation in which the legislation of an era
bears the distinct marks of a Christian influence. Under such a sit-

[9] *Literary Digest,* May 9, 1908, p. 682; see also issue of November 7, 1908,
pp. 664-665.

uation the theological effect is quite apparent because it bears a distinct biblical stamp, and the political leaders consciously and openly reveal their Christian outlook in the formulation of political policies. But in an age in which theology has come to terms with philosophical liberalism, it is quite difficult to trace the direct influence of a liberal theology on legislation and political programs in the broader sense of the word. The line dividing liberal theology and the secular outlook becomes so blurred and fuzzy, that it is difficult to discover which group has had the greater impact on the political life of the nation. Political leaders, under the influence of liberalism, are much more likely to defend their programs in terms of the democratic philosophy than they are in terms of a liberal theology. References to theology and the Christian faith as a basis for action are likely to be far less frequent in the Congressional debates of the 1920's, or 1930's, than they were in the Massachusetts General Court of 1632, or a Congressional debate of 1832, and the influence of Christian theism is barely discernible in Congressional debates, decisions of the Supreme Court and pronouncements of national political leaders in recent years.

This noticeable lack of theological reference and biblical appeal is, in itself, a mute evidence of the decline of a biblical orientation for American political thought and action. The very fact that political leaders in the various branches of government are either unwilling or unable to find a sanction for their pronouncements and actions in Christian theism is in itself an indictment of their position; and, the fact that the American people do not demand such a sanction from their leadership is an indictment of the American mind. It is, of course, true that frequently in national debates there are rather vague references to God and Christianity, but, for the most part, these references are for the purpose of justifying policies and positions already decided upon in the light of other philosophies. To give them something of a biblical sanction and a biblical veneer is the politic thing to do. It helps to prove that we are not atheistic like Russia. So the popular argument runs. The frequent identification of Christianity with democracy demands at least a polite reference to the Bible and to Christian ethics. The fact remains that Christian doctrine plays almost no part in the formulation of political and diplomatic policies by the American government today and a study of important declarations, documents, memoirs and other historical sources reveals this fact too clearly to warrant contradiction. This is not to say that there have not been staunch evangelicals in Congress, and other important governmental posts, and on occasion they have wielded a powerful influence for the right. Generally, they have been lonely voices crying in a wilderness of secularism and, at times, they have supported legislation on grounds that was something less than biblical. At other times, some of them have even been unwilling or unable to see the relationship between their Christian doctrine and political policies. As a result they have supported programs which were contrary to the scriptural position. A good illustration of this fact was William Jennings Bryan who managed to combine an orthodox position on the inspiration and authority of the Scriptures with a political philosophy and program which were thoroughly radical and which reflected a socialistic view of man and the state.

It can also be argued with considerable strength that the growth of theological liberalism in the churches greatly encouraged these trends in American political leadership. As it gained a dominance in most of the major denominations, there can be no reasonable doubt that national leaders who were members of these churches and who were rather consistently exposed to liberal preaching were influenced accordingly in their own thinking and were encouraged to support liberal policies in the state and nation as a result.[10] It is important to notice that these prominent

[10] This reasoning cannot be pushed too far lest the conclusion be drawn that all who were liberal in their theology were liberal in their political outlook and all who were conservative in theology were likewise conservative in their political thought. This is obviously not true for there were many wealthy people who were quite liberal in their religious life who were even more conservative in their political and economic views. William Howard Taft is a good illustration of this position. A Unitarian in his denominational

and influential leaders in liberal and radical movements in this country who have come from Presbyterian and Lutheran churches, had already made a clear break with the theology of their respective denominations. Norman Thomas, a graduate of Union Seminary in New York, left the Presbyterian ministry to become one of the dominant leaders of American Socialism only after he rejected practically all of his Presbyterian doctrine. The basic incompatibility between historic Presbyterian orthodoxy and socialism was quite obvious to him and he chose the latter in preference to the former as the calling to which he would devote himself. Norman Thomas is not an isolated example of this kind of development; many examples can be found in American political life during the last forty or fifty years and a strong case can be made that contemporary liberal theology has exercised an influence on national affairs much like that of social Darwinism in the decades after 1870. The dethronement of orthodoxy made possible the development of a liberal outlook in government which came into its own in the New Deal; this final culmination of a trend which had been in existence for many years was made possible by the policies sponsored and aided by the liberal leadership in organized Protestantism in the Federal Council of Churches and allied organizations; also in journals such as the *Christian Century* and the denominational publications.

It thus becomes necessary to examine the era from 1920 to 1932 and particularly the social, political and economic thinking of the major denominations during these years to see the clear parallel between the pronouncements of liberal theologians and journals on the one hand and the positions assumed by the political leaders of those years on the other. This parallel is so striking that an understanding of this interrelationship between theologi-

---

affiliation, he was rather conservative as president and jurist. It is also worthy of note that many fundamentalist churches were largely composed in their membership of lower middle class families and industrial workers. The Socialists were well aware of this fact and in their attempts to win this group to socialism they soft-pedalled the anti-Christian elements in the socialist philosophy.

cal and political liberalism becomes necessary for an understanding of this period of American history and such a study makes it quite clear that the former inspired and nurtured the latter. This influence is seen in practically every area of political interest and inquiry which engaged the attention of the American people and there was scarcely an issue which arose upon which the liberals did not make important pronouncements and take equally strong stands. In short, almost every important diplomatic, political, social and economic issue became part of the broad battle ground upon which the contending forces of conservatism and liberalism were waging an unrelenting warfare for the purpose of gaining a vantage point from which they could mold American opinion. The coming of the great depression of 1929 gave to the forces of liberalism a new opportunity to display their wares before an angry and dismayed public and provided a new, powerful appeal which they had not possessed during the twenties on such a grand scale. The panic and the ensuing depression gave to the liberal program a practical approach to the people which liberalism as a philosophy had never possessed before. The policies and programs which for many people had been the expression of a vague philosophy before 1929, now assumed a new importance and value in their eyes and seemed to provide answers which the philosophy and practices of the conservatives did not seem to have. Many Americans were not only inclined to blame conservatism for the depression, but they were also convinced that it lacked any positive answers for the dilemma. They felt it was rather unimaginative and dull. They were impatient with a theological conservatism which promised a future heaven to believers but which, seemingly, had little to offer people caught in the throes of a depression, many of whom were reduced to great want. This indictment of theological orthodoxy was unwarranted because it did have something to say to such people, but all too often they did not want to hear its message for they had been conditioned to a religious outlook which promised nothing but progress and a future on this earth filled with peace and prosperity. It is also true that many Americans confused historic Christianity with that worship of business and the exaltation of the successful business man, characteristic of the twenties. The depression, in effect, destroyed this kind of religious awe and admiration and the evangelical churches were caught in this debacle.

Thus a combination of circumstances offered to liberalism a golden opportunity to capture the American mind and the liberals were not slow to take advantage of it. They supported old causes with a new zeal and found new ones to claim their energies and devotion. In the area of domestic affairs they were generally to be found in the support of President Franklin Roosevelt and the New Deal Program of reform, and at times pressed for measures and positions far in advance of what the New Deal leaders were willing to sponsor. Although they did not give to this movement a blind loyalty which prevented any criticism or even opposition to particular measures, for the most part, the theological liberals were well aware of the fact that this reform movement was much closer to what they wanted, and had a much better chance of success, than any previous program of reform had ever been able to claim; they were well aware of the fact that in the New Deal they had a far greater hope of reforming American life in all of its aspects according to the pattern of the Social Gospel than they had in either the conservative Democrats of the South, or in the Republican Party. For these reasons, the theological liberals came into a very practical working alliance with both the theorists of the New Deal and with the politicians whose main concern was to retain their hold on as many offices in the national and state governments as possible. The advent of the New Deal did not bring about an ideological shift in liberal thought so much as it widened the opportunity for bringing its philosophy before the public. In the twenties, liberalism was unable to gain a sympathetic hearing from the party in power and its crusades were conducted in the light of this fact. It was the realization of this that caused a group of liberals to form a third party in 1924. But apart from this attempt at political action, the period of the twenties for liberalism was largely devoted to keeping its spirit alive in the midst of an unfriendly political environment and of educating the public as to its aims and projects. In this task the theological and political liberals made common cause with one another. The fact that in so doing they were generally brought into an alliance with socialists, and other left-wingers, who had little or no use for Christian theology and the church, liberal or conservative, did not seem to greatly disturb them. The burden of many of the arguments in liberal theological journals was not too different from those which appeared in the left wing of the secular press. The only distinguishing characteristic of those journals which professed to be Christian was their appeal to the Bible as a sanction for their radicalism. Apart from this rather superficial influence, there was actually little that was different.

World Peace

The most persistent attraction for the liberal mind after 1920 was the cause of world peace. Its widespread appeal was the result of the conviction that war was the greatest of all evils in modern society and that if it could be dealt with satisfactorily, the others would more readily yield to correction. In this great conviction that war must be banished from the human scene, liberals found a basis of unity and common action.

The desire to banish war was not a new theme. It had been dear to the hearts of the Transcendentalist reformers. After 1865 it had receded from first place in liberal thinking, largely because no great wars threatened American tranquility in the closing decades of the nineteenth century. But opposition to war was always a basic aspect of liberal thought and the increasing tensions in Europe after 1905 brought a renewed interest in this issue. By 1912 many American liberals were almost at the point where they felt war might be a thing of the past and that civilized nations would no longer feel the necessity of resorting to arms for the preservation of their interests or territorial integrity. The establishment of the Hague Tribunal had done much to strengthen such thinking both here and in Europe and the appointment of William Jennings Bryan as secretary of state had convinced many observers that Wilson was willing to move in such a direction in his conduct of American foreign policy. The outbreak of the war in Europe and American involvement in it brought dismay to those liberals who had fondly imagined that it was a relic of man's barbaric past, a remnant of his animal existence in the jungle, a thing of the past for twentieth century civilization. Modern man simply could not afford the luxury of the kind of destructive warfare made possible by technology. So ran the argument repeated numbers of times in many periodicals, religious and secular.

The coming of actual warfare in 1917 brought with it a readjustment in the thinking of American liberalism. Some were dismayed but preferred to look upon it as a kind of detour on the road to progress rather than a permanent change of direction. Calling it "the war to end all wars" men of this persuasion were able to retain a large degree of their optimism concerning civilization. Some who were able to convince themselves along these lines finally had to yield to the inescapable facts of the case and recast their entire thinking. Reinhold Niebuhr described men of this state of mind quite accurately:

> Some of us tried to escape the facts by regarding it as an accident or as the final adventure in the cause of righteousness. If we regarded it as an accident, we persuaded ourselves that it was a useful one which would reduce the strategy of conflict to an absurdity. If we put our faith in it as a final adventure, we imagined that it would magically purge mankind of its mania of greed and hatred.[11]

Niebuhr came to the conclusion in this article that the only way to purge mankind of these sins was by education. The war had failed to accomplish this purification which he sought and, by his own confession, he was a tired radical. But somehow or other, in

[11] *Christian Century*, Aug. 30, 1928, pp. 1046-1047.

spite of changes in his thinking which led him away from nineteenth century theology in the direction of neo-orthodoxy and in spite of his weariness with reform movements, Niebuhr managed to become involved in an endless procession of such crusades during the thirties and the forties, often being found among the leaders of these various movements.

Other liberals, chastened, to be sure, by the failure of the war to end all wars and its ghastly consequences in terms of human lives and economic costs, were, nevertheless, incurably optimistic, continuing to look for the day of peace. If alliances in a holy crusade for democracy such as World War I would not do the trick, then alliances for peace were the answer to the question. Thus the League of Nations received an almost unqualified support from every liberal leader in Protestantism; it was also hailed by many conservatives who joined their theological opponents in the belief that the League guaranteed that the war had not been fought in vain and that some good would come out of the awful carnage. The Federal Council of Churches regarded Wilson's League of Nations as the political expression of the Kingdom of God on earth and put forth a gigantic effort to create support for its adoption among its constituent members (Report of Special meeting of the Federal Council of Churches, 1918, p. 9). For the most part the larger denominations were only too ready to follow the leadership of the Federal Council in issuing statements designed to bring pressure upon the Senate to accept membership in the League of Nations as mankind's best hope for peace on earth. The General Conference of the Northern Methodist Church issued a strong plea for an effective League; the Northern Baptist Convention of 1920 took a strong stand, asking Baptists to exert effective pressure for the ratification of the League. The General Assembly of the Presbyterian Church USA (Northern) of 1919 took a decided stand in support of the League and passed an equally strong condemnation of the rejection of the League by the Senate in 1920. It is obvious that the support of the League of Nations, at least as far as official decisions were concerned, was not confined to the liberals, but the idealism of the times inspired conservatives as well to regard the League as an expression of Christian hopes and virtues, even if some of them were unwilling to follow the Federal Council in calling it the "political expression of the Kingdom of God on earth." Eminent leaders in the churches also took a similar position on this issue. Practically every prominent liberal leader was an advocate of peace through the League of Nations, such as Harry Emerson Fosdick, S. Parkes Cadman, Charles Jefferson, Shailer Matthews, William P. Merrill, Charles Clayton Morrison and others, even though some of them had grave doubts about the wisdom of other parts of the Treaty of Versailles.

The defeat of the League by the Senate for the second time in 1920 did not dim the hopes of liberals within and without the church that peace could be achieved by international cooperation of a different kind and so further attempts were made to influence the Senate to vote for American adherence to the Permanent Court for International Justice. In 1926 the Senate actually did vote for our participation in the work of this international body, but it attached qualifications of such a kind that they were unacceptable to other members of the Court and the issue lingered on until it was brought up later in the Roosevelt administration. This debate over the entrance of the United States into the World Court illustrates very clearly the drift of thought in the churches. The interest in this matter was so great and the resolutions by assemblies, conventions and conferences were so numerous that at times the denominations seemed to be in danger of losing their characters as branches of the Church of Jesus Christ and of becoming little more than political pressure groups. Theological and religious issues were often shelved, or given second place, in the debates and actions of annual meetings so that appropriate resolutions might be passed to influence the Senate to take political action desired by the churches in the interests of world peace. Resolutions, rather than the Gospel, seemed to be the more popular method of dealing with sin; personal, national and international. As usual the Federal Council set aside a World Court Sunday and a World Court Week to enhance the effectiveness of its own work and that of its denominational members.

The liberal leadership of the churches and the Federal Council of Churches probably gave an even more fervent support to the Pact of Paris (The Kellogg-Briand Peace Pact), which had been signed in Paris by representatives of fifteen countries, including those of the United States, in August, 1928, binding the signatories to the renunciation of war as an instrument of national policy. The announcement of the signing of this pact evoked an enthusiasm which was almost delirious in its joy. The United States had now broken with its isolationism to become a member of an international pact for the outlawry of war; to many observers it seemed as if this nation might now join the League of Nations by a back door. Charles Clayton Morrison wrote:

> Today international war was banished from civilization. . . . In this simple pledge are gathered up the hopes of mankind, the faith of man in his brother-man as hope and faith never before found expression in common deed. Never did the spirit of man undertake a risk so great. It must mean a new world, a world of permanent peace, on the basis of Justice.[12]

The optimism of this outburst is equalled only by its humanism. The underlying hope and faith of which this pact was an expression, according to Morrison, was not a hope and faith in God, but in man. The peace that was coming was coming from an act of man. The justice upon which the new world would be built would come from man and not from God. Salvation for man was to come not from the God of the Scriptures but from an international pact to which the United States was a signatory.

A comparison of this lyrical outburst with the editorial positions of leading liberal journals is quite revealing. In essence there is little or no difference. The humanism of the one is the humanism of the other. Thus the peace movement of the nineteen-

[12] *Christian Century,* September 5, 1927, p. 1070.

twenties offers a very excellent illustration of that coalescence of thought which was taking place between the socialists and the left-wingers in secular society and the liberal elements in the churches. The emphasis on peace as the best expression of the Kingdom of God on the earth had so seized the mind of liberal Christendom that theological considerations were virtually banished from the scene and a common cause was made with liberals of all shades of opinion.

The question arises: How effective was the support of the liberals in the final acceptance of this Paris Pact? In the matter of the Senate and the debates on the League of Nations it is quite clear from the evidence available that tremendous pressure was applied to that body to bring about our participation as a nation in that venture for international security through collective action. There is likewise no legitimate doubt that it played an important role in the thinking of some of those senators who spoke and voted in behalf of our entrance into the League of Nations. The infiltration of liberal thought is so obvious that no quotations are needed to bolster this point. But the pressure was not sufficient to offset the counter-forces working for the defeat of the League. By 1928 a change had come in American thinking and the Pact of Paris was ratified by the Senate (1929). This took place in spite of the fact that the Kellogg-Briand Pact was open to some of the same objections which had been used so effectively in the debates of 1919-1920 in the Senate against the League of Nations.

It would be straining the evidence too far to claim that all of this change in popular opinion toward American participation in such international agreements can be attributed to the influence of the Federal Council of Churches and the strong action of several of the leading denominations. But there is little doubt that a liberalism common to both of them was triumphant in the decision of the Senate to accept this declaration of national policy.

The Federal Council had been working indefatigably for the passage of such a pact for approximately six years and on December 17, 1928 (while the Pact was still before the Senate for consideration), its representatives presented to President Coolidge a memorial signed by 185,333 members of about thirty constituent churches in which they expressed their "earnest hope" that the Senate would ratify the Kellogg-Briand Pact. The Methodist Church in the North was no less active in behalf of the forthcoming millennium and, as early as 1924, had begun to use political means to hasten the coming of this great day when it formulated a plan to ascertain the attitude of every candidate for the House of Representatives and the Senate on the question of the outlawing of war and to send the information to every individual Methodist congregation.[13] Candidates for Congress were not unaware of the significance of such a move to their own political careers in the light of the fact that the Northern Methodist Church was one of the largest Protestant denominations and the fact that the General Conference of the Methodist Episcopal Church, South gave a hearty endorsement to this adventure in politics made it even more significant. At this very moment, the political strength of Methodism on the question of prohibition was so strong that aspirants to seats in Congress had to reckon with it and the threat of possible manifestations of such strength on other political questions, such as world peace, could not be safely ignored. In cooperation with the Federal Council of Churches and denominations such as the Northern and Southern Baptist Conventions and the General Assembly of the Presbyterian Church USA, they realized it was a force to be reckoned with in future elections.[14] The ratification of this pact was the only significant vic-

[13] Robert M. Miller, *American Protestantism and Social Issues, 1919-1939.* University of North Carolina Press, Chapel Hill, 1958, p. 326.

[14] In this discussion it is clearly recognized that the many conservatives in these various groups (particularly in the Northern and Southern Baptist Conventions and the General Assemblies of the Presbyterian Churches USA and US) were led to give expression to an extravagant enthusiasm for the Pact of Paris which was not truly representative of their personal theologies. This is often true in such assemblies on many issues. But the declarations themselves reveal a liberal outlook in theological matters and the content of the Pact itself reveals a similar bias.

tory which liberalism achieved in the search for world peace between 1919 and 1939, but efforts for American entrance·into the League of Nations and the Permanent Court of International Justice continued to be exerted until the outbreak of World War II. Like success was achieved in the Washington Arms Conference of 1922 and disarmament continued to be the favorite theme of those who felt that war was the greatest of evils. The publications of the Federal Council of Churches, the *Christian Century* and denominational periodicals kept up a stream of editorials on the evils of war, calling for its speedy abolition. The amount of such material is too vast to be covered or quoted; it is also exceedingly repetitious. Its significance lies in the fact that even after 1933 and the rise of Hitler in Germany the dreams of peace lingered on, showing a tremendous fascination for liberal minds which almost blinded many of them to the realities of a world that was rapidly being engulfed by totalitarianism. It was hard for them to realize that there are evils greater than war and that at times war might be a necessity, if not a positive virtue.

The coming of World War II rudely shattered these dreams and brought about a split in the ranks of secular and theological liberals as to the most desirable policy for this country to follow. Some still preferred collective security as the best possible solution to the problem of war, while others reverted to a policy of isolationism as the only answer for peace in a world gone mad. It is, of course, true that this dilemma was not peculiar to liberalism for many evangelicals found themselves in a similar quandary and were forced to choose between these two alternatives. The difficulty for many evangelicals would not have been so great if Russia had not been in a strange alliance with the West against Hitler after June, 1941. Evangelicals had no doubts that the Bible sanctioned war as a proper method for controlling human sin among the nations, but they did have doubts about the character of World War II when Soviet Russia became an ally of the West. The division in the ranks of the liberals over such questions as pacifism, collective security versus isolationism, was not one of ends, but of the proper means of obtaining the ends which all desired. These differences within liberalism were important, but not as basic as they sometimes seemed. In their insistence that war is an evil and that pacifism is the biblically enjoined national policy, there was a high degree of unanimity in their thinking. Robert Miller is probably correct in his statement that most Protestants were opposed to any changes in the Neutrality Acts of 1935, 1937 and 1939 which would weaken them in the direction of allowing American participation on "the right side" in the war raging in Europe. When war finally came on December 7, 1941, most liberals accepted it as a lesser of the evils confronting the Republic. But they could no longer pretend that it was merely another detour on a rather long road to an era of world peace. Although they still wrote articles in this spirit and gave their names to organizations supporting the formation of the United Nations after the end of the war, the old enthusiasm and vigor, the old crusading zeal of 1919-1920 was largely lacking. Many liberals gave the appearance of supporting the cause of world peace and the United Nations Organization simply because it was the thing to do rather than because they had wild expectations that the San Francisco Conference could somehow provide a solution which had been beyond the power of the Paris Peace Conference of 1919 to achieve. Liberalism, both theological and political, had no real answers for the dilemma which confronted mankind in 1945 and many, if not most, were aware of this inability.

The world which emerged after World War II presented problems of staggering proportions, greater in their import than those which greeted the peacemakers of 1919. It had been much more devastating because of the technological development of new weapons. In every aspect this war had been more total and the damage, both to property and to human personality, was beyond all calculation. The fact that this conflict made Russian communism the major system, not only in Russia, but in most of Asia and much of Europe, enhanced the other issues which the new world organization must contend with. Thoughtful observers of all shades of opinion decided they must not hope for too much from either the San Francisco Conference or from a new league which that conference would probably create.

Evangelicals were caught in this same dilemma which confronted the liberals. However great their misgivings about the efficacy of such an organization as that which was being proposed to replace the old League of Nations, they were unwilling to stand forth as unyielding opponents of such a plan to bring some semblance of peace and order to a world gone mad and they were, for the most part, ready to accept this effort at collective security as probably the best solution which could be expected under the circumstances. They realized the Charter of the United Nations worked out at the San Francisco Conference was very definitely the result of liberal influences. It was well known that the final charter embodied many of the proposals for change suggested by the Federal Council of Churches for the improvement of the preliminary charter worked out at the Dumbarton Oaks Conference in 1944. Its influence was particularly felt in the addition of the humanitarian aims in the preamble of the document and in the increased role of the Economic and Social Council in the area of human rights.[15]

The *Watchman-Examiner,* a conservative Baptist publication, took the view that the United Nations charter was a compromise, probably the best compromise that could have been worked out under the circumstances as they existed at that time. It admitted that its purpose was noble and that it would probably give the world a breathing spell from war. However, this conservative voice was not wildly enthusiastic about the new organization for peace.

Either the charter of the United Nations is a progressive historical step leading in the direction of international fellowship, economic adjustment and humanistic enterprise or it is the frame-

[15] *Christian Century,* July 11, 1945, p. 818.

work of world organization for the subjugation of peoples hitherto unequaled in human history.[16]

Neither did this voice of evangelical Baptists fall into the error of confusing the Charter of the United Nations with the Gospel of Jesus Christ.

We are quite convinced that the Charter of the United Nations is not the objective of Christianity.[17]

As a human achievement it had great promise, but there were purposes given to it which it could never fulfill and the only true hope of mankind for peace lay in the preaching of the true Gospel of Jesus Christ.

Conservative Presbyterian journals of both the Northern and Southern Churches took a moderate position on the United Nations seeing it as an honest endeavor to solve a pressing problem, but never identifying the solution with the Gospel.

The evangelical desire to support the United Nations on the principle that to do so was a Christian duty since Christians must strive for peace along with all men was seriously challenged by the presence of Communist Russia as a leading member of that organization. Evangelicals rightly suspected the intentions of the communist bloc of nations and even more to the point they were dubious as to whether a Christian nation should become entangled in such a project with a country that was avowedly atheistic. Many conservatives felt that an international organization which was acceptable to communists in its aims and purposes could hardly command the respect and support of those who held to biblical Christianity; and, their loyalty to the United Nations involved the question of how far Christian citizens can go in their support of policies which are far from the biblical world and life view. This issue was so pressing that a considerable segment of evangelical strength in this country, largely among those who

---

[16] *The Watchman-Examiner,* August 23, 1945, p. 817.
[17] *Ibid.,* September 6, 1945, p. 845.

held to a dispensational and premillennial theology, strongly opposed American entry into such an organization.

Theological liberalism, on the other hand, was almost unanimous in its support of the United Nations Organization and of American participation in its program. This is not to say that they were all of one mind as to its provisions or that they were equally optimistic concerning its ability to solve the pressing problems of the day. That certainly was not the case, but they were unanimous in feeling the necessity for such an organization. Many of them felt that it was but a step in the right direction to the only answer for the problem of war in modern society—the creation of a world government of some kind.

The *Christian Century* took a hopeful position concerning the work of the San Francisco Conference.

> It is not an ideal charter, and the organization which its adoption will call into being will not be an ideal organization. Indeed, its imperfections are flagrant. The Charter is shot through with compromises. . . . Something indeed has been achieved at San Francisco, something of genuine promise. But the world scene has not been changed. It has only been revealed. And the revelation as reflected in the Charter is both disquieting and hopeful.[18]

The editor went on to say that he found hopeful revelations of profound importance and these were a universal desire for peace and an equally universal aspiration for world cooperation; and, "in these aspirations, our hope. Our hopes, to be sure, will be tempered with anxiety; they are trembling hopes, but they must be trusted, for when hope is gone all is gone."[19]

The Federal Council of Churches was one of the first groups to act in behalf of the adoption of the Charter of the United Nations by the government of the United States. In July, 1945 its executive council called for its speedy ratification by the Senate. Its statement was somewhat more optimistic than the position of the *Christian Century*.

[18] *The Christian Century*, July 4, 1945, pp. 782-783.
[19] *Ibid.*, p. 783.

The charter offers mankind means for the achievement of a just and durable peace. . . . The churches have long held that nations can better serve God's purpose for the world as they are brought into organic relationship with one another for the common weal. The charter signed at San Francisco marks a genuine advance toward this end. . . . We believe that it is the clear duty of our government promptly to ratify the charter and thus to assure cooperation by the United States in the task of making the organization an effective agency for the maintenance of international peace and security.[20]

The debates in the Senate on the United Nations Charter reflect to a great degree this liberal position. Secular liberalism, on the whole, reflected the same kind of thinking apparent in the liberal Christian press and Federal Council pronouncements. Writing in *The Nation,* Bartley C. Crum said:

We must be realistic about the United Nations Security Organization. It is not a world state. It is not an organization to which any human being owes allegiance as against his country. It is at present an association of allied nations which have just concluded one desperate war and have determined to maintain their cooperation in peace in order that they may avoid another.[21]

Freda Kirchway, one of the noted liberal writers of the day, took a somewhat similar view:

The United Nations Charter is a mirror of the present world of national states. It represents the inner conflict of desire and fear that dominate even the strongest powers. . . . As long as this conflict exists, the new world organization is bound to be essentially a great power alliance rather than a world government.

Men who are eager to have a more democratic organization for world security will not oppose the beginning made at San Francisco.[22]

[20] *Ibid.,* p. 818.
[21] *The Nation,* June 9, 1945, pp. 641-642.
[22] *The Nation,* July 7, 1945, pp. 5-6.

These opinions are rather indicative of the liberal outlook in general. The work of the San Francisco Conference had serious weaknesses, but it was a beginning towards a genuine world organization and must be accepted for this reason. It was the best organization that could be achieved in a world still dominated by the idea of national sovereignty. Some felt that it had certain strengths which the old League of Nations did not possess; one of these lay in the fact that both Russia and the United States were members.

At first glance this restraint concerning the United Nations Charter might seem to be a lack of optimism concerning the ability of mankind to achieve an enduring peace. This is far from being the case. Many liberals doubted the ability of the present national structure to achieve peace and thus they called for some form of world government. They were realists enough to see that such an organization was not possible in 1945 and they were willing to accept the United Nations Organizations as their second choice. But they were very optimistic concerning the ability of a world government to avoid all future wars and frequently referred to the Constitution of the United States as a proof of their expectations.

Senatorial opinion, as it was reflected in the debates over the ratification of the United Nations Charter was equally optimistic. Senator Scott Lucas of Illinois, declared:

> I am convinced that there is the beginning of lasting and durable peace. And if my prophecy proves to be correct, the Charter will rank among the greatest documents of history.[23]

Equally optimistic was Senator McClelland of Arkansas:

> It is the ultimate goal, sincere hope, and the highest purpose of the signatory powers and the people they represent to eliminate and forever remove mankind's worst enemy, the scourge of war, from the face of the earth, and thus attain the fulfillment of one of the highest aspirations of all civilized peoples of the world.[24]

[23] *Congressional Record,* Volume 91, Part 6, July 25, 1945, p. 8019.
[24] *Ibid.,* p. 8082.

These samples of senatorial opinion reflect the general position of that body in regard to the potential effectiveness of the United Nations Organization in the elimination of war from the human scene. This optimism was the product of a theological liberalism. The only real difference between it and that of *The Nation* and the *New Republic* was the rather general confidence in the Senate that this era of peace could be achieved among sovereign states by such an organization and that world government was not necessary for its realization. The underlying humanism in the thinking of the day was clearly brought out by another senator who said:

> It seems to me that this charter step announces a new era in the history of mankind and new opportunities for nations and their peoples to develop the best there is in the human being without fear of aggression of the kind that enthrones might and dethrones right.[25]

A conservative approach tempered the enthusiasm of some and they were careful in their appraisals to keep from promising more for the new organization than it could possibly deliver. Senator Burnet Maybank of South Carolina sounded a cautious note in enlisting support for the United Nations and in so doing he gave a sound reason for his own position.

> The Charter is a hope. It is a plan, the best plan yet devised, to safeguard peace. It is a noble concept. It is a contract for peace, but it is not a guaranty for peace. . . . We must try for peace. The maintenance of our moral integrity requires that we try for peace and the best way is to try through this Charter. . . . I believe that this great Charter is a necessary document, a necessary plan for progress in that field (international peace). Human behavior cannot be regulated by documents, but documents which express the aspirations of mankind may help to guide human behavior toward a more peaceful world than we have known.[26]

[25] *Ibid.,* p. 8039.
[26] *Ibid.,* p. 8088.

Not too many liberals were concerned with the problem of Russian communism as an influence in the United Nations. They did not share the evangelical horror and disgust of the communist ideology. This was, in part, due to the fact that their own philosophy led them to conclusions similar to those held by the Marxists and which were often derived from similar assumptions, for American liberalism of this era was quite frequently to be found championing policies which were generally admitted to be those of the communists.

A second major reason for this indifference to, or willingness to tolerate, the presence of communist Russia in the United Nations lay in the fact that many American liberals had come to the conclusion that one of the almost inescapable results of the war would be such a modification in both the Russian and American political and economic systems that they would come to resemble each other and the two nations would thus be able to agree on a *modus vivendi* in their relations. President Roosevelt had sounded this note to his associates in his cabinet and in those preliminary conferences held during the war to determine just what kind of a peace would emerge after the hostilities had come to an end. Sumner Welles shed much light on Roosevelt's thinking at this point.

> He felt, therefore, that even though the internal systems of the two countries could never conceivably become identical, some progress toward approximation had already been made, and that this approximation made for a better understanding between the peoples of the two nations. He regarded this trend as making it more likely that no fundamental conflict between the two countries need ever become inevitable provided that Soviet Communism had permanently abandonded its doctrine of world revolution. He felt that it was indispensable that both governments should realize that in the field of world affairs their respective courses could always be parallel and need never become antagonistic.[27]

[27] Sumner Welles, *Where Are We Heading,* pp. 37-38.

There is abundant evidence that this optimistic view of the direction which Russia was taking in its domestic affairs was rather general in the Roosevelt administration and the official view seems to have been that Russia was actually becoming democratic in its policies. War-time propaganda in this country took this up in the effort to convert the American people to an acceptance of Russia as an ally in the crusade against totalitarianism. Both Hollywood and the press espoused this theme.

This theme had also been a major note in most of the secular liberal journals in this country; this attitude may explain why so many liberals who, during most of the nineteen thirties, had become so strongly pacifistic in their outlook, by 1942 were willing and even eager to accept American involvement in World War II, not merely as a kind of necessity, but as desirable. They now looked upon the conflict as a means of social progress and had come to the conviction that our participation would help in bringing about major alterations in the political, economic and social structure of this country; alterations which would aid in harmonizing the differences between the United States and Russia. This was a frequent theme in the editorials of those journals which were extremely liberal in their outlook and could find much which they regarded as good in the Russian system. In a series of editorials, the *New Republic* voiced this theme in the early months of 1942, taking the position that the war was a revolution and the real losers in such a conflict would be the pre-war conservatives. It was a foregone conclusion that a new democratic order would emerge in this country after the war and by democratic, they meant, an order which would be highly collective in its economic structure, veering toward a Russian type of communistic control. Conservatives could not stem the tide toward this for the forces in motion were too great to be controlled. Thus, they should follow the example of the British conservatives and be prepared to make concessions to this new order.[28]

This conception of the war made its way into the Roosevelt

[28] See the *New Republic* in *passim*, January, February and March, 1942.

Administration and the President himself was not free from this type of thinking. It is quite evident in his message to Congress commending to that body the report of the Natural Resources Planning Board of 1943 and it assumed something of a major importance during the campaign of 1944.

There can be little doubt that this optimistic outlook on the nature of the war played an important role in those decisions which were made at Yalta and Potsdam in 1945 for the post-war treatment of both Germany and Japan. Certain elements in the State department so openly admired the Communist regime in Russia, because of what they regarded as its great social advances, that their admiration came very close to being a kind of idolization of communism in general as a method of social salvation for modern man. In the eyes of many American liberals, Russia was a vast social laboratory in which important experiments were being carried on for the ultimate benefit of all humanity. Thus, the post-war treatment of Germany and Japan should reflect this concept of Russia. As a result of this, the decisions made at Yalta and Potsdam represent the greatest triumphs which liberalism had yet achieved in the conduct of American foreign policy, but only gradually would their significance become apparent to the people at large.

Domestic Communism and the Recognition of Soviet Russia

One of the most important, and yet unforeseen, consequences of World War I was the triumph of communism in Russia as a result of the revolution of 1917. This event was of major importance not only for that country, but for the rest of Europe and, ultimately, for the whole civilized world. It hung like a heavy shadow over the Versailles Conference and soon became a source of controversy in American politics. It had a diverse effect here much like the French Revolution had during the Washington administration. As in the days of Washington and Jefferson, so in the nineteen-twenties, the conservatives in this country were quite hostile to the revolutionary movement in Russia, regarding it as a threat to the established order and constitutional liberties in this country. On the other hand, theological and political liberals were prone to look on the movement with a considerable degree of sympathy and favor even if they did not approve of the methods which the communist leaders had used to bring the Romanov dynasty to its end. In both the conservative and liberal attitudes towards communism at home and abroad, there was a certain consistency which served to bring about a very evident division between the groups in their attitude on many political and social issues even during the nineteen-twenties, but it became much more evident in the decade of the thirties.

That communism should have proved to be an increasingly important factor in American political thought and practice was to be expected. The very success which the movement had achieved in Russia gave it a new status and prestige not only in the other countries of Europe, but in this nation as well. Communism, as a philosophy, had made its initial appearance here very soon after the *Communist Manifesto* of 1848, but at first, it was largely a philosophical rather than a popular appeal. It first gained acceptance among the lower classes during the depression which began in 1873. But it was the position of only a small minority until after 1917 when it was able to gain a much wider hearing not only among the laboring classes of this country, but among the intellectuals as well. There were many liberals, theological and political, who were not personally Marxians but who were favorably disposed toward the movement because they were in sympathy with social experiments which were in accord with the assumptions of their own liberalism. The difference between many American liberals and Marxian thought was one of degree rather than of kind, and a subtle sense of kinship gave birth to a rather widespread willingness among them to tolerate the development of the communist philosophy in this country. Some of them were not averse to having a communist regime established in the United States provided it was stripped of its totalitarian features and could be introduced by non-violent methods.

Many American liberals were in a peculiar state of mind in the early nineteen-twenties, and a great depression of spirit came upon them. The hopes and expectations which Wilson had aroused by his announcement of the Fourteen Points (the last of which was the call for the League of Nations), had been dashed to pieces by the failure of the Senate to accept the League of Nations and for many of them the Treaty of Versailles, without the Covenant of the League, was merely another treaty and not too good at that. There was also the growing realization that the war which had been fought to make the world safe for democracy had made it remarkably unsafe for that kind of government; and that the war fought to end all wars would very likely be followed by other and more ghastly conflicts. The Great Crusade had turned out to be a Great Fiasco and their former optimism had given way to a deepening pessimism. The one bright hope in a Europe in ruins was the new era in Russia. It seemed that only in Russia had autocracy given way to democracy, or at least, was in the process of giving way to it in 1919 and 1920. Only here were there some visible fruits of the conflict waged to bring the right of self-government to all peoples who desired it.

As the liberals surveyed the American scene they found little to bring them encouragement. Popular radicalism had been at full tide at home in 1919 and various schemes were being brought forward for the nationalization of the railroads and other segments of industry, the most important of which was the Plum Plan, and there were great hopes that the war would bring democratization to American business as a whole. In fact this hope had brought radical support to Wilson in 1917 when the country entered the war. The *New Republic* had written in joyful optimism at this time:

> Democracy is infectious. It is now as certain as anything human can be that the wall . . . will dissolve into democratic revolution the world over.[29]

[29] "The Great Decision," *New Republic*, April 7, 1917, quoted in A. M. Schlesinger, *The Crisis of the Old Order*, (Cambridge, 1957, p. 17).

Progressives of both the major parties were convinced that the war would bring an end to American capitalism in the form in which it had developed. They felt that governmental activity in seizing private property for public use during the war emergency had given the idea of the sacredness of private property a blow from which it would never recover. For some of these liberals, World War I brought very definite possibilities for social advance if it would bring socialism to the American scene. But in 1920 both the idealism of the war era and this radicalism declined as normalcy returned. Conservatives were genuinely and rightly alarmed at the strength of the radical movement. Wilson's Attorney General, A. Mitchell Palmer, spoke for many Americans when he wrote in the spring of 1919:

> Like a prairie fire, the blaze of revolution was sweeping over every American institution of law and order a year ago. It was eating its way into the homes of the American working men, its sharp tongues of revolutionary heat were licking the altars of the churches, leaping into the belfry of the school bell, crawling into the sacred corners of American homes, seeking to replace marriage vows with libertine laws, burning up the foundations of society.[30]

On January 1, 1920 Palmer took active steps to drive radicalism from the American home and school by ordering a series of raids on known radical centers all over the nation, as a result of which something over 6,000 people were apprehended on various charges. The liberal disillusionment with the Versailles Treaty was now enhanced with a growing pessimism concerning the Wilson administration at home, and with the state itself. Whatever hope might have remained was quickly dispelled by the 1920 presidential campaign which elevated Warren G. Harding to the presidency. The wreckage of the dream was now complete for many liberals and they began to look to Russia as the mainstay of human liberty and even of civilization itself. In 1927 a group

[30] A. M. Palmer, "The Case Against the Reds," *Forum,* Feb. 1920, quoted in Schlesinger, *op. cit.,* pp. 42-43.

of liberals, including Paul Douglas (later Senator from Illinois), Rexford Tugwell (later a prominent member of the New Deal), and Stuart Chase visited Soviet Russia. They did not return to this country as converts to the Russian version of Marxist doctrine, but they were tremendously impressed with the social experiment which they saw there. Harry Ward, Professor at Union Theological Seminary in New York, and Sherwood Eddy, one of the more popular liberal religious lecturers of the day, were more impressed with what they saw and came to the conclusion that Russian communism was something more than a mere social experiment; it was an application of practical Christianity on a vast scale and heralded a new day and a new social order for all who would dare to follow this Russian leadership toward a humanly achieved millennium.

Thus, once again, the thinking of theological and political liberalism converged toward the acceptance of common policies and goals for the evaluation and treatment of communism at home and abroad. The contemporary evidence of this meeting of liberal minds is so vast that it is impossible to present a detailed analysis, but a casual glance at the opinions of *The Nation,* the *New Republic,* and the *Christian Century* during the 1920's and early thirties, will give the reader an amazing scope of editorial agreement which existed among liberals of all hues and colors concerning communism in Russia and the United States, and what our policy should be toward this movement. Although Wilson, Harding, Coolidge and Hoover steadfastly refused to give diplomatic recognition to the Soviet regime, there was a general agreement among liberals in this country that this should be done.

Representative of liberal Christian thought was the position taken by the *Christian Century* in applauding Roosevelt's bold move in recognizing the Soviet regime in Russia late in 1933. After admitting that economic factors played a part in this diplomacy, this journal went on to deny that it could be reduced to economic factors and nothing more.

Beyond this political advantage . . . there is an even more important moral advantage. With this recognition the United States brings to an end an attempt to impose moral condemnation on Soviet Russia which has for years involved it in a position that bordered perilously close to hypocrisy. . . .

It is an earnest that the day of uninformed recrimination as between the peoples of the two nations approaches its end. It is a revelation of a new quality of humility in the American minds; a new readiness to stop merely pointing with scorn at the vast experiment under way in Russia and to acknowledge that the ends which the Russians are seeking are ends, which, in the main, the people of this country are also demanding shall be sought in our society.[31]

This position taken by the *Christian Century* did not differ materially from that assumed by the secular liberal press. The economic advantages for both countries in such a move were freely admitted, but there was much more to it than trade considerations. The recognition of Russia was simply a belated admission that the communist experiment was not only being watched with interest by this country, but that there was a great deal of value in it which could be used to our advantage. Certain aims of communism in Russia were also those of the American people under the New Deal. Utopianism was a goal which all could share even if the American version did not accept all the means the Soviet leaders might choose to bring about their own millennial society. There was no immorality involved in the recognition of a regime officially declared to be atheistic. According to the *Christian Century,* the refusal to recognize the Soviet regime in Russia was immoral because Russia was seeking ends which the American people were also seeking. According to this kind of logic, it was immoral to decry the communist philosophy simply because there was a certain identity between it and the demands of the American people for economic and social changes in this country. If this country should decide to adopt communism in

[31] *Christian Century*, November 29, 1933, pp. 1494-1495.

part, or in whole, such a decision then would somehow have a decisive effect on the nature of the movement itself.

Other liberal theological journals and groups applauded the recognition of Russia as a wise and necessary step, and, it was to be expected, that the secular publications would heartily endorse such a move. Not to recognize such a brave experiment in social planning was unthinkable and Roosevelt's action was in accord with the best interests of the country, and of humanity in general.

The Nation was in hearty agreement with the step taken by Roosevelt in regard to Russia. In fact, this journal felt that it would be one of the outstanding accomplishments of the New Deal and would be remembered long after much of the actual legislation of the Roosevelt administration had been forgotten and the depression a thing of the past.

> It means far more than new opportunities for trade. . . . It means more even than the return of common sense after the long reign of fantasy and fear. It means the creation of a new force for peace in an international situation bristling with imminent conflicts. . . . Neither Russia nor the United States wants war; indeed Russia has been pursuing a policy of peace in the face of extreme provocation. . . . We congratulate Mr. Roosevelt upon his realism and courage and good sense.[32]

The Churches and Social Reform in the Twenties

In the years between 1919 and 1932 there is a clearly discernible leftward drift in the public pronouncements of many of the larger denominations and even more outspoken were the individual ministers. For the most part their liberalism in political and economic matters was a reflection of the theological liberalism by which they were motivated. The conservative churches seldom made pronouncements on national affairs which were in sharp contradiction to their theology and those ministers who were in the vanguard of social agitation, almost to a man, had departed from the historic faith.

[32] *The Nation,* November 29, 1933, p. 607.

The denominational pronouncements were rather mild in character in the years just following World War I, but those of the ministers were more militant and reflected an unswerving devotion to socialism as their position. The denominational affirmations did not, generally, specifically endorse socialism; although the Methodist Federation for Social Action kept up a steady attack on the profit motive as the basis for economic activity, declaring it to be immoral, and calling for the substitution of Christian socialism. In 1920 the annual Convention of the Northern Baptists resolved that "industry is a social service whose ruling motive should not be the profit of the few, but the welfare of all, and that the service motive must become the dominant spirit in the method and processes of industry."[33] The 1920 General Assembly of the Presbyterian Church USA called for a cooperative spirit in industry which would take precedence over the profit motive. The Federal Council of Churches was willing to take a more advanced stand on free enterprise than most of its constituent members and at a special meeting in Cleveland in 1919, and in the next year in its statement on "The Church and Social Reconstruction," it emphasized the necessity for reconstructing society on a democratic and cooperative basis. These pronouncements of the early twenties had relatively little influence on the main stream of American politics at that time. The flood time of post-war prosperity caused them to fall on deaf ears and it was only with the coming of the economic crisis of 1929 that they gained any real hearing. The end of the era of prosperity also brought with it an increasing radicalism in denominational pronouncements. Theological liberals needed the impact of the great economic debacle to gain a wider support from the American people.

This is not to say that there was no political activity in the nineteen-twenties indicative of this theological trend. Not only the Progressive Party of 1924, but individual political leaders in both of the major parties, and such figures as Norman Thomas, very clearly reflected the influence of the Social Gospel on their

[33] *Annual of the Northern Baptist Convention*, 1920, p. 266.

own positions. But they had relatively little influence on the course of national affairs. Political and economic conservatism was too firmly entrenched to be easily threatened by their attacks. The chief function of theological liberalism in the decade between 1919 and 1929 was to supply the necessary intellectual stimulus for political discontent and to keep alive the liberal dream. It maintained both a philosophical and something of an organizational continuity between the Progressive movement of the opening years of the century and the New Deal.

The voice of liberal protest was raised on many other issues in American life, particularly on the question of labor and race relations, but in these areas there was relatively little political action which can be traced to its influence. The executive committee of the Interchurch World Movement appointed a special committee to investigate the steel strike of 1919 with Methodist Bishop Francis J. McConnell as chairman. It issued a long report which was highly praised by those friendly to labor and hotly condemned by others. In the following years the Federal Council of Churches and denominations increasingly made labor disputes a legitimate subject for official pronouncements. Likewise in 1920 the Federal Council of Churches made the first ecclesiastical statement on race relationships in this country and a study commission was created. Later, other bodies took up the problem and undoubtedly prepared the way for later action of a political nature. For various reasons political liberals were unable to secure suitable legislation in the years before the depression.

Prohibition

On the subject of prohibition much has been written and to a degree certainly lies within the scope of this study. This was probably the one issue in this era which drew as much, or more, support from evangelical circles as it did from the liberals. However, it is too much to claim that the passage of the eighteenth amendment and the legislation necessary for its enforcement were the result of liberal influence alone. On the evils of the liquor trade and on the necessity for the abolition of drunkenness both liberals and conservatives could meet on common ground.

In the matter of prohibition the pattern was much more complex than on any other issue of the nineteen twenties. In the first place, secular liberalism was not in agreement with the religious liberals on the evils of drink to the same degree as they were on such issues as the recognition of Soviet Russia, the necessity for world peace and the rights of labor over the rights of property. It should also be noted that a similar cleavage existed among the ranks of the theological conservatives. This difference of opinion among conservatives was probably both theological and political in its origins, but it must be remembered that the prohibition issue had been vigorously pushed by the religious and political radicals during the first half of the nineteenth century and, historically, it had not been a part of the conservative outlook and program. Many sincere evangelicals felt the vast powers conferred on the central government by the eighteenth amendment constituted a greater threat to Christianity than the liquor trade that was to be outlawed.

Organs of liberal opinion, such as the *Christian Century*, quite often were ardent champions of national prohibition, the eighteenth amendment and its enacting legislation, and they took a very dim view of Franklin Roosevelt's support of the repeal movement in the 1932 campaign. In like manner, theologically conservative publications did not always look upon repeal with the same degree of disapproval which characterized the more liberal journals for they were prone to find the cause of social and national sin in man himself rather than in the liquor trade. They had never considered the eighteenth amendment as an important step toward the elimination of sin and poverty and the achievement of a new high in national righteousness.

If it cannot be said that the great prosperity of the decade from 1919 to 1929 did not dull the consciences of theological liberals and advocates of the Social Gospel in American life, there can be little doubt that this awesome spectacle of a pyramiding national wealth (on paper at least), on a scale without parallel in previous American history, made their message much less attractive and the necessity of reform much less obvious to the public than it had been in the early years of the present century. A benevolent attitude toward the American scene, political, social, and economic, characterized the era and the maintenance of "normalcy" seemed to be the height of the public aspiration. Against the complacency engendered by prosperity the reformers cried out in vain. Big Business and its allies in government and the church seemed to be in an almost impregnable position. Politicians, economists and some churchmen vied with one another in giving voice to an optimism that the American economy had entered upon a new day, that depressions, such as those of 1873 and 1893, were a thing of the past, for leaders of this country in government and business had solved the problems of the business cycle. We were the masters of our economic destiny as no previous generation had ever been. But this ever-normal prosperity did not and could not last. The mystery of the business cycle had not been solved and the events of 1929 were to prove this fact rather conclusively to the American people in a way for which they were not prepared. The disastrous stock market crash of October, 1929, and the ensuing depression, replaced the optimism of the decade with a pessimism concerning the "American way of life" which had little more foundation than the previous outlook which saw nothing but rising prices and greater profits ahead for American business.

This new mood, however little justification it may have had, proved to be of monumental importance in the future development of the country and a decisive factor in the appearance of a new radicalism in political, social and economic thought without parallel in American experience. The widespread unemployment, with its consequent upheavals, in the life of so many American families not only shook the confidence of much of the working class in the invulnerability of the free enterprise system, but made it quite responsive to the appeals of those who were preaching liberal and radical social and economic theories openly and with a fervor equal to the emergency upon the nation.

7

The New Deal and Its Consequences

The depression resulting from the 1929 stock market crash and other factors at work in the American economy was a momentous event which left its mark on the nation. The decline in national productivity, the resulting decline in national income, the widespread unemployment, the many bank failures which accentuated the unemployment problem, all were real and brought unexpected and unaccustomed hardship to millions of people who were caught in a maze of mortgage and installment debt. Without sufficient resources to meet their obligations hundreds of thousands of farmers and homeowners in the cities faced foreclosure and eviction from their farms and homes. Even corporations of great prominence in the financial and business community were not immune to bankruptcy proceedings and the number of bank failures rose to frightening heights early in 1933. The combination of these factors cast such a gloom over the world of business that encouraging statements by the Hoover administration and prominent financial and industrial leaders that "prosperity is just around the corner" had little effect on the nation at large, a nation which could not forget that as late as the summer of 1929 some of these very leaders were stating that national prosperity was here to stay and that depressions were a thing of the past. Under such conditions the American mind proved to be a very fertile soil for the sowing of economic and social radicalism under the guise of a "program of recovery and reform." Thus, in retrospect, it should not be surprising that after 1930 there was a vigorous revival of theories and programs which had been discarded under the impact of the unheralded prosperity of the nineteen twenties. The depression now gave them a new lustre. There were many politicians who were willing and even eager to use them in place of the slogans and practices of the previous decade, which were now in disgrace and almost useless as a rallying cry to appeal to the voting public. In this new political leadership there were some who used liberalism as a means to the end of gaining political power and public office. There was also a significant element which not only saw liberalism as a means of gaining political control, but who looked to this liberal philosophy as the means for rewriting the whole political, social and economic structure of the nation. For them, recovery was a necessary prerequisite for that radical reform which must come as a major readjustment in American life so that such economic disasters would be a thing of the past. It is not always easy to judge the sincerity of the many leaders who came forth after 1929, but there can be no doubt that many of them were utterly captivated by a new liberalism, with its roots in the old, but which looked also to European ideologies for sanctions which it could not so easily find either in the Progressive Movement of the Theodore Roosevelt-Woodrow Wilson era, or even in its nineteenth century American antecedents.

At the same time this new liberalism was both a logical and an actual outgrowth of previous intellectual currents in this country. If it did not find all that it needed in previous American thought, it found much that it could and did apply to the current crisis. If the architects of the New Order in this country were tremendously impressed with the Russian experiment in "economic democracy," this Marxian version impressed them because they found in it similarities and parallels to their own liberal philosophy. Advocates of the Social Gospel who had long been preaching economic democracy in this country and Russia, after 1917, provided a very dramatic and extensive application of what many of them had long dreamed for America. They regretted the bloodiness of the Marxian Revolution, to be sure, but some of them were even willing to accept it as a necessary consequence of the triumph of an industrial democracy against the opposition of the stubborn capitalists.

American liberals, looking to the Social Gospel on the one hand and the Russian experiment on the other, were planning for an American version of this great crusade for economic democracy without the revolutionary upheaval and the dictatorship which marred the Russian experiment. The American approach was to take the form of a democratic collectivism and was to be achieved through legal means rather than by violence. This was the pervading frame of mind of American liberalism when the New Deal came to power as a result of the 1932 election.

Theological liberals had been quietly working toward the same general goal. The depression had given them, so they thought, their golden opportunity to unite with the secular liberal forces for the realization of the Kingdom of God on earth. It is not too much to say that they prepared the way for the New Deal both by setting forth actual political and economic programs and by giving such proposals a theological support which they found in the Social Gospel. Liberal theology not only gave a philosophical support for political liberalism during the lean years of the nineteen twenties, but after 1929 it also prepared the way for the program which emerged in the New Deal by calling for specific proposals which were often far more radical than Franklin Roosevelt and his New Deal leadership were either ready, or willing, to sponsor. Not only did they chart a course for the

New Deal to follow, but they also influenced the thinking within some of the larger denominations so that large blocks of voters in these churches were not only ready to support the New Deal, but looked upon it as an application of the Gospel to the issues of the day. Both liberal theological journals and denominational conventions and assemblies had been calling for radical reform in American life for over two years before the election of 1932 and, to a great degree, they had prepared the people for the avalanche of secular liberalism which was soon to appear in the flood of New Deal legislation.[1]

The leadership which liberal theology exercised in the preparation for the New Deal was greatly aided by the journalism which it had at its command. Among the churches at large the greatest influence was wielded by the *Christian Century*. As early as January 1932, Dwight Bradley wrote in that journal that the present crisis had brought to Protestantism an opportunity to extend the influence of democratic individualism and to "give to it a meaning which merely secular liberalism cannot bring or add."[2] A month later he wrote:

> If organized Christianity is so tied in with the capitalist order that it can offer no regenerative power, but only consolation in the day of its decline, then it cannot avoid repeating the story of those religions of the past which have gone down with the civilizations in which they grew.[3]

His solution for the problem confronting the church in the economic crisis of the day was that it should withdraw its sanction of capitalism which was so contrary to its own gospel and hasten the disintegration of the old order. The almost inescapable conclusion to such reasoning was obvious. Christianity in any kind of alliance with capitalism was doomed because the old order was

---

[1] This is not to say that all New Deal legislation was radical and undesirable, nor that its sponsors in Congress were always cognizant of the importance of the measures they were called upon to approve.

[2] *Christian Century*, January 6, 1932, pp. 12-13.

[3] *Ibid.*, February 3, 1932, p. 147.

doomed. If Christianity was to survive the cultural deluge soon to engulf the West, it must become identified with the revolutionary forces at work for the destruction of the old order. Apparently this new revolutionary order was in harmony with the Gospel and a loyalty to it would inspire a new enthusiasm for the church on the part of the American people now alienated from it because of its alliance with capitalism.

This publication took a further step toward the creation of an alliance among all liberals, political and religious, for the realization of their common goals. Its editor lamented that at the present time (May, 1932), there was no effective way in which "the liberal social convictions of a great body of our citizenship can register on the conduct of our democracy."[4] It recommended as the best solution to the problem that one or both of the two major parties should be transformed in such a way as to become a vehicle for this liberal opinion. In a subsequent issue its editor offered a political program for the proposed liberal party in which he advocated adherence to the World Court, a full cooperation with the League of Nations on the part of this country, the support of the Kellogg Peace Pact, the end of compulsory military training, the recognition of Soviet Russia ("we demand it"), the strict enforcement of the eighteenth amendment, justice for the negro, federal relief in the form of public works, old age and disability and unemployment insurance, the use of the taxing power for the equalization of personal incomes and the progressive socialization of natural resources, public utilities and basic industries of the nation and the nationalization of the entire banking system.[5] The editor observed: "This is a cautious and conservative platform for liberals to stand upon."[6] Finally, in October 1932 Paul Blanshard, writing in this same journal, openly stated what the liberals had come to believe—namely, that socialism was the only solution to the economic crisis which now

---

[4] *Christian Century,* May 25, 1932, p. 663.

[5] *Ibid.,* June 8, 1932, p. 728.

[6] *Ibid.,* pp. 728-729.

threatened the nation and that it was eminently a moral solution. Admitting that socialism is collectivism, he defended it nevertheless, because its end "is a society in which every normal human being will share in the world's wealth in proportion to service and ability."[7]

The thrust of this and similar liberal pronouncements was that socialism was not only moral but the only moral solution to the present economic crisis and Blanshard was issuing a clarion call to the churches to support a crusade which would bring socialism to this nation. It is difficult to escape the conclusion that he felt it to be the church's chief task to cooperate in this movement which would make a heaven out of this earth for the real heart of its gospel message was social in its implications. Not only must the church preach a social message adapted to the social crisis, but it must realize that this was its real reason for existence; without it, the church had no justification in a modern industrial society.

This attitude was reflected in church assemblies and meetings of ministers and theologians and during 1932 there was a growing hostility toward capitalism on the part of a large number of ministers. In January, 1932 at a conference of ministers held in Cleveland, Ohio, with over six hundred present, it was declared that a just regard for human rights had never been characteristic of the capitalistic system and that "we are driven by the very logic of the facts to look upon this tragic tide of human misery as directly the result of those principles which we cannot square with the teachings of Jesus."[8] The solution offered was an economic community built upon cooperation rather than individualism. Economic planning under government control, with a large degree of government ownership of industry, was the answer to the problem. A few months later the New York East Conference of the Methodist Church unanimously adopted a report in which it advocated that the government should take over the principle

[7] Paul Blanshard, "Socialism A Moral Solution," *Christian Century,* October 19, 1932, pp. 1271-1274.

[8] *Christian Century,* February 24, 1932, pp. 248-249.

means of production and distribution of goods, particularly the power and public utility industries. It went on to assert that "in contrast to the acquisitive motive of the present form of capitalism the Gospel of Christ offers the motive of sharing. . . . The profit motive must go. . . . We must bring our economic order, sick and wounded, to the Great Physician who can cure our social blindness and move us to love our brethren as we ought."[9]

The *Address of the Methodist Bishops* to the General Conference of 1932 was less extreme in its repudiation of capitalism, but the implication was quite obvious and they called upon the leaders of both capital and labor to "remake the whole structure of industrial life upon the teachings of Christ."[10]

At its meeting in San Francisco the Northern Baptist Convention received a report from its Social Service Committee which found the solution to the depression in a rigorous and courageous application of the social philosophy of Christianity.[11] The report did not specifically define just what this social philosophy was, but the context was clear that the framers of this report had in mind a kind of Christian democratic collectivism in place of free enterprise.

No such timidity and hesitation marked the position of the Federal Council of Churches in its pronouncements on the gathering depression. At its 1932 meeting at Indianapolis, it issued a revision of the Social Creed of 1908 in which it declared that the church should stand for the "practical application of the Christian principles of social well-being to the acquisition and use of wealth"—by which it meant the subordination of the profit motive.[12] It called for social planning and the control of credit and the monetary systems by the government and a wider and more fair distribution of wealth, a living wage and a just share of the worker in the products of industry. It also declared that the

[9] *Christian Century*, April 20, 1932, pp. 521-522.
[10] *Christian Century*, May 18, 1932, p. 629.
[11] *The Literary Digest*, September 3, 1932, pp. 21-22.
[12] *Christian Century*, January 4, 1933, pp. 34-35.

church should use its influence for the creation of a system of social insurance to cover both health and unemployment. It asserted the right of collective bargaining for labor, the abolition of child labor and economic justice for farmers. Much more radical than the actual Creed was the six thousand word statement which the Council issued on "The Social Order and the Good Life."

The liberal origin and purpose of the revised creed and accompanying statement were well recognized by both its friends and foes; it was well understood that this revision of the Social Creed of 1908 was intended to bring the churches up-to-date on economic matters and give to them a philosophy and plan of action for improving the social order.[13] Nevertheless, when taken in conjunction with the pronouncements of church conferences and assemblies and the very radical resolution of the Congregational Christian Council for Social Action of 1934 (promptly repudiated by the General Council of that church), the position of the Federal Council had considerable weight both within many of the constituent denominations, and among liberals at large over the nation. All too often the positions assumed by the Federal Council and the *Christian Century* were thought to be the voice of the church in this country.

It was almost inevitable that responsible statesmen, and other national leaders, would be influenced by declarations which they supposed were the voice of a vast majority of the members of the various denominations associated with this body. Regrettable as it may have been, it cannot be denied that this was the case and continues to be even today.

[13] Its liberalism received a scathing criticism at the hands of E. G. Homrighausen: "Frankly the theology is naive, it lacks realistic insight into the nature of the world, of the Kingdom of God, and of the ethics of the social order and the Christian ethic. Here the liberals look pretty bad,—planless, adolescent, still living in the fool's world of a sentimental world—very unrealistic and untheological. They still think of the Kingdom of God as an intensified world order which comes within the realm of time and which after all is nothing more than an intensified human order." *Christian Century*, January 11, 1933, p. 61.

During the campaign of 1932, Franklin Roosevelt gave an address at Detroit which was obviously inspired, in part at least, by Protestant, Roman Catholic and Jewish pronouncements on social justice and in which Roosevelt gloried in the fact that the 1932 Labor Day pronouncement of the Federal Council was radical, "just as radical as I am."[14] This reference to the Federal Council by Franklin Roosevelt must not be regarded as an isolated example of a strong affinity of outlook between leaders of the New Deal and the Social Gospel. To varying degrees Henry Wallace, Harold Ickes, Harry Hopkins, Frances Perkins, Arthur Morgan, chairman of the TVA, and David Lilienthal showed the influence of liberal Protestant thought on their social and economic philosophies. Henry Wallace, however, was one of the most outspoken of the New Deal group in his attempts to relate the New Deal and what he felt to be the social message of the Scriptures. Writing in the *Christian Century* he said:

The outstanding uniqueness of Jesus lay in the fact that he enjoyed an unbroken awareness of life in all its vividness. This was so real and so thrilling a thing in his life that from the very beginning of his ministry he worked eagerly to inspire other men to make this joyful discovery for themselves. To succeed in the search was to enter the Kingdom of heaven. This was the method he proposed for the establishment of a lasting happiness among men.[15]

His liberal approach to the life and work of Christ is here clearly apparent. It is a theological approach suited for the Social Gospel for it regarded the mission of Jesus to bring happiness among men and to make this earth the Kingdom of Heaven.

His liberal optimism of an evolutionary nature concerning the human race and its progress is clearly expressed in the following:

I believe at this stage in the development of humanity, it is high time for the leading people in all nations to give recognition to

[14] *Christian Century*, October 12, 1932, p. 1229.
[15] January 29, 1936, p. 188.

that which binds all humanity together regardless of race, class, creed or nation. The time is now here to do increasing spiritual reverence to the unity of mankind and to the God who is at once transcendent and immanent.[16]

Here is abundant evidence of that spiritual collectivism which lay at the heart of his economic and political collectivism. Wallace professed to see a unity in mankind which transcended race, class and creed and for which we should have an increasing reverence. Theological differences, differences between Christianity and other religions, were of small consequence in contrast to that mystical and transcendental unity which binds all men regardless of their relationship to God.

The question may well be asked: Did this theological outlook of Wallace have any practical bearing on his political and economic outlook, or was it a mere theory which was held apart from his involvement in the Roosevelt program? It can be safely said in answer to this legitimate question that Wallace, perhaps more than any other leading member of the New Deal, was very conscious of the necessity of establishing an intimate relationship between the Roosevelt program and the Social Gospel. In an address at Richmond, Virginia, in May, 1935 he said:

The Sermon on the Mount has been regarded as a spiritual law. I am now inclined to think that it is an economic law, too.[17]

He then went on to point out that the National Industrial Recovery Act of 1933 was actually an application of this spiritual law enunciated by Christ to the economic problems confronting the American people. His identification of the older Protestant orthodoxy with capitalism and theological liberalism with the New Deal is also quite evident in his writings. He insisted that his new

[16] *Christian Century,* January 29, 1936, p. 189.
[17] *Christian Century,* May 22, 1935, p. 207. It is interesting to note that this address was given just a few weeks before the Supreme Court declared this act invalid in the famous Schechter decision. It is perhaps not accidental that he chose this moment to give such a defense of this highly controversial piece of legislation.

economics of abundance, in contrast to the scarcity created by capitalism, demanded a more socialized living and a new and different set of economic virtues. To meet the conditions of a mechanized production there must be not only a new social machinery, but a "new and truly catholic religion" to give it the moral support which it needed. The truly catholic religion, he declared, was to be found in the Christianity of the first two or three centuries rather than in that of the Reformers and in Puritanism.[18]

Although Henry Wallace was probably more outspoken and open in his appeal to the Scriptures in support of his position, his attitude in general was shared by his colleagues in the cabinet and by that larger and more elusive group known as the unofficial New Dealers and the liberals in Congress. If they less frequently sought openly a biblical support for their program, they were no less influenced by that same liberal theology which Wallace proclaimed. If the Social Gospel had prepared a large segment of the American people for an acceptance of the New Deal, it is no less true that it had a similar influence on many members of the Roosevelt Administration. This kinship is not brought to view by frequent references to the Social Gospel as a definite movement in our history, or even to its more famous advocates, but rather is its impact seen in the general philosophy of those men who gave voice to it in their speeches in Congress and published articles.

It may even be questioned that all of them, or even a great majority of them, were aware that their philosophy was that of liberal theology, in the formal sense of the word. Many of them had so little contact with orthodox Christianity that they were quite oblivious as to how far they had departed from it.

Basic in the thinking of the leadership of the New Deal was an optimistic view of human nature. Roosevelt and his colleagues were aware of human greed and even of sin as a problem in

---

[18] Wallace developed this theme at length in his *Statesmanship and Religion*, Williams and Norgate, London, 1934.

social relationships and they made much of human greed as a kind of sin in their denunciation of those whom they charged with being responsible for the great depression and the general economic debacle which followed the events of October, 1929. It was not that they were unaware of the fact that there was something wrong with American society, but rather that they never located the source of the problem. Men were sinners, but not against a sovereign and righteous God so much as they were against their fellow men. Sin was, essentially, a kind of social error and dislocation, or maladjustment. It must be dealt with. There was a cure for these social ills and the cure was to be found in government and the expansion of its powers. If government could not bring forgiveness to the sins of the past, it could so re-channel human effort and economic activity that social sins could be avoided, if not completely, then certainly to such an extent that great depressions such as the one of 1929 could be brought to an end.

Essentially the outlook of the New Deal was evolutionary; society could be improved and the serious mistakes of the past did not have to be repeated. But the road to social and economic improvement was that which leads to an increasing governmental control over many phases of the life of the nation.

The question must then arise: How can this reliance upon the Social Gospel and its liberal theology explain the pragmatic character of the New Deal? Does not the Social Gospel itself make such a pragmatism a virtual impossibility? Are not these two outlooks on life so utterly incompatible that a political program, such as the New Deal, could not possibly embrace both of them at the same time? At first glance, it would seem that these questions would have to be answered in the affirmative. It certainly must be admitted that the early exponents of the Social Gospel held to a very high view of morality in general and law in particular. Pragmatism was foreign to their thinking and they believed that the right was absolute, as was the law which embodied the right. Certainly a belief in the inviolability of the moral law, its absolute nature and unchanging requirements was a characteristic of many, if not all, of the early members of the Social Gospel Movement.

This early attitude toward the moral law and the law of the land was not destined to remain a dominant note in this school of thought. The abstraction of this concept of the moral law from the biblical view of God on which it depended would eventually sound the death knell of this high view of the ethical life, ultimately undermining the belief that the moral law was absolute and unchanging in its demands upon men. The twentieth century had hardly gotten under way before it became evident that great changes had taken place in liberal thought, religious and secular, concerning the nature of morality and the law. The pragmatism which was inherent in the basic postulates of theological liberalism began to make itself felt in the whole ethical position of the Social Gospel and in liberal thought in general. In the person of Justice Oliver Wendell Holmes, Jr., it gained admission to the Supreme Court itself. By 1932 contemporary political and economic liberalism was well saturated with the pragmatic outlook; thus, it should not be surprising that pragmatism was a prominent characteristic of the New Deal. The Roosevelt administration not only showed a willingness "to try anything" to bring an end to the depression, but it also reflected the growing liberal conviction that law itself was not an absolute, but must be ready to accommodate itself to social change and not prove to be a reactionary force against the wishes of the democratic majority.

It was this pragmatic conception of law which ultimately brought the Roosevelt administration into head-on collision with the Supreme Court and the Constitution in its historic interpretation. But even before the open conflict came, theological liberalism had already declared war against the view that the Constitution was above the popular will and that all social legislation must be judged in the light of that document rather than by its social utility. It has often been alleged that the eighteenth amendment and the Volstead Act were major factors in the undermining of government according to the Constitution in this country and there is much truth to this statement, but it is very doubtful that prohibition did as much harm to the conviction that we are a government of law rather than men, as the growing prevalence of pragmatism which brought about an erosion of the foundation of the whole legal system.

The historic conception of the Constitution as fundamental law was also greatly weakened by the development of the democratic philosophy which insisted that the will of the people, or at least a majority of them, as it is expressed at any given time, must take precedence over a constitution formed a century and a half ago. This doctrine of judicial and legal relativity was part and parcel of the development of liberalism in theology and it was not a difficult matter for the advocates of the Social Gospel to join forces with the pragmatists of secular culture in a demand for the revision of the Constitution to meet modern economic and social conditions. William Key Wallace, a member of the American delegation to the Paris Peace Conference of 1919, gave voice to this philosophy of law:

> Our American institutions of government give form and substance to the cultural habits of a people concerned with the maintenance of a special brand of liberty—political liberty. . . . The institutions of private ownership flourished under the system of capitalism which was developed as a concomitant of political liberty. . . . The institutions of political liberty are no longer pertinent. A new form of liberty is being offered: a liberty undreamed of in the days when our constitution was framed.[19]

This new form of liberty, according to Wallace, was economic liberty and by this he meant that purchasing power is the right of the people. But this new form of liberty was not possible under the Constitution as it had emerged from the hands of the founding fathers, because technology has rendered the Constitution obsolete and, as a result, America was witnessing the final phase of

[19] *Christian Century*, March 22, 1933, pp. 390-393.

the struggle between the older concept of liberty as political liberty and the new ideal of economic liberty. His conclusion was that our whole frame of government must be revised in such a way as to provide for this new concept of economic liberty.

> We must frame a new constitution if we are to be in a position to afford the guarantees of economic liberty, essential to the smooth functioning of a society that has achieved our level of automatic machine power production.[20]

His position is open to many objections, historical, logical and theological, but it is not within the purpose of this study to examine them in detail. The main point to be observed is this: this demand for a new constitution rests upon a pragmatic conception of the nature of law and of the Constitution, one which was quite congenial to the theological liberalism of the day and also to its secular counterpart.

Although this pragmatic and essentially relativistic conception of law was frequently discussed in liberal journals and by philosophers of law, it did not make too much headway in the federal courts, except with Justice Oliver Wendell Holmes, Jr., until President Franklin Roosevelt made a determined effort to bring the Supreme Court into line with the philosophy of the New Deal in 1937. It was, in fact, the refusal of the court, under Chief Justice Charles Evans Hughes, to accept the administration's interpretation of the Constitution and the resulting decisions from 1934 to 1936, which struck down much of the legislation passed since March 20, 1933 which led to an open break with the court and the "court packing" plan of 1937. There was a basic difference of opinion between the court and the Roosevelt administration over the nature of the Constitution which Roosevelt could not resolve except by a drastic change in the thinking of the nine justices of the court. He rightly saw that the adherence of these jurists to the political philosophy of the Convention of 1787 placed the whole New Deal program in judicial jeopardy

[20] *Christian Century,* March 22, 1933, p. 392.

and threatened both his programs for economic recovery and reform.

Although some early decisions against the New Deal had irritated President Roosevelt, the decisions of 1935 and 1936 (see footnote 21) brought the issue to a head. After the election of 1936 had given him what seemed to be overwhelming majorities in both the House and the Senate, President Roosevelt, early in 1937, sent a message to Congress for the reorganization of the federal judiciary, one section of which would have allowed him to appoint six new justices to the Supreme Court under certain very specific conditions. His stated position at this time clearly indicates that he expected the justices to adopt a pragmatic attitude toward the Constitution which would allow a great deal of leeway to the administration in its legislative policy looking toward a kind of social and economic experimentation quite foreign to the Constitution according to its historic interpretation.

The frontal attack on the court which took place early in 1937 had not been clearly foreshadowed during the campaign and the Democratic platform gave no indication of the storm that was brewing.[22]

The first real admission by the Roosevelt administration that the problem of the Supreme Court was to be faced came in Roosevelt's annual message to Congress on January 6, 1937.

> During the past four years there has been a growing belief that there is little fault to be found with the Constitution of the United States as it stands today. The vital need is not an alteration of our fundamental law, but an increasingly enlightened view with reference to it. Difficulties have grown out of its interpretation, but rightly considered it can be used as an instrument of progress and not a device for the prevention of action. . . . With a better

[21] The most important of these decisions were: *Schechter* vs. *United States; Carter* vs. *Carter Coal Company; Butler* vs. *United States.*

[22] Liberals, however, were much more outspoken in their attitude toward the Supreme Court. *The Nation* stated that the Supreme Court was the real issue of the 1936 campaign for the Court was blocking national efforts to achieve security for the American people and all attempts to regulate business.

understanding of our purpose, and a more intelligent recognition of our needs as a nation it is not to be assumed that there will be prolonged failure to bring legislative and judicial interpretations to the actual present national needs of the largest progressive democracy in the modern world. . . . The judicial branch also is asked by the people to do its part in making democracy successful. We do not ask the courts to call non-existent powers into being, but we do have a right to expect that conceded powers or those legitimately implied shall be effective instruments for the common good.[23]

In this address Roosevelt clearly revealed his basic position in regard to the courts and the Constitution, namely, that the Constitution must be so interpreted by the court that it would become an instrument of New Deal progress and not a means for delaying, or preventing, such a victory for the people. It was unthinkable that legislation should be framed to be in accord with that historic document; rather the charter of American liberties was to be given a new interpretation which would be in accord with the best interests of the American people as they were interpreted by the Roosevelt administration. Thus, by judicial fiat, the Constitution would be changed to meet the demands of pragmatic liberalism and the influence of liberal theology is quite evident. A theology which was willing to subject the law of God to popular interpretation and the will of the popular majority logically led to a view of law which was just as elastic. Relativism in theology is surely followed by relativism in legal and political theory.

It could not be expected that the Supreme Court itself could long remain immune to the infiltration of this pragmatic philosophy of law. During the height of the battle in the Senate over the court bill in 1937, the court did reverse its former position to a degree and upheld New Deal legislation. This shift in position did not so much represent a change in philosophy on the part of the members, as it was a part of the strategy of Chief Justice Hughes to soften the agitation for the bill which would have permitted,

[23] *Congressional Record*, Volume 81, Part 1, p. 85.

what was popularly called, a packing of the court. However, a more basic change in the outlook of the court did come with the changes in membership which began shortly after the defeat of the bill in the Senate. Within a few years resignations gave Roosevelt an unusual opportunity to revamp the court without the necessity of resorting to the defeated bill. The new appointees, to varying degrees, accepted the pragmatic philosophy of the law, but in Felix Frankfurter it had a most devoted candidate. In the years after 1937, the court abandoned one historic interpretation of the Constitution after another in favor of those which seemed to be more in line with the needs of the hour. The underlying relativism of these opinions was not always openly admitted, but it is there to be observed by the discerning reader. In a decision rendered in 1951 there is a glaring example of this relativism which sheds a great deal of light on the philosophy which guided the court in much of its judicial work.[24] In this case the further deterioration of rights supposed to be inviolable becomes evident.[25] However, this case is only one of many in which relativism and the pragmatic temper of the court become obvious to such an extent that the decisions which it renders are actually jeopardized thereby.

This relativism and the willingness to consult with sociologists and psychologists in the writing of opinions characterizes nearly every recent decision of the Supreme Court to such an extent that the decisions which it renders are of very doubtful legal significance and at best can hope to have only a temporary legal authority. To a great extent these decisions are merely an acceptance of what the court thinks is the majority opinion of the moment and thus they seek to buttress them with references to sociological and

[24] It is the triumph of this philosophy which explains why the court has surrendered the principle of *stare decisis*. As a result, on more than one occasion the court since 1937 has reversed its own stand taken in a previous case and predicting what the justices will do has become a most hazardous undertaking.

[25] *United States vs. Jeffers, United States Supreme Court Reports*, Lawyers Edition, Vol. 96, No. 3, December 17, 1951.

psychological dogma. It is very doubtful that the justices themselves intend that their decisions should have a lasting value, but
should simply be regarded as way-stations on the long road toward what they hopefully call new insights into the Constitution
which will make that document more suitable for the needs of a
democratic society.

This trend has come into its own in the cases dealing with the
relationship between church and state, particularly in those dealing with the intricate problem of religion in the public schools.
The reliance upon sociologists and psychologists produced the
decisions in the segregation cases of the last ten years, and this
was notably true of the famous decision of 1954 which declared
that segregation in the public schools was unconstitutional. In
this decision great reliance was placed upon the psychological
effects of segregation on Negro children in such a manner that
previous decisions of the Supreme Court were set aside as having
no real bearing on the case because of the present state of development of psychology as a study.[26]

This departure from legal precedents has proceeded at such a
pace that the recent decisions themselves are of such doubtful
legality that they can easily be set aside by future courts on this
ground, or on the ground that the insights provided by sociologists and psychologists are no longer valid. This resort to psychological and sociological opinion has been disastrous to the historic
concept of law as it has been held in this country.

The New Deal and Liberal Theology

Although many theological liberals had grave misgivings about
the repeal of prohibition as a necessary or justifiable measure
and although some of them held serious reservations about
Roosevelt himself, doubting whether he had what it took to lift
the country out of the depression and to bring needed social and
economic reform, they soon recognized the intellectual atmosphere of the new administration as being very congenial to the

[26] *Brown* vs. *Board of Education of Topeka,* 347, U.S. 483.

demands of the Social Gospel for the creation of a democratic collectivism in this country and they soon fell in line behind the New Deal and gave it their hearty support.[27] Very soon, both individually and collectively, they were passing resolutions in support of the program; church conventions and assemblies even went beyond the announced aims of the administration and openly called for a high degree of socialism in this country. The dramatic answer to their long years of planning and agitation seemed almost too good to be true. Their prayers had been answered and many liberals were ecstatic in their belief that the Kingdom of God was about to break in on the American people through the medium of this political program; many of them began to look on the 1929 crisis and the depression as a positive good in the sense that they made possible the introduction of a radical political and economic program which might never have been possible apart from the crisis psychology of 1932-33.

Churches in annual conferences and assemblies hastened to go on record that they welcomed the Roosevelt program and could give to it a biblical sanction. One of the first of these was the Quadrennial Statement of the Bishops of the United Brethren Church given at the General Conference of 1933, in which they declared that individual capitalism, as a philosophy of life, had undermined the entire structure of American life and that there "must be a more equitable distribution of the wealth of the nation" and that the "whole system of our economic life must be changed" and "must be buttressed by the high ideal taught by Jesus in the Sermon on the Mount."[28] This statement was not only one of the first, but it was also one of the more conservative affirmations of the need of economic reconstruction in a direction away from individualism to a collectivism.

The *Christian Century* was much more forthright and less guarded in its greetings which it extended to President Roose-

[27] *Christian Century*, November 11, 1936, p. 1488. The *Christian Century* later admitted that it had supported practically every Roosevelt proposal.
[28] *Ibid.*, June 7, 1933, p. 763.

velt's program. In an editorial entitled, "The Regimentation Bogey," it declared:

> There can be no doubt that a new philosophy both of government and of economics is taking form at Washington. It is a philosophy of whose outline Mr. Roosevelt gave no hint when he was a candidate. . . . The fact that this new President had brought a new theory and a new policy into being which is intended radically to alter American life in its political, industrial and financial aspects. The essence of Mr. Roosevelt's policy is the abrogation of the theory of free competition for business, the abandonment of the laissez faire theory of the relation of the government to business and the adoption of the theory that the supreme function of government is to act as an umpire with authority to see that the play of the profit motive shall be regulated in the interest of the people as a whole.[29]

The *Christian Century* then went on to say that the profit motive could be regulated in such a fashion, insisting that capitalism would upset the best laid plans of statesmen and "corrupt the best bureau set up to administer it."[30] If this is the case the question could well be asked: Why should liberals endorse an effort at the regulation of business which they felt was doomed to failure from the beginning? The editors of the *Christian Century* were not at a loss for an answer, justifying the program in the hope that it would open the way for an even better economy, by which they meant state socialism. But in all of this there was no real danger of regimentation simply because "the government is the people's instrument and it is the people themselves who regulate it."[31] Thus, if all the people were involved in the regulation, this kind of centralization was not a danger as all of the people were a part of the centralization. Sometime later the editors of this journal voiced the optimistic belief that not only a great majority of the people at large, but most of the enlightened lead-

[29] *Christian Century,* June 14, 1933, p. 870.
[30] *Ibid.,* p. 870.
[31] *Ibid.,* p. 871.

ers of business would welcome an attempt on the part of the Roosevelt administration to set up a system of national economic planning.[32] However, they did admit that such a program was of very doubtful constitutionality.

The direction which liberal theology was taking became increasingly clear in an editorial in this same journal a few weeks later when the New Deal was acclaimed as a definite departure from the traditional form of economic activity in this country.

> The New Deal thus points distinctly in the direction of a final break with the capitalistic system, and has already by its adoption, gone far on the path of socialization. But it has not gone far enough to determine whether its future will move toward socialism or toward fascism. That will be determined by the success or failure of the New Deal. If it works moderately well during the first year, it is reasonable to expect that its further development will be peaceable and in the direction of a most consistent socialism.[33]

The New Deal could not be expected to bring about this highly desired consistent socialism without the aid of the church and the theological liberals were quite willing to bring the church to the aid of this secular device for realizing the secularized Kingdom of God on earth. The *Christian Century* insisted that the Christian Church must come to the aid of this noble project and produce the new economic man needed by the New Deal; it went on further to delineate what this new kind of man must be, insisting that the theology of conversion had never been profound or thorough and that it was psychological rather than social in its nature. Thus it had never been able to effect a new birth in the economic man. The New Deal brought to the church a new responsibility to send forth into the new economic order a new economic man. Thus, the Christian Gospel was to be subjected to the demands of a secular movement. The preaching of the Gospel of redemption was to be replaced by an ecclesiastical pro-

[32] *Christian Century*, June 21, 1933, pp. 806-808.
[33] *Ibid.*, August 30, 1933, p. 1078.

gram which would bring the church into an open alliance with a program for collectivism of the economic order.[34]

Justin Wroe Nixon was just as forthright in his affirmation of what the church must do in the new age which was dawning in this country. Convinced that the Puritan use of the Old Testament and the Lutheran-Anglican retreat from economic thought were no longer adequate responses to the needs of society, because the America of 1933 was undergoing a kind of "Copernican revolution" in ethical values, he declared that the church could not hope to fashion character unless it was willing to attack the basic problem of the changing forms of social organization.

> The churches will have to decide what kind of religion they will dispense. But there are sound reasons for believing that only when they are able to bring the intimate personal idea and the larger social relations of men into some kind of practical accord will they be able to satisfy the urge of the world toward wholeness and compete successfully with the new totalitarian faiths.[35]

The liberal theology of this writer is obvious in almost every phrase. The belief that the church has within its power to decide what its message will be is a far cry from the view of the church and its mission which is found in the Scriptures. But the belief that the church will really come into its own when it tries to satisfy the urge of humanity toward a new collectivism or wholeness is no less a repudiation of the historic Christian message. Professor Jerome Davis of Yale Divinity School took this kind of reasoning one step further when, after his return from a visit to Russia, he declared that in Russia they found religion vital, "a socialized faith, being translated into the collective life in terms of social and economic justice."[36]

It is not only interesting, but very important to notice the basic agreement between liberal Christian journals, such as the *Christian Century*, on the one hand, and liberal secular journals and

---

[34] *Christian Century,* October 11, 1933, pp. 1262-1264.
[35] *Ibid.,* October 25, 1933, pp. 1330-1333.
[36] *Ibid.,* 1933, p. 1239.

thinkers, on the other. When President Franklin Roosevelt declared in his address before the Federal Council of Churches in December, 1933, that it was his purpose to create a state "built on spiritual and social values," one of the first to hail this declaration was Oswald Garrison Villard, who said:

> Certainly when the President declares that he is for prosperity "socially controlled for the common good" and for "collective effort which is wholly in accord with the social teachings of Christianity," he states again the idea of liberals and Socialists, and even of those further to the left.[37]

Secular liberals, for the most part, were quick to claim the Social Gospel as being part of their own movement and they were no less eager to claim political and social theories and programs emanating from this philosophy as reflections of their own philosophy of society and economic life. In fact, liberal theology was the only version of Christianity with which they were willing to have their own movement become identified, or from which they were willing to accept support. They were well aware of the basic incompatibility existing between their own liberal social and economic programs and historic Christian orthodoxy. Theology had a message for this life only and the church must be solely concerned with proclaiming a message for the improving of life on this earth.

As the New Deal program began to take shape and its outlines became more visible, many churches began to come to its support with enthusiasm and some even began to demand a more radical attempt at national reform. In December, 1933, about one hundred representatives from the presbyteries of the Presbyterian Church USA, in and around New York City, held a meeting at which Adolph Berle spoke and the National Recovery Administration was the focal point of attention. The conference came to the conclusion that the NRA embodied so many of the social ideals of the churches that is deserved their loyal support.[38]

[37] *The Nation,* December 20, 1933, p. 697.
[38] *Christian Century,* December 27, 1933, pp. 1649-1650.

This was a timid position which the Presbyterians assumed in comparison to that which other groups took. Later in 1934, the New York East Conference of the Methodist Church declared that the New Deal was essentially correct in the direction which it was taking, but that it had not gone far enough and that it would have to eliminate the profit motive from American society and socialize the banking system and all natural resources except the soil itself.[39] A convention of Ohio ministers from several denominations, meeting early in 1934, hailed the National Recovery Administration as a fine example of the social implications of Christianity and declared that the value of the NRA codes lay in their thrust as a movement toward the public ownership of the basic industries of the nation and the kind of democratic control for which they stood. But they added: "We do not believe that under a profit economy the NRA can succeed."[40]

Denominations, as well as groups of pastors, were also taking the same direction toward a radical economic collectivism. In April, 1934 some five hundred delegates from forty-one conferences of the Methodist Episcopal Church, South adopted a Social Creed which called for a practical application of the Christian principle of social well-being to both the acquisition and use of wealth which involved social and economic planning and social control of business enterprise for the common good, for the purpose of bringing about a wider distribution of wealth.[41] While the specific means of achieving these aims were not spelled out, the import of these resolutions was quite apparent and all concerned were well aware of the fact that the southern branch of Methodism was placing itself in the same camp with the northern wing of the church. A far more radical step was taken by the General Council of the Congregational Church at its meeting in Oberlin in 1934, at which it repudiated war and condemned capitalism as an economic order because it depended "for its

[39] *Christian Century*, January 2, 1934, p. 18.
[40] *Ibid.*, February 14, 1934, p. 211.
[41] *Ibid.*, May 16, 1934, pp. 670, 678.

existence upon the exploitation of one group by another" and "created industrial and civil strife and international war" and precipitated "periods of unemployment, insecurity and all its attendant miseries." They also accused it of "destroying human, moral and spiritual values."[42] In place of capitalism the Congregationalists called for the "inauguration of a genuinely cooperative social economy democratically planned to adjust production to consumption requirements" and for the modification or elimination of the "private ownership of the means of production or distribution of goods whenever such ownership should interfere with the social good."[43]

That the theology lying behind such affirmation was liberal and even radical cannot be successfully refuted. This liberalism was coming to power in many, if not most, of the larger denominations and was making itself felt in their official meetings. In an editorial entitled "A New Protestantism," the *Christian Century* hailed this development, declaring it to be the most significant movement going on in religion.

> Every true concept of religion now seems to be a social concept.
> . . . The conviction is growing among us that the individual truly can be saved only in organic relation to his world. Thus the world itself becomes the true subject of redemption.[44]

The conclusion was logical; Christianity must broaden its basis, for the Kingdom of God in the eyes of the theological liberals was the growing society of justice and good will.

> Here in the Kingdom of God we shall find God. This was where Jesus found Him. This is where modern social insights direct us to seek Him.[45]

Kirby Page took this logic one step further and found in the social conception of the Kingdom of God the justification for

[42] *Ibid.*, July 11, 1934, p. 919.
[43] *Idem.* The editors of the *Christian Century* felt that the direction which this Oberlin meeting took was the direction which all Protestant churches must take.
[44] *Ibid.*, October 17, 1934, pp. 1304-1306.
[45] *Ibid.*, p. 1305.

social revolution. He argued that the necessity of economic revolution in the creation of this divine society, the Kingdom of God, could be easily demonstrated. Capitalism could not be reformed and private competition in economic life must go, to be replaced with a different economic order. In order to accomplish this end, instruments of social compulsion must be found.[46] Page professed to find a biblical sanction for this approach in the Lord's Prayer.

> Every time we pray the Lord's Prayer, with discernment and sincerity, we are praying for revolutionary changes to be made in the present economic order.[47]

During 1935 ecclesiastical endorsement of the New Deal was just as frequent as it had been in the two preceding years, but in the pronouncements of 1935 another note was sounded. Liberals were only too glad to endorse the program of the Roosevelt Administration as far as it went, but there seemed to be a growing conviction that it was not going far enough and needed prodding from theological liberals if the Kingdom of God was to be realized in the United States under the aegis of the New Deal. The Committee on Social Relations of the Board of Directors of the American Unitarian Association made a report in February of that year which recommended that Unitarians support the New Deal, but it also called for the government control and ownership of public utilities, means of transportation, banking, coal and other natural resources, and it also called for the use of the taxing power of the federal government for a more equitable distribution of wealth in this country. It was frankly admitted that the report was based on the assumption that salvation must come to man through his own efforts.[48] About the same time the Methodist Federation for Social Service issued a report which found fault with the Roosevelt Administration for

---

[46] However, he did concede that a peaceful solution must also be sought and he seemed to favor compensation for private property rather than an outright confiscation. *Christian Century,* February 20, 1935, pp. 234-235.

[47] *Christian Century,* February 20, 1935, p. 234.

[48] *Literary Digest,* February 23, 1935, p. 26.

betraying the forgotten man and retaining the profit system as an essential feature of the American economic system.[49] A few months later the New York East Methodist Conference, following the lead of the Methodist Federation for Social Service, received a report from a special committee which openly called for the abolition of capitalism and the creation of a planned economy. It asserted: "Nothing less than the ultimate establishment of a cooperative Christian commonwealth can satisfy a genuine following of Jesus Christ."[50]

It would be both tedious and unnecessary to offer to the reader further quotations from the liberal ecclesiastical press. Statements similar to those presented here could be duplicated again and again in the liberal denominational and inter-denominational journals. Although both theological and political liberalism had its greatest strength in large denominations which drew their greatest support in the North, it must not be supposed that this radicalism was confined to them. Some of the smaller groups were infected with this virus to as great, or even a greater, degree than the large churches. It was also evident in those denominations which were generally regarded as conservative. Although the Northern Presbyterian Church never went to such lengths in its official declarations as those included above, nevertheless, its leadership and general assemblies felt compelled to issue statements demonstrating the "social awareness" of the church. Most of the Lutheran groups used more constrained language but they did not remain immune to the liberal social and political influences at work in the America body politic. Even the Southern Baptist Convention and Southern Presbyterian Church, generally regarded as the most conservative of the larger denominations both in their theology and social and political outlook, felt the urge to take cognizance of the existence of social and economic problems and urged that the Scriptures should be the basis of their solution.

[49] *Ibid.*, February 16, 1935, p. 17.
[50] *Christian Century*, May 29, 1935, pp. 716-717.

The Political Reflections of Liberal Theology

There is abundant evidence that theological liberals not only welcomed the New Deal for what it was, but for what it promised to bring to the country in the form of an even greater degree of radicalism in the economic and social spheres. The question may well be asked: To what extent did they actually influence the course of public affairs, and to what extent did the legislation of the New Deal era reflect this liberal theology? Did the leadership in Congress, responsible for the passage, if not always for the formulation, of New Deal measures show any acute awareness of the liberal implications of their position and did this liberal position in turn, reflect a definite philosophy which found its nurture in these liberal theological currents?

Such questions are basic to the thesis of this book and are pertinent at this point. They can be answered, not in the sense that it is possible to find frequent references to theological positions during the debates in Congress; a study of Congressional debates, and other pertinent material, of the Roosevelt era reveals very little, if any, definite biblical theological material apart from references to some of the better known biblical stories, the Ten Commandments, the Sermon on the Mount, and the ethical teachings of Jesus Christ. The issues confronting the Roosevelt administration were generally considered to be political, economic and social in nature and were treated accordingly.

This refusal, or failure, to realize the broader implications of the issues confronting the American people during the thirties is, in itself, quite revealing and gives some insight into the thinking of those who were content to deal with the pressing problems of the day simply in terms of their social and economic aspects. The failure to realize that the crisis was, to a great extent, the result of a national departure from biblical norms for social, economic and political conduct testifies to the fact that the great doctrines of orthodox theology were no longer considered a significant frame of reference for the discussion and conduct of national affairs.

The idea of sin as an offense against a holy and sovereign God was almost entirely absent from the thinking of the New Deal leadership and was almost never seen in Congressional debates. The presence of evil in American society was freely admitted, but usually regarded as a social maladjustment on the part of the wealthier classes in their relationship with the masses; very seldom was there any clear recognition that all men are sinners. In line with this superficial idea of evil, largely derived from psychology rather than from the Bible, was its corollary: that evil could, and must be, corrected by appropriate governmental action. Since the emphasis was now on social rather than individual sins, the correction was to be social rather than individual repentance and regeneration. The proper approach to the problem was legislation, not in the older sense of the word, but a new type was appearing, a legislation which was drafted by economists, sociologists, psychologists and professional reformers. Almost inevitably the historic concept of the purpose of the law and the legislative powers gave way to a new philosophy which regarded legislation not so much as a means of establishing norms for the conduct of society under common grace in the light of the biblical revelation, but for the reformation of society according to the thinking of those in sociology, psychology and economics who were greatly influenced by Marxian philosophy and who had little regard for the American constitutional system or heritage. By such an approach it was their aim to bring about a virtual revolution in American political, social and economic life.

All this is not to say that all of the Democrats in Congress were fully aware of this revolution which was going on under their very eyes, or that they would have approved of it if they had been aware of it. Neither is it any more accurate to insist that those Republicans who opposed the New Deal did so for theological and idealogical reasons. There were many evangelicals in the Democratic Party who were aware of the implications of the New Deal, but who were powerless to change the political currents. There were evangelicals among them who frequently supported many, if not most, of the New Deal measures, apparently unaware of the idealogical cleavage existing between their evangelical theology on the one hand, and the liberal outlook of the Roosevelt program on the other.

Here again, the failure of evangelicals to evaluate the legislative program, in terms of their Christian faith, and to bring the contradictions between it and the basic assumptions of the New Deal philosophy to the attention of Congress and the people at large, is also of significance. Their reticence in regard to this issue stems from the failure on the part of many of them to relate their evangelical convictions to the actualities of political life. A Christian world and life view no longer was dominant in their thinking.[51] It is a sad fact that the Scriptures no longer occupied a vital place in the American scene so that legislators would consider them relevant to the issues of the day.

However, the influence of liberal theology on the Roosevelt program cannot be, and does not have to be, measured solely in terms of the lack of theological references in Congressional debates. This silence is significant, but the intimacy existing between theological liberalism and the New Deal program could hardly be established simply on the basis of the fact that there was almost no conservative evangelical emphasis in the political literature of the day. At most it would do little more than show that evangelical theology was losing its grip on the American mind.

A study of the vast amount of literature emanating from both within and without the administration in support of its economic

[51] It is true that the crisis psychology of the day was a strong factor. There was fear on every hand and the New Deal seemed to be the only way out for many members of Congress whose own private convictions brought much misgiving to them concerning the methods and ultimate purposes of the program. Many conservative Democrats, in particular, were under tremendous pressure from the Roosevelt Administration and the people to render a solid support to all New Deal measures. It is also true that in 1933 many members of Congress, by their own later confessions, voted for bills which they had not read and of which they had but a faint apprehension.

and social program reveals that the liberal leadership, both in Congress and in the inner circles of the New Deal, was keenly alive to the political, social and economic aspects of theological liberalism and were only too willing to claim them in support of their policies. Increasingly, after March, 1933, supporters of the Roosevelt program adopted the same philosophy of society which appeared in liberal theological journals and denominational declarations and the phraseology used was often identical. If practical politicians were not always willing to go as far as the Federal Council of Churches and other groups wished them to, it does not mean that they were not fully cognizant of the implications of the social philosophy which they were following in their recovery and reform programs.

The first evidence of this close relationship existing between the liberals of the Roosevelt administration and theological liberalism is found in the debates of 1933 over the Agricultural Adjustment and National Industrial Recovery Acts of that year which, at that time, were widely regarded as two of Roosevelt's most important legislative proposals of that session of Congress. They lay at the very heart of the New Deal program for initiating recovery and reform and little attempt was made to conceal the fact that they constituted a kind of revolution in American life. On the contrary, the fact that they were revolutionary in character was a source of delight for many in the New Deal and a cause for boasting. The outcome of the 1932 Presidential election, and the 1934 Congressional elections, had convinced the liberals of the administration that the temper of the American mind was favorable for this kind of a revolution and that the philosophy of the New Deal was in harmony with the thinking of the majority of the voters.[52]

[52] This attitude stands in sharp contrast to the cautious statements made by Roosevelt during the campaign of 1932 when little was said which would indicate a radical political philosophy or a revolutionary approach to the problems of the depression. The Democratic Party platform of 1932 had been quite conservative, emphasizing a constitutional approach to the problems of recovery and reform. This platform was so conventional that most of it was adopted by the Republicans in 1936 in their opposition to Roosevelt's New Deal.

By 1934 the philosophy behind the Roosevelt program was frankly that of social revolution and there can be little doubt that the concept of social evolution achieved by governmental planning was dominant in New Deal circles. It was an adaptation of the old Progressive philosophy of 1912, and the social and economic theories of Lester Frank Ward, brought up to date to meet the problems of the nineteen thirties. Although most of his major addresses during the campaign were not concerned with political philosophy, the Constitution and the role of the Supreme Court, Roosevelt did give an important insight to his political thought in one address, the Commonwealth Club Address, given at San Francisco on September 23, 1932.

> I think that every one who has actually entered the economic struggle which means every one that was not born to safe wealth —knows in his own experience and his own life that we now have to apply the earlier concepts of American government to the conditions of today.

> The Declaration of Independence discusses the problems of government in terms of a contract, perforce, if we should follow the thinking out of which it grew. Under such a contract rulers were accorded power and the people consented to that power on the consideration that they were accorded certain rights. The task of statesmanship has always been the redefining of these rights in terms of a changing and growing social order. New conditions impose new requirements upon government and those who conduct government.[53]

It has always been a source of wonder and amazement that this speech received so little attention at the time for it contains the germ of the New Deal and reveals the pragmatic character of Roosevelt's own approach to the issues of the day. The position which he assumed here was a flagrant denial of the thinking of Jefferson and those who supported the Declaration of Independence. Neither Locke nor Jefferson would ever have conceded for a moment that under the social contract rulers accorded cer-

[53] Franklin D. Roosevelt, *Public Papers* (1928-1932), pp. 742-756.

tain rights to the people. Such a doctrine was abhorrent to them and contrary to the whole philosophy by which they were motivated. Essential to both Locke and Jefferson was the idea that all people by nature had certain inalienable rights and that government was instituted to preserve and protect these rights. Never did they contemplate the idea that government conferred rights. Equally foreign to their political philosophy was Roosevelt's corollary of his first error—that it was the task of statesmanship to consistently redefine human rights in terms of the changing social conditions. Both Locke and Jefferson agreed that these inalienable human rights were beyond the power of any government to define, interpret or change. The whole spirit of the writings of Jefferson, and the other leaders of the American Revolution, breathe the inviolability of these inalienable rights. One can only imagine what prompted Roosevelt to make such assertions during a political campaign; it is quite amazing that so little was made of this serious departure from democratic dogma by one who was its professed apostle.[54]

The doctrine that the economic emergency frankly required new methods and means of controlling the economic life of the nation came out into the open with a new vehemence in the debates over the Agricultural Adjustment Act of 1933. When this bill was introduced into Congress on March 16, 1933, Roosevelt said:

> I tell you frankly that this is a new and untrod path, but I tell you with equal frankness that an unprecedented condition calls for the trial of new means to rescue agriculture. If a fair administrative trial is made of it and it does not produce the hoped-for results, I shall be the first to acknowledge it and advise you.[55]

[54] The trend of Roosevelt's thinking did not go entirely unnoticed. David Lawrence, the eminent Washington observer, wrote: "Radicalism or constitutionalism? This is the choice the voters will be asked to make, though to be sure, the Democrats will deny that they intended radicalism while the Republicans will insist that they ought not to be classed as reactionaries. The Democrats will call themselves Progressives and their opponents the champions of reaction; while the Republicans will not hesitate to proclaim themselves as liberal conservatives and their opponents as true radicals."

[55] *Congressional Record,* Vol. 77, Part I, p. 578.

To which Representative James M. Beck of Pennsylvania replied:

> I think of all the damnable heresies that have ever been suggested
> in connection with the Constitution the doctrine of emergency is
> the worst. It means that when Congress declares an emergency
> there is no Constitution. This means its death. It is the very
> doctrine that the German Chancellor is invoking today in the
> dying hours of the parliamentary body of the German Republic;
> namely, that because of an emergency it should grant to the
> German Chancellor absolute power to pass any law that contra-
> dicts the Constitution of the German Republic. . . . We pay
> the Constitution lip service but the result is the same.[56]

Beck admitted it still lived so far as it prescribed the mechanics
by which the government was to be conducted.

> But the Constitution as a restraining influence in keeping the
> federal government within the carefully prescribed channels of
> power is moribund, if not dead. We are witnessing its death
> agonies, for when this bill becomes law, if unhappily it becomes
> a law, there is no longer any workable Constitution to keep the
> Congress within the limits of its constitutional powers.[57]

This warning fell on deaf ears and the House passed the bill by
a vote of almost three to one. The doctrine of emergency took
precedence over that of the supremacy of the Constitution as the
fundamental law of the land.

The debates over the National Industrial Recovery Act of
1933 brought out in sharp focus the extent to which the doctrines
of legal relativism and emergency permissiveness had penetrated
the Congressional mind. In a radio address, Senator Robert Wag-
ner of New York defended the legislation on the ground that its
whole purpose was to give every deserving American a permanent
opportunity to earn a comfortable living and "to accomplish this
we have enacted twentieth century law to help twentieth century
economic and social problems." The fact that a national emergency was the sole justification for the passage of such danger-

[56] *Ibid.,* p. 754.
[57] *Ibid.,* p. 755.

ous legislation was clearly expressed by Representative Marland of Oklahoma:

> No law has been written which so much affected human rights, human happiness and human destiny since the writing of the Magna Carta on the field of Runnymede 718 years ago as will the passage of the National Industrial Act. It may mean that by the passage of this act we shall have repealed the great charter of human rights which guaranteed government by law instead of government by discretion which had hitherto prevailed. By this National Industrial Recovery Act we will confer upon the President of the United States wider discretionary powers of government than have ever been held by any but an absolute monarch. The saving grace of this renunciation lies in the fact that a national emergency exists and that the powers granted to the President shall cease to exist at the expiration of two years.[58]

An even more radical attitude is illustrated in the position assumed by Hugo Black, a senator from Alabama.

> I am not complaining about this bill being too reactionary. I admit that it is revolutionary. There is no question about that. It is a departure from the settled forms of government which we have followed in the past. I am not complaining about the fact that the President of the United States, with conditions as they are, has seen with open vision a situation which demanded bold and aggressive action. I applaud him with all my heart for being willing not to stand on the outmoded, antiquated formulas of past ages to meet past conditions, but being willing to step forward boldly and aggressively in an effort to cure the economic unbalance, which exists in this nation.[59]

Here is an even more forthright statement of the emergency doctrine, but here there is no regret that such steps are necessary and will exist only so long as the crisis continues. Rather did Hugo Black rejoice in this bold action and state his belief that

[58] *Ibid.,* Vol. 77, part 6, p. 5698.
[59] *Ibid.,* Vol. 77, part 6, p. 5845. Later President Roosevelt appointed Black to the Supreme Court in which position he frequently gave voice to this philosophy in his judical opinions.

the formulas of the past (the Constitution as historically interpreted), should be set aside in favor of new formulas which would
meet the issues of the twentieth century and its peculiar problems.

The present era demanded a revolution in political thought
and practice to meet the conditions of the industrial age and the
older concepts of political liberty must give way to the newer
idea of security at almost any price. Basic to Black's position is
the assumption that law is little more than the crystallization of
public opinion at any given time as that opinion, in turn, is produced by the economic and social issues of the day. A second
assumption in his position was the inadequacy of the Constitution and that this inadequacy was the result of the fact that it was
the living voice of a former political philosophy which no longer
had any real meaning for the American people.

The same kind of thinking can be seen in the debate which
broke out in Congress following the decision of the Supreme
Court in the famous Schechter decision which brought an end
to the National Industrial Recovery Act on the ground of its
unconstitutionality. Representative Hildebrandt, a very liberal
New Deal Democrat, was most vocal in his condemnation of this
important decision:

> Neither property rights nor antique documents should ever ob-
> struct human rights. The rights of the whole people precede the
> rights of any corporation complaining about regulation and any
> mortgage holder who wants to evict a helpless and broken
> farmer. The rights of the whole people take priority over any con-
> stitution penned in any age or country—even our own.[60]

This highly emotional appeal for the correctness of New Deal
policy shows great human warmth on the one hand, and dangerous fallacies on the other. In the first place, it falls into the fatal
error, so common to liberal thinking, of drawing a distinction
between human rights and property rights, as if there were some
magical division between them. Actually it is a very false distinc-

---

[60] *The Congressional Record*, Vol. 79, part 8, p. 8470, May 31, 1935.

tion: human rights are property rights or rights of human beings to property. There is no abstraction known as "property rights" in the sense that somehow property has rights in and of itself, divorced from human beings in whom alone rights may reside. It will be remembered that liberal theologians and journals fell into this same error. Just as erroneous is the assumption, on the part of Hildebrandt, that the rights of all the people take precedence over the rights of the individual or constitution. He seems to forget that rights do not lie in the people at large apart from individuals, but in individuals alone. Hildebrandt was holding a view of human rights which was very far from that taught in the Scriptures.

Also prominent in his thinking was the idea of the necessity of securing the passage of radical social legislation, and of the incompatibility of such legislation with the Constitution as it was interpreted by the Supreme Court at that time.

> If new social legislation can be enacted that will not be declared unconstitutional, well and good. But the chances are that it will be so characterized by the present Supreme Court, and most people will starve while we are waiting for a change in the Court's personnel. Perhaps temporary statutes may be drawn up that will get by this tribunal with its openly reactionary attitude. But in the long run two permanent methods of relief seem to be the only ones. First, amend the Constitution sufficiently so that the Government can take any steps it finds necessary to assure every able-bodied, full-grown citizen engaged in useful labor the comforts of life as well as to assure the same to the disabled, sick and minors. Second, amend the Constitution so that the Supreme Court will never again have the power to block humanitarian enactments by branding them unconstitutional.[61]

Representative Hildebrandt was willing to take an even more drastic step to assure the continuation of the New Deal. He also urged an amendment to the Constitution which would "leave no doubt as to the government's authority to socialize any industry,

[61] *Idem.*

whether it be the railroads . . . or others . . . If the Constitution is to be amended let us play safe and draw up an amendment that will unmistakably establish the right of the people to have both an industrial democracy and a political democracy."[62]

This extreme position did not characterize the thinking of the majority in the House, to be sure, but the doctrine of emergency as a justification for legislative acts which were known to be unconstitutional was the dominant note in the debates of the day and the logic of this pragmatic approach to the Constitution led the more extreme liberals into socialism itself even as it had led the theological liberals to the same destination.

This is not to say that all the legislation of the New Deal era was either unconstitutional or injurious to the American political tradition and heritage. Some of it was needed and even long over due. Because the approach of the administration to the problems of the day was pragmatic, its very pragmatism sometimes led to actions which were highly desirable and even contrary to its professed liberalism. Some of the more consistent liberals in Congress, like Senator Norris of Nebraska, attacked the National Industrial Recovery Act as this very point.

On the whole, however, most of the legislation passed between 1933 and 1939, to varying degrees, reflected the basic liberal philosophy of those who actually guided the destinies of the New Deal in Congress; and this liberalism was voiced again and again in the debates in Congress and in the public utterances of prominent members of the administration to such an extent that an exhaustive presentation of them would be tedious and unnecessary. There can be little doubt that the liberal social philosophy of the Federal Council of Churches and of those large denominations which in turn dominated its decisions, was both a preparation for, and an underlying support of the social, economic and political liberalism and radicalism of the era of the New Deal. The kinship is too deeply rooted and the parallels are too obvious to be successfully refuted. There are some who argue that this

[62] *Idem.*

revolution known as the New Deal would have come without the aid of liberalism in theology and this may be true, in the sense that a small group would have accepted its implications, but it is rather doubtful that it would have gained the popularity it did achieve without the preparation it received from the Social Gospel.

8

World War Two and After

The unsuccessful battle of 1937 in Congress to increase the size of the Supreme Court, and the even more unsuccessful attempt in 1938 of the Roosevelt Administration to purge from the Democratic Party those members of Congress who had taken the lead in the Congressional defeat of the Court bill, seriously impaired the strength of the New Deal in its legislative activities. The developments in both Europe and Asia assumed a new gravity and claimed the attention of President Roosevelt to such a degree that in 1939 and 1940 comparatively little in the way of controversial legislation was passed that did not have to do, either directly or indirectly, with diplomatic events abroad. At the same time, American liberal forces were split by a violent controversy over pacifism and whether complete pacifism was a desirable or possible policy in the light of the rise of the dictatorships in Germany, Italy and Japan. The announcement of the signing of the pact between Hitler and Stalin in August, 1939 gave American liberalism a rude jolt from which it did not easily recover; some liberals began to be aware of the fact that Russia, under Stalin, was as much a dictatorship as Germany under

Hitler. This very discovery in its own peculiar manner had a tremendous effect on liberal opinion in the United States and eventually enabled many liberals to abandon their pacifism and come to accept the war as a new kind of crusade in which this nation not only could, but should, participate. This new-found conviction was strengthened with Hitler's attack on Russia in June, 1941; and, by the time of Pearl Harbor, some liberal journals had already become impatient with Roosevelt for not throwing off his policy of neutrality and embarking on this great new crusade against totalitarianism.

However, this conversion to the use of force was not as foreign to the liberal position as it might seem at first glance. American liberal thought had always contained an element of pragmatism, with its corollary that the end justifies the means, and there can be little doubt that this pragmatism had a great influence in this change from pacifism to an acceptance of war as a legitimate instrument of national policy. It must not be imagined that the endorsement of our involvement in World War II was strictly for the purpose enunciated by the Roosevelt Administration in the propaganda which began to flow from official sources even before Pearl Harbor, but which became a veritable deluge after December 7, 1941. Indeed, if the advanced liberals, both within and outside the administration, had not seen in the war something more than a mere international struggle against Hitler and Mussolini, it is unlikely that they would have come to its support with as much enthusiasm as they actually did muster.

The *Christian Century* began its quest for a foundation on which it might support a war which it had previously condemned as being contrary to the Gospel of Christ as early as January, 1942 when it declared that God was trying to speak to his people in this war since "every event is a Word of God." Even this could only mean a kind of conditional acceptance of the war and by no means did this journal regard it as a righteous conflict at this time.

War is the collapse of the divine order for which God is striving, with man's cooperation, to establish in the world. The collapse of this order is due to man's disobedience. The collapse itself is God's judgment. God does not command us to fight. He condemns us to fight.[1]

The dilemma in this attempted solution is apparent. The God who failed because man had failed now condemns man to fight as a kind of punishment in which both are involved. It seems that God who lacked the power to prevent man from failing was somehow strong enough to bring about a war as a condemnation for failure and to guide that conflict in this direction. This is the inevitable intellectual quagmire which attends all forms of synergism in the vain attempt to evade the biblical doctrine of the sovereignty of God.

It soon became apparent that liberal theologians were now determined to call upon a church and an American people who, up to this time, had been powerless to prevent depressions and war, to adopt the proper methods by which they could avoid both in the future, and the war would thus become a new vehicle for realizing the Kingdom of God on earth. This is a far cry from the pacifism of the nineteen thirties, a pacifism which, at that time, was supposed to be the *sine qua non* of the projected Kingdom. The war which signalized the collapse of the divine order was now to become the means for its restoration on a more biblical basis than had ever before been true.

In order to formulate the proper procedures for the realization of this goal, the Federal Council of Churches called a National Study Council to meet at Delaware, Ohio early in March, 1942. The theme of this conference was the realization of a just and durable peace as the result of the present conflict. It decided that economic security is as necessary as political security for the realization of such a goal; it also affirmed that it was the supreme responsibility of the church to bring in such a state to the world. This economic security was a right of the people and

[1] January 14, 1942, pp. 38-41.

thus they have a duty "to prevent cyclical trends in business by regulatory methods." The report called for more industrial democracy as a necessary basis for political democracy; this call for an industrial democracy was little more than a thinly veiled plea for a much greater government ownership of, and control over, American business.[2]

The Methodist Federation for Social Service a month later called for the social (governmental) ownership of all industry necessary to win the war and it was imperative that the government take over the automobile and steel industries at once, if this war was to help bring about the Kingdom of God.[3] At a meeting of this organization in May, 1942, Harry F. Ward declared that collectivism would be the next step in society and that the task of the Protestant church was to see to it that this collectivism was democratically controlled, that it would not be fascist in its nature, and he suggested that the dialectics of Karl Marx should be used to determine the direction in which society was then moving.[4] He saw the present war as another stage in a world wide revolution.

Early in 1943 the Methodist Church held a conference at Delaware, Ohio to study what the aims of the nation should be in the war and just what the church could contribute to the realization of those aims. The conference insisted that it was the duty of the church to make the Christian principles of the sovereignty of God, man as a child of God, society as the family of God and nature as the creation of God effective in the midst of world revolution.[5] The *Christian Century* added that this conference made its greatest contribution to the discussions of post-war planning

[2] *Christian Century*, March 18, 1942, pp. 349-350; also March 2, 1942, pp. 389-397. The leaders of this conference were: Charles J. Turck, President of Macalester College, a Presbyterian USA school; Earnest F. Tittle, a Methodist pastor from Evanston, Illinois; Luther Weigle of Yale Divinity School; John Mackay, President of Princeton Theological Seminary. The American Unitarian Association, the Northern Baptist Convention and the National Baptist Convention were also represented by delegates.

[3] *Christian Century*, April 1, 1942, p. 430.

[4] *Christian Century*, July 1, 1942, p. 814.

[5] *Christian Century*, March 24, 1943, pp. 351-352.

when it turned the face of a great denomination again toward its faith in God and saw the Christian message in its religious rather than sociological terms.[6] Just how the *Christian Century* could call its deliberations theological in the light of its affirmations that all men are the children of God and that society as a whole is his family is hard to understand. This theology, whatever else it might have been, was certainly not that of the Scriptures, but of the liberalism which was part and parcel of the Social Gospel movement.

The Presbyterian Church USA by 1942 was willing to join in with the Federal Council and the other churches, to a degree it had not been willing to accept before. Its Committee on Social Education and Action declared that "Ours is the duty to build a people's Christian loyalty into the social order and to open their imagination and loyalty to all the implications of world citizenship."[7] Preparation for peace was a major responsibility of the church and America must accept her responsibility for building a better world that would square with the teachings of the Master. Both the Presbyterian General Assembly of 1942 and the Northern Baptist Convention voted to support the war effort, but they refused to bless it as they had in 1917.

In the various resolutions and public pronouncements of liberal theologians in this period there runs the note of the ecumenical movement. The church must train for an industrial democracy; the church must train and prepare for a world citizenship that would result from the present conflict; but, it would be the church and not the churches. Such leaders as E. Stanley Jones, Rufus Jones, Charles Clayton Morrison, and Herman Rauschnig called for a united church to meet the demands of a United Nations after the war. The realization of the Kingdom of God was dependent on the union of the churches. Even a united church was not to be identified with the Kingdom of God, but without this, the goal of history would not really be fulfilled.

[6] *Ibid.*, p. 352.
[7] *Ibid.*, June 10, 1942, p. 762.

Even as the Federal Council of Churches had been conceived in the first decade of the twentieth century as the means for realizing the Social Gospel as it was then defined, so an ecumenical church was an absolute necessity for its fulfillment in the days after World War II. The oneness of all humanity under the United Nations demanded the oneness of the church as a symbol of an undivided human race, in which truth would mean little and all differences, theological and other, merely unfortunate blemishes on the solidarity of man. The great task of the church was to prepare its membership for such a desired conclusion to the war. If the church could not give an unqualified blessing to the war which men had been condemned to fight, they could at least look with favor upon it for the realization of a goal which theological and political liberalism had decreed to be the aim of the conflict.[8]

Secular liberalism was not slow to pick up the refrain shouted by the ecclesiastical liberals. They soon began to see in the war the possibility for the realization of their own secular version of the "more spiritual" Utopia which the Federal Council and the Methodist Federation for Social Action believed to be the logical results of the war. Indeed, it was this same hope which made it possible for the more secular pacifists to break with their own conviction for the necessity of an absolute pacifism in order to accept a position which would allow them to preach its desirability but which, at the same time, would allow them to assume a more practical approach and support a war which promised to usher in the long-awaited liberal millennium. Secular liberal periodicals in their own way duplicated the mental gymnastics of

[8] This paragraph is an admittedly brief summary of a voluminous literature of the day found not only in the *Christian Century* but in the official, or semi-official, organs of the more liberal denominations and in the pronouncements of self-appointed spokesmen for the churches, as well as in the official pronouncements of the Federal Council of Churches and the various conferences which it sponsored from time to time. The *Christian Century* was so sure of the results of this war that it officially declared itself in favor of a policy that would allow Stalin to take over all of Germany in the interests of a post-war peace. September 29, 1943, pp. 1094-1096.

the ecclesiastical liberals and assumed a position which would allow them to give a qualified endorsement of the war effort; and, their solution was startlingly similar to that of the *Christian Century* and the liberal churches. Hitler's treacherous attack on Russia had in part helped them in this change of direction for they could now justify Soviet participation in the war and, at the same time, it helped to erase the painful memory of the 1939 pact between Germany and the Soviet regime. The events of June, 1941 gave to the conflict a kind of halo which the liberals could see even in the midst of the smoke of bursting bombs and ruined cities. The Japanese attack on Pearl Harbor gave the liberals an even greater reason for coming out in support of the conflict in which the United States was now actively engaged. Liberalism could now claim war as its own, as an instrument for bringing to this nation a new radical social and economic program which had not been possible from 1933 to 1940. Not only would our involvement bring added power to the federal government to a degree beyond the fondest hopes of the extreme liberals of 1933, but it would also bring a certain compulsion to conservatives to support the program made necessary by the war for they would seem to be obstructing the war effort if they should attempt to moderate this trend toward centralization of power in the hands of the federal government. The nature of the conflict played into the hands of the radicals in the Roosevelt Administration and they were not slow to recognize this fact and take advantage of it. The subordination of the domestic New Deal to the successful prosecution of the war was, at best, only a temporary policy, for victory would make possible a better New Deal not only for the United States but for most of the world.

The similarities between the secular and the religious radicals in their hopes for the war are too obvious to need much comment. They both accepted the war as part of a vast popular upheaval or revolution which would usher in a new democratic order and which would mean, as far as the American people were concerned, a federal government with vastly increased powers and with a high degree of socialism as the ultimate goal of this new order.

Some writers attempted to disguise the collectivism and socialism of the new order by painting it as a device for maintaining full employment and productivity after the war by preventing what they feared might be a disastrous period of deflation once the impetus given to our economy by the war was removed.[9] Henry Wallace gave great prominence to the concept of a people's revolution in his public statements at that time and he saw in it the great hope of the future, declaring that it offered the only real opposition to Hitler and that it could ultimately achieve success in this country in spite of the opposition to it from the reactionaries. Wallace professed to see in this people's revolution seeds of the Utopia for which he had long been seeking.[10] However, it must not be imagined that Wallace was the only member of the Roosevelt Administration who looked with favor on the war as a means of centralizing power, both political and economic, in the hands of the federal government as a necessary prerequisite for the achievement of the new democratic order. There were others who were perhaps less vocal, but no less dedicated to this goal and no less excited by the pleasing prospects of its attainment. Indeed, it is hardly too much to say that military victory would be almost meaningless if it were not accompanied by a victory for democracy at home, by which they meant the triumph of a planned economy.

It must be admitted that these hopes were not without a real foundation. The very fact that we were, as a nation, engaged in total war made it very difficult for the conservatives to oppose measures which were put forward as necessary for the successful prosecution of the war effort. The tremendous costs of the conflict made heavier taxation necessary and yet the heavier taxation was

---

[9] See *The Nation*, January 10, 1942, pp. 32-36 and for March 20, 1943, pp. 406-407.
[10] *Ibid.*, May 16, 1942, p. 562.

a legalized confiscation of wealth. Yet to finance the war largely by the sale of heavy bond issues would result in an inflation so disastrous that it could wipe out the accumulated savings of the people. It was not an easy decision to make which confronted the supporters of the Constitution and free enterprise. Participation in the war seemed to mean the destruction of the American heritage of constitutional freedom in its widest and finest sense. Rationing of foods and goods, the control of man power to assure its wisest use and the regulations of other precious freedoms which circumscribed American liberty could all seemingly be justified as part of the struggle against the totalitarian states. Many of these regulations were necessary, but underneath this realization of the necessity of these war measures there was a lurking fear in the minds of many conservatives that they were part of a post-war program also, and that in the war-time legislation the foundations were being laid for a post-war planned economy.

These fears were not groundless as events were to prove. The fears of the conservatives were, at the same time, the hopes of the liberals and early in 1943 Roosevelt gave to Congress the blueprint of what form the new Democratic order was to take in this country. It was contained in the report of the National Resources Planning Board, a body which had been appointed before the war, for the purpose of planning for the better use of national resources, both human and natural. In transmitting this report to Congress, Roosevelt gave voice to the same philosophy which we have met in the theological liberals and the organs of secular liberalism. When the President undertook to transmit this program to Congress and then to ask for its consideration and passage, the whole question of a planned economy was no longer merely one of liberal theory and pious hopes. It was now a political problem of tremendous importance for it had reached the place where it could become the law of the land. In March, 1943 the new order seemed to be on the verge of achieving a victory here in the United States. That Franklin Roosevelt was now converted to this mode of thinking seems clear from the message which he sent to Congress at the same time in which he strongly urged the passage of this revolutionary proposal.

> Because of their basic importance to our national welfare during and after the war, it is my earnest wish that Congress will give these matters full consideration during this session. We must not return to the iniquities and fears of the past, but ought to move towards the promises of the future.[11]

The National Resources Planning Board reflected this same basic confidence that this nation could, and would, march forward to meet the challenge and promises of the future. It was confident that "this upsurging of human personality, even in the terrible grip of war, looks for the new heaven and the new earth." The Board was equally confident that it had found the formula for the achievement of this American millennium.

> Peacetime activities can be found big enough to keep people employed to the extent necessary both to create the market through effective demand and to create the goods and services to maintain the national income at a hundred billion dollars or higher . . . . Government can and should underwrite effective demand for goods and services.[12]

The report gave the impression that such a goal could be achieved without any serious departure from the Constitution, but a closer examination of this document reveals that its framers were actually advocating a radical departure from the historic, if not from the contemporary, pattern of American social, economic and political activity. It reiterated the belief that future depressions could be avoided by huge expenditures of government funds obtained by borrowing. Thus, after the war the national debt was to be increased, rather than decreased, at the first signs of a possible depression, or, if the national income should fall below the hundred billion dollar mark. By a mathematical

[11] *The Congressional Record,* Vol. 89, part 2, p. 1792.

[12] This report was in two parts, the first containing 640 pages, had been given to President Roosevelt before Pearl Harbor, and the second, containing some 50,000 words, in December, 1942.

process all of its own, the Board had somehow determined that this was the magic figure which would sustain the hoped-for Utopia.[13]

In addition to the spending aspects of the report, the Board went on to make specific recommendations for the economic life of the nation in the post-war era which would help to guarantee an economic stability. It recommended a partnership between the federal government and private enterprise, particularly in those industries in which federal funds had been used to finance expansion for the purpose of aiding the war effort. Such a partnership was specially recommended for the aluminum, magnesium, shipbuilding and aircraft industries. It also proposed that the controls imposed over man power, wages and prices, as war emergency measures, should be continued after the end of the conflict. The Board was also of the opinion that manufacturing plants should be more evenly distributed in each region of the country and that such an equitable distribution could be achieved through a post-war method of retaining specifically selected industries and that the federal government should have a dominant voice in deciding just which industries should be retained. It also recommended that the reconversion of industry to peace-time production should be aided by the federal government by supplying industry with forecasts of the probable demand for consumer goods. It also called for a vastly expanded electrification program for the nation as a whole, based on the Tennessee Valley Authority, and for the creation of a National Transportation Agency to coordinate federal activity in this area of economic activity. In a previous report it had already suggested the advisability and urged the necessity of government ownership of the railroads.

It is little wonder that *The Nation* called this report the American Beveridge Plan for it was actually suggesting a program of

[13] It is amusing but also disconcerting to note that this figure has been far surpassed on many occasions in the post-war era and yet the millennium has not yet arrived.

security from the cradle to the grave on a much more sweeping basis than any previous suggestions placed before the Congress of the United States by a federal agency. It represented the formulation of a new New Deal more drastic and more collective than any proposed between 1933 and the coming of the war. Its ideal was a society in which planning for economic and social reform was to become one of the chief functions of the federal government.

The Board did have the grace to say that there would still be room in this scheme for private property, but it did not indicate how much room they might be willing to leave for an institution which the liberals increasingly felt was an outmoded vestige of an economic life that was passing from the American scene.

The report undoubtedly reflected the liberal optimism that, out of the carnage of the war, out of the slaughter and destruction which had two continents in its grip, the best was yet to be and was soon to break in on a humanity that was fighting for its very life against totalitarianism. The answer which liberalism gave to men was more totalitarianism, democratically controlled.

The *Christian Century* rose to the defense of this remarkable document, denying that it was socialistic in its intent and asked Congress to act on it, adding that if Congress should fail to act, and that if Parliament should fail to pass the Beveridge Plan for Great Britain, the revolution would surely come.[14]

The Nation adopted virtually the same attitude, declaring that what was envisaged in the report was not socialism, but that kind of mixed state in which alone capitalism could hope to remain progressive. But this journal also added:

> Laissez fair capitalism is dying, and it is up to this generation to see whether the new controls will be democratic or monopolistic.[15]

The Nation, however, was quite pessimistic about the success of the mixed economy which the report called for and made it quite plain that it wanted a much more drastic collectivism than even the liberals of the New Deal seemed to be pressing for. Maxwell Stuart

[14] March 24, 1943, pp. 350-351.
[15] March 20, 1943, p. 401

lamented that "as long at we retain private enterprise, our planning cannot be complete."[16] It was quite clear that the liberals desired nothing less than a democratically controlled collectivism. They settled for less only because the administration could not, or would not, press for more.

Fortunately for the American people this bill was referred to a Senate Committee of which the late Walter George of Georgia was chairman and it died in committee. This was not the case with other bills which had more to do with the war effort and when opposition to them seemed to be an opposition to the successful conclusion of the war. As a result, many bills were passed from 1942 to early 1945, the effect of which was to so centralize power in the federal government that their influence would remain long after the peace was declared. Not many of these presented the issues of the post-war era so clearly or stressed the nature of American society which was desired by the liberals who were using the war to obtain their ends. The debates on this particular report of the National Resources Planning Board brought out very clearly the close relationship existing between the thinking of the theological liberals and the advocates of the Social Gospel on the one hand and the advocates of a secular millennium on the other.

The Post-War Era

World War Two had brought profound changes not only in American life in general, but to the Christian Church in particular. If the Utopia which the liberals had been expecting failed to materialize, so did the great depression which they feared. Their insistence that the federal government must make provision for some sixty million jobs, either in private industry or on some governmental programs once the army was demobilized, proved to be as unnecessary as it was embarrassing since that figure for employment was soon surpassed by the employment provided in private industry. The demand that the economy should be so planned by the federal government as to produce a gross national

[16] *The Nation*, March 20, 1943, p. 337.

income of one hundred billion dollars seemed almost ridiculously pessimistic in view of the fact that private industry began to produce such a volume of goods and services that the gross national income soon exceeded the wildest expectations of both liberals and conservatives.

The fact that private industry was able to perform at a rate which exceeded not only the expectations of the liberals, but also that figure which they had decided would be the one which would justify the creation of a controlled economy left their plans with no validity. The great success of the private sector greatly weakened the liberal argument that such a federally dominated economy was an absolute necessity if the needs of the nation were to be met. Only the stubborn doctrinaires could maintain their demand for the creation of a controlled economy with a large mixture of socialism. That some of them did insist upon this is either a tribute to the strength of their convictions or a proof of their inability to recognize what was taking place in post-war America.

A study of the religious journals reveals that a similar dilemma was confronting the liberal leadership of the major Protestant denominations. Theological liberalism was facing an embarrassment strikingly similar to that which was confronting their political counterpart. The very millennium which these liberals in the churches had been preaching and calling for through the Federal Council of Churches, the columns of the *Christian Century,* and other journals had been surpassed by private industry operating under the free enterprise system, and they were at a loss as to how this phenomenon should be explained and handled. The economic Utopia had arrived, but the Kingdom of God which was supposed to have followed in the wake of this abundance of consumer goods had failed to make its appearance. Something had gone wrong with the program advanced by the advocates of the Social Gospel. The ills and evils which were supposed to vanish with the appearance of this high standard of living were still a part of the American scene. While it cannot be maintained that economic and social radicalism declined after the advent of peace, a hasty evaluation of the situation might have given such an impression. It was not as vocal among the rank and file of the workers but it was kept alive by Henry Wallace and the Far Left in the political life of the nation.

There was even the evidence of a certain degree of political conservatism not only among the rank and file of political leaders but among some religious leaders as well. The intrusion of neo-orthodoxy into many pulpits of major denominations brought with it something of a division in the liberal ranks and this division tended to bring a setback to their cause for a few years. Because of its nature neo-orthodoxy shook some of the favorite assumptions of the older theological radicalism, assumptions which were necessary for a rational approach to social and economic problems. Without the belief that the world was rational and could be rationally comprehended, a social gospel program would, and did have great difficulty in communicating its belief to society at large. Because neo-orthodoxy was rooted and grounded in Kantian philosophy and existential thought it, by necessity, denied the biblical doctrine of common grace and thereby destroyed the theological basis for a meaningful and effective social and political program. Without such a conception of God's sovereign grace over all of human history and the ensuing meaningful reality of the historical process in all of its various aspects, both the world and all human activity must necessarily lose that meaning and purpose which God has assigned to them by the exercise of His holy will. Neo-orthodoxy with its retreat to and delight in *heilgeschichte* tended to ignore the historical process as such. Neo-orthodox thinkers thus found it necessary to concentrate their attention on the acts of God through which He revealed Himself in the stream of events. Although this retreat from the aggressive social and political action which had characterized liberalism in the previous decades proved to be of short duration, it did provide its leadership with a time to rethink and regroup for that kind of action which would appear during the nineteen fifties and become a major force in the life of the nation in the nineteen sixties.

9

Conservatism and Liberalism, Theological and Political: Their Ebb and Flow, 1950–1980

The nineteen fifties witnessed a remarkable revival of evangelistic zeal and efforts by many groups and individual evangelists, unprecedented in American history. The advent of television soon after the close of World War Two, and the widened use of radio, offered to both the denominations and independent evangelists the opportunity and means for reaching the largest audiences in the history of preaching.[1] Many conversions were reported and it seemed as if one of the products of the revival of patriotism and religious fervor which took place during the war would be a resurgence of a vital Christian faith in the nation, a faith which would bring new strength to the church during the decade for the realization of the hopes for post-war America which had been aroused during the previous decade.

[1] While Billy Graham was the best known of these evangelists, he was by no means the only one to seize the opportunity presented for reaching the nation with the Gospel. Large denominations, like the Missouri Lutheran Synod also began to use television very effectively and Charles E. Fuller commanded a large radio audience with his "Old Fashioned Revival Hour." The National Council of Churches also maintained an ecumenical series on the radio.

However, this evangelical revival soon met a series of tests in new theological and political movements which threatened to destroy these expectations. Although the evangelistic revivals continued with an apparent unabated zeal as the decade of the 1950s advanced, it cannot be said in retrospect that they changed the mainstream of national affairs to any great degree. Nor did they bring to the country a more biblical outlook and character to its political or economic life. The reason for this ineffective impact on our national life lay, in part at least, in the nature of the evangelical effort itself and in the new and more virulent spirit which characterized American political and social liberalism during the 1950s.

In the first place, these evangelistic efforts and revivalism tended to be somewhat superficial in their theological outlook. The preaching all too often was concentrated in its effort to produce conversion to the neglect of the other aspects of the conversion experience and of the whole counsel of God. Too little emphasis was placed upon what conversion should mean in the hearts and lives of the converts; it was too often assumed that if people were only converted, growth in the understanding and practice of the Christian life would come as a matter of course. This development itself was, to some extent, the result of the increasing use of television as a means of reaching vast audiences and the ensuing temptation to use the programs as a kind of "sanctified entertainment" for the people of this nation.

The failure of the evangelistic endeavor to make a greater impression on the American public during these years cannot be blamed entirely on the weaknesses of the preaching. Even as evangelicals were striving to win the country for Christ with an "old fashioned message," liberals in the major denominations were girding for battle against them and preparing to present a new version of the old Social Gospel which they felt would be the answer to the needs of the day. Political and social liberals were also organizing to capitalize on the problems of the day for their own purposes and were in no mood to surrender the fort to the resurgent evangelicals. They clearly recognized that conservative preaching of any kind must, by its very nature, bring in its wake conservative political and social fruits already in evidence in the life of the nation.

The narrow victory by which President Truman defeated Thomas Dewey in the election of 1948 was a convincing indication that the Roosevelt era, marked by decisive Democratic victories at the polls, was coming to an end.[2] The conservatism which was beginning to emerge was, however, based for the most part on pragmatic grounds rather than on a philosophical or theological foundation. Thus, while it claimed the Constitution as its inspiration, it cannot be said that the philosophy which inspired that doctrine guided the thinking of those who were leading this movement. There was a growing conviction, however, that the liberalism of the Roosevelt era was not suited to the needs of post-war America and that the nation needed a new vehicle to meet and solve the problems of the day.

On the other hand, many Americans had become so accustomed to the presence of the welfare state and many forms of governmental intervention in the economic and social life of the people that even conservatives were unable to shake off the lure of its presence and the belief that the government should play an important if not a decisive role in shaping the destinies of the nation. It is evident that this conservatism lacked a firm theological foundation, and these conservatives were inclined to conduct their political activities on the basis of the claim that conservative Republicans could and should administer the liberal programs already inaugurated in the Roosevelt and Truman era because they could make them more effective and, at the same time, hold in check their potentially dangerous consequences.

That such claims were not only contradictory but even bordered upon the absurd never seem to dawn upon those making them and upon the so-called ''moderate'' Republicans who assumed leadership in the Eisenhower era. As a result, these moderates found it very difficult to withstand the popular clamor for more and more government intervention in the economic life of the nation,

---

[2] In this election Truman was able to garner just under fifty percent of the popular vote, although in the electoral college his margin was 304 to 189.

and for more welfare programs. Like their liberal predecessors they adopted policies which quite often were diametrically opposed to the American constitutional tradition and the Christian heritage of the nation. These contradictions gained new force during the administrations of John F. Kennedy, Lyndon Johnson, and Richard Nixon and reached their epitome during the presidency of Jimmy Carter, who more openly than any other presidential candidate in recent American history identified himself as a "born again" Christian and who, at the same time, consistently followed a liberal pattern in his conduct of the office which more frequently than not was in open contradiction to the Christian heritage of the nation and the faith which he professed.[3] Such a theological ambivalence has become a major souce of weakness for those who sincerely desire to recall America to its constitutional foundations and Christian heritage.

Although conservatives seemed to be gaining the upper hand in the life of the nation, their strength and promise were more apparent than real and were soon to meet a very real challenge from liberalism. Both theological and political liberals were girding for battle and had no intention of losing what they felt had been significant gains in the Roosevelt-Truman era. In 1950 they strengthened their ecumenical stronghold by replacing the Federal Council of Churches with the National Council of Churches of Christ in America.[4] There had been a growing conviction among liberal churchmen that the organizational form of the Federal Council made it an inadequate vehicle for the creating of that type of society which they envisioned. Charles Clayton Morrison, a long-time leader in the ecumenical movement and an early advocate of the Social Gospel, supplied the incentive for a stronger council in the columns of the *Christian Century*, of which he was the editor for many years.

---

[3] President Carter is by no means alone in his inability to square his political activity with his proclaimed biblical position. In the Senate, Mark Hatfield of Oregon has consistently followed a very liberal pattern of political conduct which is quite contrary to biblical Christianity.

[4] For a discussion of its formation, see C. Gregg Singer, *The Unholy Alliance*, New Rochelle, N. Y., Arlington House, 1976.

Protestantism has not learned to live in the modern world. It has carried over from the era of individualism its structure of organization and its simple procedures that seemed appropriate to them. Everything around it has changed, the whole structure and psychology of society, but Protestantism proceeds as if it were still living in the middle eighteen eighties.[5]

Having virtually condemned the older ecumenical movement for its inability to shed itself of the vestiges of an undesirable individualism, Morrison then called on Protestants to surrender their heritage for the alleged blessings of a democratic collectivism and conform to the modern world. Such a change of heart and conformity were very dear to the hearts of the liberals in control of the major denominations, who were determined to convert America to the support of their radical cause. Morrison declared that the remedy for the problem was not to be found in the Federal Council of Churches, but in some form of organization above and beyond sectarian cooperation which had characterized both the purpose and the history of the Federal Council. His solution was an ecumenical church, a union of all the major denominations of the nation and, hopefully, some of the smaller ones as well. A secular collectivism must be paralleled and strengthened by its ecumenical counterpart.[6]

The stepping stone for the realization of this utopian dream was to be the formation of the National Council of Churches, which would be a transitional kind of organization. It would find its greatest strength in its constituent denominations along with the interdenominational agencies which would also join it, but had never been a part of the Federal Council. The avowed objective of this new council was the realization of the Kingdom of God through the strengthened proclamation of the Social Gospel. If America was to become truly Christian, it must first become socialistic and collectivistic.

In his inaugural address the first president of the new Council, Bishop Henry Knox Sherrill of the Protestant Episcopal Church,

[5] *Christian Century*, May, 1951, p. 618.
[6] Singer, *op. cit.*, pp. 178-180, and *Christian Century* in *passim*, pp. 146-195.

declared that "there can be no artificial distinction between the sacred and the secular. The Gospel has to do with international relations, with peace and war, with the atomic bomb, with economic conditions, with family life for nothing human can be alien to the love of God in Christ." [7]

The whole tone of the organizational proceedings of the council made it quite clear that the council was to pursue thoroughly secular goals under the guise of applying biblical principles to national and international problems. The proceeding disguised a thinly masked plan to unite the ecumenical movement with secularism, political, social, and economic, for the purpose of restructuring American life into a collectivist state.

Although its design was to have the council join hands with the political and social liberals to achieve this goal, the new council, at first did not have much of an impact on the course of American development. Necessarily its first concern was the development of its own internal structure and the development of a harmonious relationship with the constituent denominations. However, there was no lack of issues to claim its attention, for they soon began to appear on the political horizon. [8]

National Issues and the Liberal Stance in National Affairs 1950–1960

The emergence of Communist Russia after World War II as a powerful, if not dominant, force in the affairs of Europe and in many other areas of the world posed not only a threat to American leadership, but also a distinct threat to the survival of those freedoms for the preservation of which we had entered that conflict. [9] The Berlin blockade in the summer of 1949, the civil war in China,

[7] *Ohio State Journal*, December 2, 1950.

[8] For a complete presentation of the aims of the Council, see "The National Council Views Its Task in Christian Life and Work." May 16, 1951, in *Pronouncements Issued by the National Council of Churches in the United States of America Through February, 1961*, pp. 9.1 to 9.1-6.

[9] The rise of Russia to a position of such power had been greatly facilitated by the agreement which President Roosevelt had made at Yalta in February, 1945. President Truman had confirmed, even making more specific, these agreements at the Potsdam Conference in July of this same year.

which eventually brought about the downfall of the Republic under Chiang Kai-chek, and the ensuing rise of the communist-controlled Peoples Republic of China in this same year brought home to the American people the greatest awareness of the meaning of Russian communism. By 1950 this had become a national as well as an international development in establishing a threatening problem. Americans began to see communism as a threat to the domestic peace and tranquility of the nation. Conservatives were much alarmed by this rising development, while the liberals were inclined to look upon this scene with a certain degree of complacency and tended to minimize the danger which it might pose to this country. The more radical liberals were even ready to welcome the emergence of Red China as a kind of rebuke to the West and to what they regarded as the dictatorial and corrupt practice of the regime of Chiang Kai-chek.

The attack on South Korea by the forces of North Korea and the obvious support given to them by both Russia and Red China further alarmed many, if not most, Americans and heightened the growing cleavage between liberals and conservatives in America. This development became an important factor in the determination of both the domestic and foreign policies. By early 1951 the war in Korea and the growing conviction that communism had secured a stronghold within the State Department and other branches of the federal government brought about a resurgence of conservative strength in political life on the one hand, while, on the other, it also sharpened the determination of the liberal elements to regain a decisive control over the machinery of government which they had held in the previous decade. They were determined not to let either the dream or the promises given to the people during the Roosevelt era vanish from the American scene. The conservatives were equally determined to rid the government of the sinister forces threatening the nation, and they were reinforced in their determination by the results of the congressional elections of 1950. These developments confronted liberalism, both secular and theological, with a tremendous challenge. The conservative religious forces were preparing to do battle with the recently organized National Council of churches while the political liberals looked to stronger ties with organized labor, but they did not disdain any help which might come from their theological allies.

The Election of 1952 and the Eisenhower Era

The invasion of South Korea by the North Korean communists in June, 1950, caught the American people by surprise. It stunned the liberals, who had been insisting that Russian communism would now be in this new postwar era a peaceful force in world affairs. They were not prepared to rush to the defense of North Korea, and they were equally unwilling to be found in the ranks of those who condemned Truman for his prompt action in sending military aid to the South Koreans. Because of its avowed dedication to pacificism, the *Christian Century* faced great difficulty in handling this problem, although it did admit that the Russian occupation of the territory north of the 38th parallel was a "hard boiled and bellicose act."[10] However, the editor managed to combine this criticism of Russian policy with a criticism of American military policy by declaring that the Russian action would make practically all of the South Koreans believe that anything would be preferable to Russian occupation.[11]

The National Council of Churches was strangely silent at this time (1950–1951) in regard to the war in Korea. When the conflict broke out, the council had not yet been formed. But even in 1951 it refused to take a strong stand in opposition to the conflict, contenting itself with a statement by its general council that the Truman Administration should not close the door to further negotiations with Russia.[12] The major denominations were, at the moment, also rather silent in regard to the war.[13]

[10] *Christian Century*, July 5, 1950, p. 811.

[11] *Ibid.*, p. 831. The editor also managed to maintain some semblance of loyalty to pacifism by issuing a warning that if the United States was not careful it could find itself in the same place as Russia.

[12] *Pronouncements Issued by the National Council of Churches Through February, 1961*, p. 22.1-1.

[13] *The Christian Century* and other liberal periodicals, both secular and religious, were

Not until the end of hostilities in 1953 and the beginning of the peace negotiations did the liberal religious leaders dare to speak up. The National Council of Churches called the meeting of the Fourth National Study Conference, which met in Cleveland, Ohio, in October of that same year. This conference renewed the liberal plea for universal disarmament and opposed the adoption of the Bricker amendment to the Constitution on the ground that it was a threat against international cooperation by this country.[14] The basic thesis of this conference was little more than a dreary reiteration of that theme which the liberals had so often accepted and voiced, that once Hitler was defeated, Russia would become a democratic, and therefore a friendly, power. Although the invasion of Korea obviously was a repudiation of this theme, the leaders of the National Council, in conjunction with *The Christian Century,* the *Nation,* and *The New Republic,* continued to call for national disarmament in the expectation that if the West should choose this policy, Russia would also. As difficult as it is to defend, this basic optimism in regard to Russia has continued to dominate our foreign policy from 1953 until today and lies at the heart of the Salt I and Salt II Treaties, and the willingness of the Carter Administration to either abandon or postpone the construction of modern weapons of warfare. This liberal optimism was considerably chilled for the moment in 1956 when Russia again proved that she was neither friendly nor democratic when she invaded Hungary. The pessimism was of short duration, however, for by 1958 liberals were not only displaying a new optimism in regard to Russia, but were also busily at work mapping out new programs for cooperation between the East and the West which would not only demand the reconstruction of our foreign policy, but of our domestic policy as well.

The Fifth World Order Conference, sponsored by the National

---

more outspoken against the war. The liberal leadership of the major denominations could not afford that luxury. Liberal journals were generally supported by those of like mind. But within the major denominations there were many conservatives who were in sufficient strength to make the leaders wary of voicing their true feelings in regard to the conflict.

[14] This amendment provided that treaties and executive agreements with foreign powers should not become effective until they had been duly enacted by both branches of the Congress.

Council of Churches, met in Cleveland again in 1958. It clearly set forth the development of liberal thought in regard to the problem of communism. Although it still used veiled language to state its position, there could be no doubt as to the substance and implications of the report.

> Stronger efforts should be made to break through the stalemate and find ways of living with the communist nations. Sometimes this is called co-existence. But we are concerned with something more than the minimal meaning of the word. Our relationship with the communist countries should combine competition between ways of life and cooperation for limited objectives. . . . We should avoid the posture of general hostility to them [the communists] and cease the practice of continual lectures by our leaders.[15]

The members of this conference were quite confident that such a policy toward Russia posed no great difficulties and would actually pay great dividends.

> There is a real hope that new generations within the communist countries will be less fanatical in their ideolgical convictions, and that they will be more preoccupied with peace, with economic well-being and with tentative experiments in cultural freedom than with attempts to dominate over other nations. It is not expected that they will formally renounce what we consider to be their errors. It is enough for the kind of living described above if their emphases and priorities change.[16]

Such optimism may sound hopelessly naive and utterly unreal in the light of what has taken place since 1958 in world affairs, but it had a tremendous impact upon liberal thought at that time, and to the extent that it penetrated official thinking it also influenced our foreign policy and those aspects of domestic policy which were closely related to it. This optimism had no theological foundation of any kind and the report pointedly refrained from denouncing communism as an atheistic ideology; neither did it condemn Russia for its communism.

The ruthless invasion of Hungary should have alerted the liberals as to the foolishness of their policy and its demands. The next rude

[15] *National Council Outlook*, December 21, 1958, p. 21.
[16] *Ibid.*, December 21, 1958, p. 21.

awakening did not come until the Cuban missile crisis under President Kennedy in July, 1962.

The Domestic Scene 1950–1961

We have already noted that the closing months of the Truman Administration were not particularly favorable to the passage of any liberal or radical legislation which was not regarded as necessary for winning the war in Korea. Because of this conflict Congress was in no mood to listen to the pleas of the liberals who wanted more Fair Deal legislation. A conservative mood was in the making and the liberals were regrouping for the 1952 election. Thus, the Republicans were searching for a candidate who would place them back in control of the nation's government in Washington.

The election of Dwight Eisenhower in the 1952 election was a kind of victory for conservatism in that it removed the Democratic liberals from the control of the White House. But this new administration was not actually conservative in the traditional meaning of the word. If Eisenhower's program did not meet with the approval of the liberals of the New Deal tradition, neither was it able to please the conservatives. During the election there was little mention of a truly conservative political philosophy and program which was based on an orthodox philosophy. As a result, this program was more pragmatic than philosophical or theological in character and outlook. Neither the secular nor religious press paid very much attention to this lack in the Republican approach to the problems of the day, but some astute observers were aware of the contradictory position which the administration was assuming and exposed its pragmatic character.

Writing in *Newsweek* Earnest K. Lindley gave an excellent analysis of the kind of conservatism which Eisenhower represented as he set it forth in his Annual Message to Congress in January, 1954. Lindley declared that President Eisenhower "ratified most of the major tenets of the New Deal and rejected completely the thesis that depressions are a natural phenomenon which from time to time must be endured. . . . He embraced the idea that the Federal Government has responsibilities for the welfare of the individual citizen. The direction of his domestic policies is not surprising. It reflects the philosophy of the wing of the Republican Party which was primarily responsible for his nomination as well as a large sector of the Democratic Party. The Eisenhower program is designed to sap the strength of the Democratic Party and to annex the independent voters necessary to keep the Republican Party in power."[17]

Lindley also made a further interesting and important observation:

Mr. Eisenhower's economic philosophy is essentially conservative. By any broad test his social program is conservative. But both involve the use of methods which were generally opposed by conservatives twenty years ago and are not endorsed by some today. . . . Together they set forth a new conservative program.[18]

Lindley endeavored to clarify his own position by stating that Eisenhower was liberal in human affairs, but conservative in economic matters. In doing so he committed an error which has been engrafted into American thought by its exposure to communist philosophy. Lindley was trying to distinguish between economic affairs on the one hand, and human interests on the other. This is a distinction without meaning for they cannot be separated.[19]

Henry Hazlitt was perhaps even more acute in his assessment of the political scene and more pointed in his criticism of the Republican program set forth by the Eisenhower Administration:

When it comes down to dealing with relationships between the human in this country and the government, the people in this administration believe in being what I think we would normally call liberal and when we deal with economic affairs of the country we believe in being conservative.[20]

Hazlitt came to the conclusion that "this seems to take over from

---

[17] *Newsweek*, January 10, 1980, p. 33.

[18] *Ibid.*, February 8, 1954, p. 32.

[19] This distinction has gained such currency today that it lies at the heart of nearly all political rhetoric and is commonly accepted in modern educational theory and practice, often times without any realization as to its origin by those who use it.

[20] *Ibid.*, February 16, 1954, p. 80.

the New Deal the essence of the Keynesian ideology—the belief in compensation spending—the belief that any decline from a peak of inflationary prosperity can and should be offset and rectified by an increase in deficit spending.''[21]

Lying at the very heart of the Eisenhower program was the philosophy of John Maynard Keynes, the noted English economist, who had gained the ear of Franklin D. Roosevelt with the result that the New Deal legislation from then on reflected this approach to the problems of the nation. For a long time Keynes had been a member of the Fabian Society in England, a socialist group in that country.[22] Like most of his Fabian colleagues, Keynes erected his philosophy on the basic assumption that Christianity was not and could not be true and that new principles of human action must be found in a form of socialism which was very close to communism. Roosevelt's first contact with Keynes seems to have been a letter which Keynes published in the *New York Times* on December 31, 1933, and which apparently influenced him to abandon the gold standard a few months later. In a personal interview with President Roosevelt in 1934, Keynes was able to persuade him that he should adopt deficit spending as the policy which would lift the nation out of the depression. That there was a radical intent behind the writings of Keynes and the tone of his later compared with his earlier works is not difficult to demonstrate. He wrote:

> Lenin is said to have remarked that the best way to destroy the capitalist system was to debauch the currency. . . . Lenin was right. There is no subtler, no surer means of over-turning the existing basis of society than to debauch the currency.[23]

That such an idea was not an incidental reference, but lay at the heart of his whole approach to economic issues is quite evident, and he had given it much thought. He wrote: ''The debauching of the currency is a process that engages all the hidden forces of economic

[21] *Ibid.*

[22] Keynes had set forth his philosophy in his *Treatise on Money* and *General Theory of Economics*, the first in England in 1930 and the second in this country in that same year. In 1936 his *General Theory of Employment, Money and Interest* was published.

[23] *Essays in Persuasion*, New York, Norton, 1963, p. 77.

law on the side of destruction and it does it in a manner which not one man in a million is able to diagnose.''[24]

Thus, this Keynesian approach to combating depression became the standard monetary policy for the succeeding administrations. It is doubtful that all those who have espoused such an approach, or even those who continue to support it today, are aware of the Marxian origins, or of its almost inevitable results. It was with good reason that Henry Hazlitt called the Eisenhower program a ''Mini New Deal.''

The debauchery of the currency through the persistent policy of encouraging inflation was and remains the standard radical attack on the fiscal soundness and integrity of the United States Government. Very few Americans are aware that it has its origins in a radical philosophy which was, and is, necessarily anti-Christian in both content and outlook. But liberals from the days of Franklin Roosevelt to our own day have, to varying degrees, been aware of its radical background and have sought to conceal it from the people. They have defended their inflationary programs on the ground that we must provide foreign aid for our friends abroad and an ever-widening social welfare program at home. Not only does such a program give an appearance of prosperity, but it also is an ideal way of redistributing the wealth of the nation according to a Marxian formula.

The liberal leadership within the major denominations and the National Council of Churches eagerly embraced such a policy on the ground that it was a necessary application of the principles of the Social Gospel. The leadership of the National Council has at times been willing to go further and faster into the area of creating a total social welfare state than the politicians have seen fit to tread.

The momentum achieved by this policy of planned inflation by the time of Eisenhower had become a popular national disease because money was so abundant and many people interpreted this vast supply of money as an indication of an increasing and virtually endless time of national prosperity. From 1952 on, both Demo-

[24] *Ibid.*

cratic and Republican presidents have felt the compulsion to continue the inflationary process even though during their campaigns they would make valiant, if unrealistic, pleas for a balanced budget even while pleading for more and more federal expenditures for various welfare projects, some of which have had dubious value, while others have proved to be very harmful, not only to the nation at large but to the recipients of the federal grants.[25]

The Election of 1960 and the Resurgence of Political Liberalism

Except for the reaction in the South to the decision of the Supreme Court in the segregation cases and the ensuing upheaval in Little Rock, Arkansas, the Eisenhower Administration proved to be the calm before the storm. The off-year elections of 1958 were an indication of the political changes which were in the making. The closeness of the race between Richard Nixon and John Kennedy tended to conceal the significance of the Kennedy victory. Liberals, however, both secular and theological, were jubilant with the outcome of the election and had been working diligently for just such a change in the political life of the nation. They had not been idle during the Eisenhower years. The combined voices of the *Nation* and the *New Republic,* with the help of the influential *Christian Century,* had given liberalism an imposing place in national affairs quite disproportionate to the rather small truly liberal element in the population. The National Council of Churches by 1955 was beginning to give to the movement an institutional leadership by which religious liberals could join forces with various other like-minded groups such as the National Education Association, the labor organizations, the National Association for the Advancement of Colored People, the League of Women Voters, and an assortment of more radical groups, all loosely allied in their common opposition to the continuing influence of historic conservatism in American life. By 1961 the major television net-

[25] Today many observers have come to the conclusion that this inflationary spiral is almost irreversible apart from stringent political and fiscal policies which no president or Congress could put into effect without very serious consequences.

works had also joined this crusade against the American heritage.

The National Council of Churches was particularly active in the formulation of liberal positions on various issues of the day and in presenting them before Congress and the Washington hierarchy.[26] By 1955 the council had broken its self-imposed silence and was busily at work preparing an agenda for action when the time seemed ripe. As early as 1952 the council had laid the foundations for its entry into the mainstream of political action when it sponsored the publication of *Goals in Economic Life*, the first in a series of six volumes bearing the title, *The Ethics of Society*. This project was the result of a three-year study by a grant from the Rockefeller Foundation.[27] The general thesis for the first volume was that welfare economics (the welfare state) was certainly the best, if not the only, solution to the problem of finding a balance between the individual and the economic group. Underlying this thesis was another one not openly stated, to the effect that free enterprise could not achieve this much-needed balance. That this document should contain strong communist strains should not have been surprising in view of the radical theological and political philosophies of those who composed it.

In October, 1954, the General Board of the council overwhelmingly accepted the basic principles of these statements, although in so doing it attempted to modify some of them in an effort to head off some of the severe criticism which they knew they would invite.

During the election year of 1956 the National Council undertook

[26] In contrast to this united religious liberalism, the evangelicals lacked a strong editorial voice for their position. Journals devoted to the cause of Christian orthodoxy and its accompanying political and economic conservatism were not lacking, but they were unable to command the attention of a significant number in the churches. This situation was not rectified until the appearance of *Christianity Today* in 1956. This journal soon became a major influence for evangelical Christianity although it never entered upon the political arena as did its liberal rivals. Although it was not political in character, it did seek to create a Christian concern for political issues and to delineate where Christians should stand in regard to them.

[27] This group was composed of Charles P. Taft, chairman, Arthur Fleming, at that time president of Ohio Wesleyan University, and Waldo Beach of the Divinity School of Duke University. Among those who contributed to the first volume were Kenneth Boulding of the University of Michigan, Ralph Linton of Yale University, and John C. Bennett and Reinhold Niebuhr of the faculty of Union Theological Seminary in New York. The liberal, if not radical, character of these volumes was thus assured from the beginning of the project.

its most important intrusion into the economic and industrial life of the nation when its Department of Church and Economic Life sponsored a conference at Pittsburgh in conjunction with the major denominations. This conference followed the usual ecumenical approach by drawing up a *Message to the Churches* in which it set forth its economic philosophy:

> We are entering a new age in the history of mankind. For the first time in human experience it appears possible that enough can be produced to meet the basic needs of man. We may refer to this new period as the age of abundance in contrast with past ages of economic scarcity. The promises of this economy are great, but its perils are so real that we cannot evade the challenge which this age brings to the Christian conscience.[28]

The underlying assumption and only partially concealed implication of this opening paragraph are rather clear. The challenge in making the promised economic abundance available to all is so great that our economic system must be restructured to meet it. This restructuring must lead to some sort of collectivism since free enterprise had already failed to meet the needs of the people.

This 1956 conference was the beginning of a new crusade by the National Council to achieve its goal of social justice for the nation. This is seen in its invitation to all liberal and radical groups to take part in this grand crusade. This conference was to be the means by which all liberals, secular as well as theological, could band together to bring about the realization of their demands in American political and economic life. From 1956 on, it became increasingly difficult to distinguish between the aims of the secular humanists as they were stated in the columns of *Nation* and the *New Republic* and those of the religious humanists as they were stated in the liberal religious journals. Whatever hesitance the National Council may have felt in the early years of the 1950s about openly declaring its humanistic stand had pretty well disappeared by the end of the decade. In his report to the triennial meeting of the council at Denver in 1960, Roy Ross, the associate general secretary of the

[28] C. Gregg Singer, *op. cit.*, pp. 202-203.

council, called upon it to engage in the great task of reforming every aspect of American life.[29] Although he masked this appeal in terms of a "redemptive endeavor," the real thrust of his message was quite clear and the National Council at this same meeting created the necessary committees to initiate the various projects which would realize this "Grand Reform."[30]

Liberalism was thus ready for the election of 1960, which gave the victory to John F. Kennedy and the Democratic Party. The *Christian Century* hailed the party's platform even though it had some reservations about the convention which produced it. Agreeing that the Republican Convention was a better show than the Democratic, it also insisted that "a fog of self righteousness" hung over both of them. It also conceded that both Nixon and Kennedy were secularists and would not be bound by any theological restraints since both were ruled by their brains and not by their hearts.[31] It concluded its rather cynical observations on the conventions and their candidates with the observation: "Our choice is not between messiahs and devils, but between men like ourselves. It is not between one platform which is a blueprint for utopia and the other which is a formula for certain ruin."[32] Nevertheless, it managed to achieve a certain degree of satisfaction with the platform of the Democratic Party, even going so far as to admit that the best thing about this party was its platform.

Other observers, however, were much more aware of the implications of the platform and what it portended for the American people. Henry Hazlitt, as usual, read between the lines of that document and concluded that it invited the American people to accept what he called the New Collectivism, the purpose of which was to force them to spend their money in a manner which the government would dictate through higher taxes. The underlying theory, according to Hazlitt, that the government would spend the money on those things which the people would want if they were

[29] *Triennial Report of the National Council of Churches, 1960*, pp. 140-143.
[30] *Ibid.*
[31] *Christian Century*, August 10, 1960, p. 915.
[32] *Ibid.*, p. 916.

competent to know their own best interests. Naming Kenneth Boulding as the chief spokesman for this group, he offered a very piercing analysis of what they really believed. "The essence of collectivism is to belittle the purposes of the individual in favor of those of some mystic collectivity."[33] It is obvious that this New Collectivism was strangely like the older forms and was nothing less than an offer to introduce to this country the corporate state.[34]

The election of 1960 proved to be the end of an era and the preview of what was in store for the nation in the decades ahead. The shallow conservatism which had characterized the Eisenhower Administration had not offered the people that kind of leadership or thoughtful approach to the basic issues which would invite an enduring commitment to those principles which had undergirded orthodox conservatism in the past history of the nation. The closeness of the race tended to conceal the real nature of the contest and what it portended for the nation. Kennedy's devotion to liberalism was a question mark. Because he was a Catholic many liberals feared that on such issues as birth control the papacy rather than the desires of the American people would tend to dictate his position. But the theological questions proved to be a peripheral issue in the campaign and were not often discussed. Collectivism was the dominant note in the platforms of both the major parties. If it was more openly stated in the Democratic platform, it appeared in a more timid manner in that of the Republican Party more by expression in the republication in its appeal to the voters through promises of federal aid of various kinds rather than through an open endorsement.

Following the example of Franklin Roosevelt, Kennedy chose a slogan for his program, calling it the "New Frontier." This was an effort to catch the public's imagination. The winds of change were blowing, and they became very apparent in address. In August, 1960, the *New Republic* had correctly interpreted the outcome of the election, three months before it took place, when it said that "whoever wins in November we shall have a change—a moderate change with Nixon and a great deal of change with Kennedy." This

[33] *Newsweek* July 18, 1960, p. 75.
[34]*Ibid.*, p. 75.

proved to be a very accurate analysis of the platforms and the candidates of the two major parties.[35]

After Kennedy's inauguration, however, the pattern predicted in August became a reality, at least as far as Kennedy's intent was concerned. Raymond Moley quite accurately evaluated the trend of political affairs when he pointed out that there had been a pattern estblished during the days of the New and Fair Deals of Roosevelt and Truman and that over that twenty-year period there had been a government of four types in which liberals had been contending among themselves for power.

> At first there were people who favored over all national planning. Then there were some who wanted government to get into business competition, especially in the electric power industry. There were those of the money magic ilk who believed in making everybody rich by swelling the volume of money. Finally, there were those who believed in more drastic regulation over all business.[36]

Moley pointed out that the appointment of James Landis, a disciple of Felix Frankfurter, as the one who would reorganize the various commissions which had emerged since March, 1933, was the key to an understanding of what the Kennedy program would be—namely, an increasingly drastic regulation of American business by the federal government. Landis was to have the power to regulate the regulators, and this type of centralization would be the order of the day for the New Frontier.[37]

There can be no doubt that the philosophy of Kennedy's New Frontier was that of a pragmatic liberalism. This reliance on a pragmatic approach to problems stands in strong contrast to the admonition which he gave to the American people in his inaugural address when he said: "Ask not what your country can do for you,

[35] See K. Porter and D. B. Johnson, *National Party Platforms, 1840–1964*, Urbana, University of Illinois Press, 1970, for these platforms along with those of the minor parties in this election.

[36] *Newsweek*, January 23, 1960. Moley had been an original member of the Roosevelt "Brain Trust" and was a very acute observer of the American political scene. Breaking with Roosevelt rather early in the New Deal era, he became an increasingly active critic of virtually the entire New Deal program.

[37] *Ibid.*, p. 88. It should be noted that with the help of the Speaker of the House, Sam Rayburn, Kennedy was able to have the Rules Committee of the House of Representatives stripped of much of its power.

but what you can do for your country.'' If this admonition had been heeded by the new president, the history of his and succeeding generations would probably have been very different from what it actually was. Although his philosophy was quite liberal, and even radical at some points, and although his cabinet appointments reflected his liberal bent, the Kennedy Administration was actually not able to accomplish very much towards achieving its announced goals. The Bay of Pigs fiasco of April, 1961, the Berlin crisis of that same year, and the Cuban crisis of 1962, which brought us to the brink of war with Russia, turned the attention of the administration toward our pressing foreign problems and weakened Kennedy's hold on the popular imagination. As a result, in spite of his great hopes and dramatic promises, Kennedy was actually losing control of Congress and had little to show in the way of important domestic legislation when he was assassinated in November, 1963. Nevertheless, in spite of the loss of political power and the growing inability to have a positive influence on the legislative program in the manner in which he desired, Kennedy had a great impact on American political life. His influence in this area cannot be measured in terms of legislative enactments. Rather it is to be seen in the changed atmosphere which enveloped the national scene. This development cannot be proved beyond dispute by footnotes on the bottom of a page, nor by appeals to the usual historical sources. But its presence was widely felt soon after he assumed office.

A moral and intellectual deterioration became evident and proved to be the source and inspiration for much of the student unrest and turbulence which was rampant in many of the large cities during the remainder of the decade.

One of the consequences of the assassination of President Kennedy was the fact that Lyndon Johnson, his successor to the office, was able to capitalize on this event to introduce his program, the ''Great Society,'' into the political, economic, and social life of the nation, even though he finally weakened his own leadership because of his involvement in the war in Vietnam.

The Election of 1964 and the Great Society

Soon after his accession to office, President Johnson set in order the machinery necessary for carrying his Great Society into effect, but he needed both the time and the momentum which a victory in 1964 would give him to secure the needed legislation.

Even before the campaign of 1964 had officially begun, the importance of this election was clearly perceived by liberals of all hues and institutional allegiance. Nor was its decisive nature lost to the conservative political leadership of the nation. On the other hand, theological conservatives either were less quick to recognize the philosophical foundations of the Johnson program or were unwilling to give voice to their fears.

The theological liberals suffered from no such inhibitions, and their support for Johnson was vehemently expressed, as was their determined opposition to Barry Goldwater, the Republican nominee. It is very difficult to discern any real theological cleavage between the two candidates. As a matter of fact, Goldwater's conservatism was as clearly pragmatic in its background and character as was Johnson's liberalism and lacked any solid philosophical or theological foundations. It is true, however, that many of his stated positions on important issues did reflect the convictions of many theological conservatives, and liberals were quick to seize upon this practical agreement when they took up the cudgels against the Republican candidate. At the same time they also realized that the pragmatism underlying his conservative stance was in many ways quite similar to their own position. As a result, the editorial position assumed by the *Christian Century* in 1964 stood in sharp contrast to that which it had shown four years earlier. Many liberals did not seem to realize that Lyndon Johnson was as secular in his outlook as John F. Kennedy or Richard Nixon. The assassination of Kennedy in 1963 produced a profound shock all over the country, but it stunned the editor of the *Christian Century,* who wrote: ''A blast from the trumpet of the Angel Gabriel announcing the end of time could have hardly affected us more than the news of the assassination of John F. Kennedy.''[38]

By 1964 this weekly journal had shed all traces of that neutrality which had characterized its attitude toward both parties in 1960 and turned sharply against Barry Goldwater, and was strongly in favor of Lyndon Johnson.

It is clear that behind this support of Johnson there lurked some doubts and questions on the part of the theological liberals. A careful reading of the liberal religious journals and pronouncements of the major denominations in their annual assemblies and conferences reveals some uneasiness concerning the direction which Protestantism was taking. The editor of the *Christian Century* lamented the apparent aimlessness of contemporary Protestantism and traced this and other disturbing factors to the diversity existing in the movement and its sharp division into fundamentalism, evangelicalism and liberalism. The remedy was to be found in the ecumenical movement and ending the traditional emphasis on the right of private judgment (in religious matters) which, in the opinion of the writer, has been the cause of much folly.[39] Reinhold Niebuhr raised his voice in an even more bitter attack on American Protestantism, declaring that the crisis which it faced lay in the intense individualism which characterized it and professed to find the root of the trouble in the Social Creed of 1908, the basis of which, according to him, was drawn from a moribund Calvinism ''which regards wealth as the reward of virtue and poverty as the punishment for drunkenness or laziness.''[40]

Although these articles were written in 1963, it is evident that the liberals were preparing for battle in 1964 and that the election campaign of that year was to be used as the vehicle for bringing a new sense of purpose to Protestantism, a sense of purpose which would be channeled to the support of an avowedly liberal party, led by an avowedly liberal candidate. That this was the case can also be

[38] *Christian Century,* December 4, 1963, p.1480.

[39] Bernard Eugene Meland,''Modern Protestantism, Aimless or Resurgent?'' *Christian Century,* December 4, 1963, p. 1496.

[40] *Ibid.,* p. 1498. In this approach Niebuhr was endeavoring to revive the long-exploded Troeltsch-Tawney characterization of Puritanism. It is difficult to believe that Niebuhr was not aware of the collapse of this theory.

seen by the position assumed by the *Christian Century* and other journals of like mind in 1964.

In 1964 the *Christian Century* renewed its plea for the revitalization of Protestantism and its theology which would make the church more relevant to the needs of the twentieth century and bring its thinking into conformity with modern humanism. William Ferm, the dean of the chapel at Mount Holyoke College, called on the church to declare its independence of its outworn dogmas, such as the idea of a personal God over history, and "the Creed of Chalcedon since it is meaningless for our day."[41] His solution for the dilemma confronting Protestantism was to have the church declare the interdependence of the human race.

The triumph of Lyndon Johnson over Barry Goldwater in this election has frequently been regarded as a victory for political and economic liberalism, or radicalism over conservatism. This is undoubtedly true, but the size of the vote given to Lyndon Johnson did not accurately reflect the strength of liberalism any more than did the relatively small vote given to Goldwater indicate that conservatism was that weak. The triumph of Nixon over Humphrey four years later hardly supports this thesis. The Republican chant of 1964, "in your heart you know he is right," could hardly compete with the unfounded, but widely accepted, charge that if Goldwater were to be elected he would lead the nation into war. Yet, it must also be admitted that the profound theological changes which were already under way helped to prepare America to accept the profound political, economic, and social upheavals which would shake the fabric of the republic to its very foundations before the decade should come to an end. Morally, socially, and economically the thinking of the American people was being transformed and prepared to tolerate a new era. Robert E. Fitch, dean of the Pacific School of Religion, lamented that "a common sense code of morality is all that is left for young people today." He called for bigger and better inhibitions and declared that "there is a need for a reservoir of personal responsibility."[42]

[41] *Ibid.*, July 15, 1964, pp. 903-906.
[42] Robert E. Fitch, "A Common Sense Sex Code." *Christian Century*, October 7, 1964,

There is no doubt that the moral climate of the country was changing in a dramatic manner, a change for which evangelicals and liberals of the old school were quite unprepared to meet. The older liberalism, for the most part, had been intent on maintaining a Christian morality and ethic within the context of liberal theology, but this was no longer true of the new brands of liberalism. Evangelical orthodoxy was also on the defensive, for it was confronting a new and more radical theology and a new evangelicalism which was rising within its ranks. Confusion had gripped the evangelical movement. Many new ethical theories, advanced by the extreme liberals, were attracting the attention of those evangelicals who felt the lack of a biblical ethic in their own thinking. Carl F. H. Henry, editor of *Christianity Today*, rightly observed that a new brand of social ethics was emerging and that some evangelicals were becoming entangled in the snares which were being artfully laid to entrap them by the ecumenical leaders, who were "rolling out the red carpet for them when they marched at Selma, or when they joined organized picket lines in demonstrations, or when they joined ecclesiastical pressure blocs on Capitol Hill or at the White House, or when they engineered resolutions on legislative matters through annual church meeting."[43]

In such activities these evangelicals were following the lead of the liberal religious leaders, who had put together an effective lobbying force in Washington and were frequently found in the forefront of social and labor agitation. The National Council of Churches had set up an office in Washington for the specific purpose of lobbying in behalf of liberal programs of various kinds,

pp. 1233-1235. The total thrust of the many articles written in the *Christian Century* in 1964 was toward a politically motivated humanism in which the church should play a role. See issues of July 1, 1964, pp. 851-852; July 8, pp. 879-883; July 29, pp. 955-957; September 2, pp. 1079-1083; September 9, pp. 1099-1101; and November 11, 1964, p. 1367. I have cited the *Christian Century* because it was, and is the most influential liberal religious journal and generally reflects rather accurately the thinking of the leaders of the major denominations.

43 Carl F. H. Henry, "Evangelicals in the Social Struggle," *Christianity Today*, October 8, 1965, pp. 3-11. This article is an extremely important pronouncement by a noted evangelical who charged that for two generations a liberal social ethic had been markedly influential in American public life in the areas of education, government, and labor, p. 4.

and it was proving to be very effective for promoting liberal legislation. In December, 1965, Edward Espy, the general secretary of the National Council of Churches, gleefully reported to the General Board that:

> It is striking to note that many of the general policies advocated by the National Council across the years have been incorporated into federal legislation. This was true during the Truman, Eisenhower and Kennedy Administrations, particularly in international policy, and it has been especially true in domestic legislation under the Johnson Administration.[44]

However, the influence of the National Council was not confined to the halls of Congress, and Espy exuberantly declared:

> The Supreme Court has handed down numerous decisions in keeping with the position of the National Council. Cases in point are civil rights ruling, the decisions on legislative reapportionment and rulings on prayer and Bible reading in the public schools.[45]

That these were no idle boasts if fully attested by a comparison between the acts of Congress in various fields, the decisions of the courts, and the pronouncements and resolves of the National Council in its triennial meetings and General Board declarations. There can be no doubt that the liberal theology of this body and the network of liberal leadership which brought the major denominations into its political camp lay at the heart of the legislative programs during these and succeeding administrations. On the other hand, the National Council and its ecclesiastical allies should not be given all the credit or receive all the blame for these acts of Congress and decisions of the Supreme Court. These activities of the Congress and decisions of the courts reflected the liberal political thought of our day and had the support of other organized groups. Yet, at the same time, it remains true that much of the legislation passed since 1960 can be traced to the liberalism, theological and secular, of the leaders in Congress and in the courts of the land. It is also true that most of this legislation was directly

---

[44] *Minutes of the General Board of the National Council of Churches,* Matthews, December 2, 1965, n.p.

[45] *Ibid.,* December 2, 1966.

opposite to the biblical view of the functions and powers of the government because it did reflect a liberal theology which was not only hostile to Scriptures, but also inevitably hostile to the whole idea of the American constitutional tradition.

The biblical doctrines of the holiness and the wrath of God were replaced in our legislative and judicial proceedings by a concept of divine love which confused the mercy and justice of God and left little place for the biblical teachings in regard to the judgment of sin and sinners and what the Scriptures require of rulers in the maintenance of justice and political order in the state. Lacking any understanding and appreciation for covenant theology, this liberalism has consistently refused to see the devastating results of the fall into sin and the need of sinners for redemption through the atoning work of Jesus Christ.

The inadequacies of liberal theology and its political derivatives have not only allowed the National Council to enter into the political arena on the side of radicalism, but it has encouraged the supporters of the ecumenical cause to join hands with humanistic seculars in that political world to seek a utopian kingdom on earth which, by its very nature, must embrace all nations of this earth in a vast communist experiment, a vast collectivist state, in which all human liberty would perish in a vain quest for world peace.

With such support from religious and secular liberalism, it is no wonder that Lyndon Johnson was able to bring about a veritable revolution in American life with his Great Society. A series of acts dealing with race relations, education, social security, and medical insurance made this upheaval a reality in American life. But his Great Society not only threatened the continuing influence of the Constitution as the mainstay of our political activity, it also was designed to bring about a redistribution of wealth through a plan of high taxation and an inflationary budget.[46]

[46] There was scarcely an important piece of legislation in the Johnson era which could withstand the test of a close scrutiny as to its constitutionality. The liberal majority on the Supreme Court meekly followed the leading of the administration in its decisions after counseling with their sociologists and psychologists. The Constitution seemed to have but a limited influence on their thinking.

Liberals exulted in the fact that this was the case. The *Christian Century* proudly exclaimed that Johnson had prevented the take-over of the federal government by a rightest-racist coalition and had also prevented a plunge into a world war.[47] The Johnson victory over Goldwater in November, 1964, encouraged the liberals to push the administration even further to the left in its domestic policies. Thus the *Christian Century* was emboldened to call for the abolition of the House Committee on un-American Activities against which liberals of all varieties had been waging war for a decade or more.[48]

The apparent success of Johnson's Great Society and its un-doubted popularity with the masses of Americans placed a strain on theological conservatives. During the 1950s and early 1960s it was rather widely accepted that a theological consistency demanded that evangelicals should pursue a conservative course in political, social, and economic matters while liberals should logically follow a liberal pattern in their political outlook. However, this general pattern changed during the latter half of the sixties and the social disruptions of the day along with our involvement in the conflict raging in Vietnam brought with them a growing diversity of opinion within the evangelical ranks on such issues. A growing number of evangelicals, particularly those of an Arminian outlook, began to feel that they should develop a social concern and offer a biblical answer to these pressing problems. Calvinists were like-wise feeling the pressures brought upon the church by the social upheavals, but they were anxious to develop answers which would be in harmony with their theological position and were quite un-willing to accept the answers which secular liberals were demand-ing of the church as well as those offered by Arminian evangelicals.

Many of the younger evangelicals felt that covenant theology was a kind of strait jacket which placed limitations on their involve-ment in these struggles. Many of this school of thought actually

[47] *Christian Century,* November 11, 1964, p. 1387.
[48] *Ibid.* Among those who supported this call were John C. Bennett of Union Seminary in New York, Martin Luther King, Jr., James Pike, Episcopal bishop of California, and John A. Mackay, president of Princeton Theological Seminary.

became impatient with Calvinism and conservative orthodoxy in general and were looking with great interest at a new brand of evangelicalism, which they felt could come to terms with the Social Gospel and yet not cause them to surrender their commitment to the great truths of the gospel. Some of them even came to the place where they were willing to embrace an evangelical Social Gospel which could hardly be distinguished from the secular liberalism so rampant around them. To achieve this goal they were willing to modify their own theological conservatism to a point where it could come to terms with the secular humanism of American liberal thought.

The stage for the emergence of this New Evangelicalism had been set in the domestic and diplomatic events of the decade, 1960–1970. The younger evangelicals had been increasingly disturbed by what they considered to be an unwarranted reluctance of many conservatives to deal with the race issue. Likewise, many had been embarrassed by the conservative support of what they felt was a totally unnecessary war in Vietnam. They did not accept the thesis that it was being waged to prevent a communist expansion from taking over that part of Southeast Asia. Senator Mark Hatfield of Oregon, a confessed evangelical, took a strong stand against this war and beckoned to other evangelicals to follow him into the fold of political liberalism, not only in regard to the war, but on other matters as well.[49]

This awakening social conscience was in itself a healthy development, but it was also fraught with great danger for the evangelical cause, and the danger became quite evident after 1970. An awakened evangelical conscience, guided by Reformed theology could be, and should be, a powerful factor in any program of true reform in the national life. A social conscience which was guided by a biblical world and life view was exactly what was needed then and what is needed today. But after 1970 there was a very strong temptation and tendency for evangelicals to accept the secular

[49] The war in Vietnam broke over party lines and drove a sharp wedge between liberals and conservatives in both the Democratic and Republican Parties.

program of liberal reform as that which was in accord with the biblical ethic and one, therefore, which they could accept as their own. They failed to heed the strong warnings of Carl Henry as they appeared in the columns of *Christianity Today* between 1965 and 1973. In 1973 this journal issued a plea for a well-informed evangelical concern which would be based on a sound knowledge of the institutions and practices which were in need of reform and an equally sound insight into the principles involved in a program of social reform truly biblical in character.

> Many evangelical teachers are completely befuddled when confronted by demands for answers to questions that are not exhaustively dealt with in Scripture. . . . In their bewilderment they frequently resort to paraphrasing worldly opinions. Occasionally interpolating a pious thought or two. Thus many evangelicals come close to sounding like utilitarians, situation ethicists or even Marxists when confronted with hard questions from the contemporary world . . . questions of war, capital punishment, abortion, revolution, exploitation.[50]

Pursuing this line of thought to a logical conclusion the editor insisted that evangelicals once again need to make contact with the solid substance of the Christian ethical tradition and then do some new and systematic and creative thinking in order to face the powers of this world with a consistent and biblical world and life view. This sound advice went unheeded by many of the leaders of the New Evangelical Movement, who apparently were more interested in demonstrating some kind of a Christian social concern which would gain the attention and respect of the secular humanists because of its similarity with their own outlook. Fifty evangelicals met in Chicago in November, 1973, and issued *A Declaration of Evangelical Concerns.*[51] Although this document was primarily a call for evangelical action in regard to racial injustice and the plight of the poor, it also contained phrases which were decidedly radical in nature and came very close to placing the signers of this document in a position which bordered on communism. It declared that "we must attack the materialism of our culture and the maldistribu-

---

[50] *Christianity Today*, October 12, 1973, p. 38.
[51] *Ibid.*, December 2, 1973, p. 38.

tion of the nation's wealth and services. . . . Before God and a million hungry neighbors we must rethink our values regarding our present standard of living and promote a more just acquisition and distribution of the world's resources.''

This document concluded with a disclaimer that its formulators were preaching a new gospel or that they were endorsing any political ideology. Those who signed this document may well have believed what they were asserting, but it can hardly be denied that a careful reading of the whole declaration would lead to such a conclusion. It would seem that it was a clarion call to evangelicals to join in with liberals and radicals in support of causes which bore little resemblance to a biblical ethic. Although it was not stated openly, it is significant that those who signed it were urging evangelicals not to allow their theological presuppositions to interfere with their plans for political, social, and economic action. In effect, this document gave an almost *carte blanche* permission for those who regarded themselves as evangelicals to enter into the social and political conflicts of the day and join hands with the secular liberals and radicals in the pursuit of social reforms which were the product of a secular humanistic philosophy rather than an expression of the true biblical ethic. It might also be noted that there was a tendency among the members of this group of younger evangelicals to be rather critical of those who held firmly to the inerrancy of the Scriptures and to find an alliance with those who held to a weaker view of scriptural authority in an effort to justify their alliance with secular humanism.

This group is now facing the same temptations and dangers which those evangelicals of the closing decades of the nineteenth and the opening years of the twentieth century faced, namely, to accept an ecumenical approach to social problems with liberals in the vain hope that they retain their evangelical position untarnished and unimpaired. But the evangelicals of 1908 found themselves bound with unbelievers in the emerging Federal Council of Churches and involved in various social and political schemes which have no place in an ethical system which is faithful to the plain teaching of the Scriptures.

The Johnson-Nixon Era, 1964–1974

Although liberal secular and religious leaders had greeted the election of Lyndon Johnson to the presidency in 1964 with great enthusiasm and had rallied to the support of the Great Society as it continued to unfold in legislative actions after 1964, many of them became disillusioned as the nation plunged more and more deeply into the war in Vietnam. In his inaugural address Johnson had announced the coming of the Great Society as his program. It was, in essence, the promise of abundance and liberty for all citizens: ''a place where every child could find the means to enrich his mind and enlarge his talents, where leisure is a welcome chance to build and reflect . . . where the city of man serves not only the necessities of the body and the demands of commerce, but the desire for beauty and the hunger for community, where men are more concerned for the quality of their goals than for the quantity of their goals.''[52]

There was very little material in the address which was original with Johnson. Both the title of his program and the philosophy underlying it were derived from Graham Wallas' book, written fifty years earlier.[53] Graham Wallas had been a hard-core socialist, and beneath the seeming noble phrases which Johnson borrowed from him there can be detected the strident tones of a call for a new approach for introducing collectivism into the American scene. Johnson also borrowed heavily from Franklin Roosevelt's New Deal to erect his own foundation for this new approach. Basically this new movement was little more than the humanistic vision of the city of man which stood out in sharp contrast to St. Augustine's City of God.

There can be no doubt that this program was quite popular until the American people rose against the involvement in the war in

---

[52] *Public Papers of the Presidents of the United States, Lyndon B. Johnson,* Government Printing Office, Washington, 1966, pp. 71-74.

[53] Graham Wallas, *The Great Society,* New York, Macmillan, 1914.

Vietnam. Their early optimism gave way to disillusionment, and many of the younger generation loudly and violently protested against the war. Accompanying these protests was also a cultural decline, which was accentuated by a moral disintegration. Riots in the cities and on college campuses, the rise of various semi-religious and philosophical cults, and the widespread use of "soft" and hard drugs arose in many segments of American society and were accepted as the order of the day. There was a widespread alarm for the future of the country as concerned citizens watched the increasing use and public acceptance of abortion as a desirable means of avoiding the births of unwanted and unloved children. Homosexuality and sex without marriage were gaining a respectability which had never been accorded or approved previously in the history of the nation. There was an impressive amount of evidence that America was suffering from a moral decline unparalleled in our history.

Liberal theology which spawned the "God is dead" movement and the New Morality as it was presented in Situation Ethics gave nurture and comfort to these sexual deviations, the drug movement, and to the movement for the legalization of abortion.

By the middle 1960s liberalism had so undermined the meaning and contemporary validity of the biblical ethic in the eyes of the younger generation that many of them came to the conclusion that the biblical moral code had little relevance for their day.[54]

The campaign of 1968, between the Democratic nominee, Hubert Humphrey, and Richard Nixon, the Republican choice for the presidency, revolved usually around our participation in the war in Vietnam as the chief diplomatic concern and the restoration of law and order at home as the dominant domestic theme. While Nixon

---

[54] Not all liberals condoned the use of drugs. The practices of abortion and sexual deviations were also not condoned by all liberals, but they had lost the authority necessary for any successful opposition to these practices, which were the logical offspring of their own theological position. Liberal religious journals often condoned active opposition to the war in Vietnam and activism in regard to racial segregation, but they usually avoided giving any specific endorsement to the other aspects of the social revolution. Conservative evangelical publications viewed these movements with alarm and took a strong stand against abortion, the drug cults, and sexual immorality.

can be regarded as more conservative than Humphrey, it cannot be successfully maintained that theological issues played an important role in the outcome of the election. The conservatism which Nixon claimed as his own and which gave him the victory in the November election was basically pragmatic in character and lacking in any fixed political principles derived from the original Constitution or a biblical world and life view. Humphrey's liberalism was a mixture of political and social pragmatism on the one hand, and a consciously held theological liberalism on the other.

The legislative history of Nixon's first term in office gives no evidence of any devotion to any historic concepts of the nature and role of government or of private and public ethics. It could also be maintained that, so far as the conduct of the government is concerned, in actual practice Nixon was as liberal as Humphrey promised to be if he had won the election.

In his signing of the Salt I Treaty and in his unceasing efforts to promote *detente* with Russia, and in his promoting closer relations with Red China, it is clear that Nixon's foreign policy was decidedly liberal and contrary to the biblical view of government. In his administration secular humanism seemed as dominant, both in Washington and over the nation, as it had been in the days of Lyndon Johnson. The decadence of American popular music and literature and the continuing decline of American public education as it fell into the hands of humanists all bore witness to the fact that humanism was permeating nearly every aspect of American cultural activity and its institutions.[55]

The election of 1972 must be regarded in the same light as that of 1968, as far as its theological implications are concerned. The one major difference between George McGovern and President Nixon would be found in the more radical stance by McGovern, the Democratic candidate. He could command the respect of neither the Democratic regulars nor the moderate liberals. As a result, Nixon was able to win a rather decisive victory in this election, the

[55] Charles Gregg Singer, *From Rationalism to Irrationality*, Phillipsburg, N. J., Presbyterian and Reformed Publishing Co., 1979.

fruits of which were destroyed in the ensuing Watergate and related scandals. The main thrust of the Nixon years was toward a moderate, or even radical, liberalism at times, particularly in regard to his foreign policy.

In some respects the 1976 campaign was decidedly different from those of 1968 and 1972, on the surface at least. The leadership of the Democratic Party was determined not only to avoid the errors which had brought defeat to the party in the two previous campaigns, but also to find a candidate who would present a different image to the voting public.

By 1976 the American people were thoroughly weary of the repeated scandals which had rocked official Washington and were rather suspicious of all professional politicians.[56] They found the man they wanted in James Earl Carter, former governor of Georgia (1970–1974), but who was virtually unknown outside of his own home state. He could appear before the voters as one who was unsullied by any contact with the politicians in Washington and whose political record was thought to be without blemish.

The rise of Jimmy Carter to a place of political prominence in the Democratic Party was not as accidental, or incidental, as it might have seemed at the time it took place. He was not without ties to the bureaucracy he seemed to oppose, for they had been forged even while he was governor of Georgia. The fact that he openly confessed a conversion experience and professed to be "born again" made Carter a most attractive candidate at a time when the party desperately needed just such a man.[57] In a series of complex moves in which Milton Katz, a professor of law at the Harvard School of Law and an official of the leftist, pacifist Carnegie Endowment for International Peace, and Averill Harriman played a major role, Carter was introduced to the proper political leaders within the party who would groom him for the

[56] Several sexual scandals had rocked Congress. In fact, the decline of the liberal ethic was increasingly evident in government, in business, and other aspects of life.

[57] Although no one should question the reality of Carter's conversion, we can only wonder about the depth of his understanding of the Scriptures when he also announced that his religious reading had been largely centered in the theology of such noted liberals as Reinhold Niebuhr and Paul Tillich.

1976 campaign. Averill Harriman had a long record of friendship with Soviet Russia and involvement with left-wing diplomatic and domestic causes too numerous to mention. Harriman actually introduced Carter to Zbigniew Brezinzski, who then took Carter to meet David Rockefeller. By 1973 Carter had been prepared for working with the recently formed Trilateral Commission. This commission, an off-shoot of the Council on Foreign Relations, had just been formed with Rockefeller's financial backing, for the purpose of advancing liberal diplomatic policies. The basic purpose of both of these Rockefeller-sponsored organizations had been, and remains, the creation of a one-world government. The liberals within these groups created a team to work for the election of Carter, one of whom was Peter Bourne, the English-born psychiatrist who had worked hard for the defeat of the United States in the Vietnam conflict. It is no wonder that after his inauguration President Carter appointed many members of the Trilateral Commission to key positions within and outside his cabinet, notably Brezinzski, who became National Security Adviser, Cyrus Vance, Secretary of State, and many others.[58]

As a result of his indoctrination into the philosophy of the Trilateral Commission and the influence of the liberals holding many high places in the administration, President Carter conducted a foreign policy which was based on the assumption that Russia would honor all of the agreements included in Salt I, and which advanced policies which favored Russian communist interests with an amazing consistency. Perhaps the climax of this underlying approach to diplomacy was the signing of the Panama Canal Treaty, which surrendered the canal and the Panama Canal Zone to the ultimate ownership of the Republic of Panama, which was

[58] It is appropriate to point out that the Trilateral Commission fathered a Declaration of Interdependence in 1976, which was scheduled to be read in Philadelphia on July 4, at the mammoth celebration of the 200th anniversary of American independence. However, sober judgment prevailed among enough members of this group to cancel the proposed reading. In essence the document declared that the time had come for this country to surrender its independence and be prepared to enter into a world government which would rest upon the interdependence of its members. This was a thinly disguised appeal for a communist-dominated world.

governed by a communist dictator. Carter also decided to delay the building of the B 1 bomber which would have brought much-needed strength to the United States Air Force and make it more competitive with Russian military might. The climax of these decisions came with the signing of the Salt II Treaty in 1979, an agreement which went even further than the Salt I Treaty in allowing Russia to go far ahead of this country not only in the strength of its air force, but in naval and other strategic areas necessary for the defense of this country against Russian attack.

Not until Russia had invaded Afghanistan were Carter's eyes apparently open to the growing reality of the Russian military strength and threat, and only then did he, temporarily at least, back away from asking the Senate to pass the Salt II Treaty.

This predilection for radicalism and communism in his foreign policy was accompanied by inexplicable zeal for the passage of anti-Christian legislation on the domestic scene. His support of the Equal Rights Amendment, his tacit support of abortion as a legitimate principle of ethical action, and his creation of a separate Department of Education with an avowed humanist as its first Secretary (a cabinet ranked office) were all in accord with the humanistic liberalism of the Democratic Party. And, all of these positions depended upon and aided the further centralization of political, economic, and social power in the hands of the federal government and were accordingly unconstitutional.[59]

From 1977 to 1981 the Carter Administration was thus characterized by a consistent support of anti-Christian causes generally supported by evangelical Christian and political conservatives who were deeply concerned with the maintenance of constitutional government in the nation and the preservation of the proper balance of power between the state and federal governments.

---

[59] During the Carter Administration there was also a series of efforts on the part of the Department of Health and Welfare and the Department of Internal Revenue to force private and Christian schools to accept federal control. The excuse was that such control was necessary to insure the high standards of scholarship, but the real reason was the liberal zeal to insure that all young people would be exposed to humanism in all of the schools of the nation.

The Election of 1980

Both major parties held their conventions in the summer of 1980 and both conventions were rather painful experiences for the television viewer. The Democratic Convention was the scene of a bitter contest between President Carter and Senator Ted Kennedy which threatened to split the party from stem to stern. It was settled when President Carter capitulated to the Kennedy forces and allowed three of Kennedy's main planks to be incorporated into the party platform.

The Republican Party was the scene of a high degree of harmony except for the maneuvering which nearly brought former President Gerald Ford on the ticket as former Governor Ronald Reagan's running mate. Neither convention provided very much in the way of political leadership, and statesmanship was conspicuously absent for both of the conventions.

The Republican Convention, however, did draft a platform which was remarkably conservative. While it did not openly profess any theological stance, there was an evangelical tone to the whole convention, and this was reflected in the provisions of the platform. In fact, this platform was the first for many years to support those measures which were distinctly evangelical in outlook and to condemn those which were openly contrary to the biblical ethic.[60] In making such affirmations the party also placed itself in support of maintaining the Constitution, although both parties were remarkably silent on the question of the Constitution itself. The Republican Party platform solidly opposed the so-called "right of abortion" and pledged itself to seek a constitutional amendment to overturn a decision of the Supreme Court of 1973 which permitted women in the early stages of pregnancy to have legal abortions.[61] Unlike the 1976 Democratic Convention, the 1980 convention was quite silent in regard to Carter's "new birth"

---

[60] For the first time since 1940 the Republican Party did not come out in support of the Equal Rights Amendment, but contented itself with an affirmation that it supported equal rights for women.

[61] *Roe v Wade*, 410 U.S., 113.

and evangelical outlook.

However, although neither party in its platform placed any great emphasis upon Christian orthodoxy as a guiding principle, the campaign proved to be quite different, and a new force entered the political scene, the Moral Majority, a loose coalition of conservative religious groups composed of those who had become alarmed by the tendencies which were becoming increasingly evident in the federal government toward an open hostility to Christian morality; in some cases, even to the Christian church itself. This Moral Majority proved to be a new and powerful factor in the election. Its leadership, for the most part, came from the Christian ministry, and they took a strong stand against legalized abortion, the legalization of homosexual practices, the use of drugs, the Equal Rights movement as it found expression in the Equal Rights Amendment, and an equally vigorous stand in favor of capital punishment. In all of these areas the arguments which it marshalled either for or against these issues were theological in character and reflected an evangelical outlook.

For this reason, along with the fact that the Republican Party platform favored such stands, in the election of 1980, in which former Governor Reagan of California decisively defeated President Carter, theological factors played the most important role which they had attained in American political history sinced 1900, perhaps the most important role in the history of the American Republic. At this juncture it is impossible to tell whether this development will be temporary in nature, a product of a particular crisis in the history of the nation, or whether it will lead. to the formation of a permanent evangelical action group which will play a role in future elections. The election of 1980, however, was a unique expression of the operation of theological influences in our political history.

The Liberal Theology of the Supreme Court and the Departure from the Constitution

No discussion of the infiltration of liberal theology into the political history of the nation would be complete unless the role of the Supreme Court in the decline of constitutional government was given due consideration. Mention has been made of its growing influence as it appeared in its decisions rendered in the Roosevelt era. These earlier decisions set the stage for the later enlargement of the powers of the federal government and the reduction of those of the states, but not until after World War II did the "small cancer in the Constitution" become a malignant tumor which would drastically change the whole direction of constitutional law and bring the document to the point of death, where it would no longer be the supreme law of the land.[62] The growth of this cancerous tumor in constitutional law was the result of a series of decisions which re-interpreted the Fourteenth Amendment in such a way as to give it precedence over the first eight amendments and virtually negate the Tenth Amendment, which reserved to the states, or the people thereof, all powers not specifically named in the body of the Constitution to the federal government. These decisions have virtually merged the Bill of Rights with the Fourteenth Amendment, and also particularly the First and Fifth Amendments as they apply to religion, life, liberty, and property.

It was this process of enlarging the scope of the Fourteenth Amendment and reducing the power of the Tenth Amendment which laid the foundation of the alleged power of the courts to re-interpret the rights of the states in the areas of religion in the schools, capital punishment, abortion, and related matters. It was not, however, merely a matter of enlarging the powers of the court and the federal government at the expense of the historic role of the states in such legislation, but it was also the problem that these developments took place within the context of re-interpreting the Constitution in such a way as to reinforce the demands of the liberal humanists that all religious activities of any kind be removed from the public schools of the nation and that Christian religious symbolism also be removed from governmental activities. Along with

[62] For an authoritative discussion of this sweeping change in the direction of the development of constitutional law see Clarence E. Manion, *Cancer in the Constitution*, Shepherdsville, Ky., Victor Publishing Co., 1972.

this was the insistence that the laws of the states be re-written to allow unbiblical practices of various kinds. To be sure, this basic purpose was not openly acknowledged in the various decisions of the Court, but their thrust was unmistakably clear, even though it was cloaked in language which looked to human rights and the democratic philosophy for their sanction. The thinking of the Court was also increasingly influenced by the opinions of those sociologists who were gaining the ears of jurists, not only on the Supreme Court but on inferior federal and state courts as well. The trend towards psychological and sociological decisions also meant that the Supreme Court was increasingly unwilling to abide by previous decisions and set out to blaze new trails in the interpretation of the Fourteenth Amendment, as well as other sections of the Constitution, which it was tacitly regarding as being outdated and in need of judicial revision. Implicit in this decision to seek new directions for the process of judicial review was the conclusion that the Court must become a kind of legislative body if the law of the land was to be brought up-to-date and outworn interpretations of the Constitution were to be set aside.[63] Although this trend in the thinking of the Court was not confined to such issues as segregation, capital punishment, pornography, abortion, and homosexuality, it was so frequently used in cases involving these issues that it has become almost axiomatic in the thinking of the Court to use it as its basic guide in deciding such cases.

Public education furnished the excuse for the first invasion of the Court into the reserved rights of the states and not only to extend the scope of the Fourteenth Amendment in this manner, but also to give to it a new meaning which was not intended by those who wrote it. In *People of Illinois ex rel Vashti McCollum*[64] the Court held that it was unconstitutional for a state (in this case Illinois) to facilitate the giving of religious instruction to public school students in public schools during school hours for sectarian purposes. In essence it

---

[63] Thus the principle of *stare decisis* was virtually set aside and held to be no longer a safe guide in rendering decisions.

[64] U.S. 203.

was a decision against the growing practice of allowing released time for religious instruction during the school day.[65] The position of the Court (an 8-1 decision) was that the action of Illinois violated the requirement of the First Amendment that there can be no establishment of religion in this country and that the Fourteenth Amendment transferred to the states the prohibition contained in the First. As Clarence Manion and other legal scholars have pointed out, this insistence that the Fourteenth Amendment has made such a transfer is historically and legally inaccurate and most certainly was not the position of the Court before 1940.[66]

Equally weak was the insistence of the Court that such abuse of public property was a violation of the establishment clause. In a decision rendered as late as 1930 the Court had held that the use of public funds to purchase school textbooks and deliver them free to students in public schools was not a violation of the Fourteenth Amendment since the benefit of this action was directly to the children and only incidentally to the schools.[67] Unlike the released time program in Illinois, this program actually involved the expenditure of public funds for the benefit of parochial school students.

In 1962 in *Zorach v Clausen,* a case arising in New York, the Court retreated somewhat from the position which it had assumed in the McCollum Case and agreed that an action by a state to permit students to go to religious centers for religious activities during school hours was not a violation of the Fourteenth Amendment.

In the cases cited thus far it is apparent that the Court was endeavoring to preserve the concept of a "wall of separation" which Jefferson had laid down as the guiding principle in the problems of religion and the state schools. In an educational and political world which was becoming increasingly humanistic and secular, such a position of neutrality became very difficult to uphold, not only in the area of religion and the schools but on a

---

[65] In Illinois the cost of this instruction was borne by the religious groups involved (Protestant, Catholic, and Jewish), and the one class hour a week was given over to this voluntary activity.

[66] See Clarence Manion, *op. cit.,* for an excellent discussion of this problem.

[67] 281 U.S. 370 (1930).

much broader level as well.

In an effort to provide some kind of religious character and inspiration each day for the students of the state, the New York Board fashioned a very simple prayer, supposedly acceptable to Jews, Protestants, and Catholics, and which would meet the demands of the Court. But in *Engel v Vitale* in 1962 the Supreme Court held that an action by a public authority in adopting a prayer that acknowledges a dependence upon God, and further invokes God's blessing on parents, teachers, and the nation, which prayer is to be repeated by school students each day, was a violation of the freedom of religion clauses incorporated into the Fourteenth Amendment.[68]

The trend of the thinking of the Court in regard to religion in the schools became even more clear in a case in which the Court held that the state and local rule requiring the recitation of the Lord's Prayer and the reading of a selection of Bible verses at the start of each school day violated the provisions of the Fourteenth Amendment. In this case the anti-Christian intent of the ruling by the Court was quite apparent. Christian practices were to be banished from the scene of public education throughout the nation. Here the Scriptures themselves were outlawed from the educational process and humanism was given a place in the schools as a religion.[69]

Humanism as a religion was taking the place of Christianity in the public schools of the nation, and the religious liberty of Christians was, and is, being violated in its behalf. There can be little doubt that the growth of immorality, the use of drugs, the general lack of discipline in the schools of the nation, and the rapid decline in the academic development of the students can be directly attributed to the religious vacuum which these decisions have created in public education. In fact, a dramatic decline in discipline in the schools was almost an immediate product of these decisions.

[68] *Engel v Vitale,* 370 U.S. 421 (1962). Although this decision raised a storm of protest, this compulsory nature of this New York statute would seem to be something of an infringement on religious liberty, even though it could hardly be regarded as an infringement of the establishment clause. The prayer in question was nebulous in character, so much so that it lacked almost any real religious significance.

[69] *Abington School District v Schempp,* 374, U.S. 203 (1963).

The Supreme Court and Criminal Justice

The new interpretation which the Court has given to the Fourteenth Amendment has not been restricted to the problems of the relations of church and state, but has invaded much of the legal life of the nation as well. This impact has been very serious in the area of the administration of criminal justice and the treatment of crime and criminals.

Increasingly, the decisions of both the lower and higher courts in the various states and the Supreme Court have been largely framed by sociologists and psychologists who have gained the ear of too many jurists and have swayed their thinking away from the biblical concept of crime and punishment toward a philosophy of criminal justice which is a mixture of Freudian psychology, liberal theology, and sociological confusion. Many judges have become so preoccupied with the so-called "rights" of the criminals standing before them that they have nearly forgotten not only the violated rights of the victims, but the eternal principles of right and justice as they have been enunciated in the Scriptures for the conduct of human government. In its most extreme form this concept of the nature of crime and guilt led some jurists to the bizarre conclusion that since society is the cause of criminal conduct on the part of some of its members, society itself is to blame and the criminal should not be held guilty.

Two decisions rendered in 1964 and 1966 constituted a virtual overthrow of the enforcement of the criminal laws of the nation and made it possible for many guilty criminals to go free because they were able to escape judgment on some flimsy pretext that the law enforcement officers had not followed a prescribed course of arrest.[70]

In 1967 the Supreme Court took a further step to the left and away from sound jurisprudence and the biblical view of justice in a decision which set aside virtually all of the laws of the various states

[70] 378 U.S. 478 (1964) and 384 U.S. 436 (1966). However, the court restricted the scope of these two decisions in three later ones: *Michigan v Moseley* (1975); *Beckworth v U.S.* (1976); and *Doyle v Ohio* (1976).

providing for capital punishment in certain serious criminal cases.[71]

In *Furman v Georgia* the Court struck down two capital punishments, holding that in these cases the imposition of the death penalty constituted a violation of the Eighth and Fourteenth Amendments because it constituted a cruel and unusual punishment. Although hanging and the use of the firing squad were the usual methods of applying the death penalty when the Constitution was adopted, the Court decided that more modern methods such as the use of the electric chair and the gas chamber were somehow cruel and unusual. Although in *Gregg v Georgia* this decision was modified to allow the use of the death penalty if it were applied proportionately and with other safeguards, there has been a reluctance to return to the use of capital punishment in many states. A close study of the opinions of the justices in each of these decisions makes it quite clear that they gave almost no consideration to the biblical principles underlying the use of this penalty and were largely guided by sociological principles in rendering these decisions except possibly in their insistence that the punishment must be proportionate to the crime.

One other case must be mentioned for its importance in showing how far the Supreme Court has wandered from its original purpose as stated in the Constitution and has become the mouthpiece of the most radical elements in the country. This is the famous, or infamous, Keylishian Case, which declared unconstitutional a New York law which sought to prohibit communists from either teaching or holding administrative positions in the schools of that state.[72] In speaking for the court in this decision, Justice Brennan gave as the excuse for the over-ruling of a previous decision of the Court that "pertinent constitutional doctrines have since 1952 rejected the premises upon which the conclusion rested."[73] Actually no new constitutional doctrine worthy of the name had been developed since 1952 which would justify such a reversal. The truth of the

---

[71] *Furman v Georgia*, 408 U.S. 238 (1972); *Georgia v Gregg*, 428 U.S. 153 (1976).

[72] *Adler vs the Board of Regents*, 1952. Curiously enough, the Supreme Court had upheld this very same act.

[73] *Ibid.*

matter was that the Court was determined to drive God out of the classroom and replace teachers who believed in Him with communists and give them permanent tenure. It is now clear that the whole course of decisions by the Supreme Court since the Vashti-McCollum case of 1948 has been to remove the God of the Scriptures from the government and educational system of this country. Thus, through this Court, even more than through the Congress or the Presidents who have served since 1948, humanism has been crowding our Christian heritage out of the picture. The Supreme Court, at one time the citadel of Christian orthodoxy and political conservatism, has now become the vehicle through which both our Christian and constitutional heritages are being destroyed.

In 1973 in *Roe v Wade* the Supreme Court took another and possibly the most significant step away from a recognition of the Christian foundations of our government and legal system when it so interpreted the Fourteenth Amendment and the use of the word "person" to legalize abortions as a means of terminating undesired pregnancy during the first three months.[74] Although in its decision the Court held that the initial and basic constitutional issue is the scope of constitutional personhood and rejected the contention that it was "when life begins," the desire of the Court to avoid the admittedly difficult question as to when life begins and to concentrate on the problem of "personhood" led it into accepting a view of the origin of life which is directly contrary to the Scriptures and therefore legalizes the murder of the unborn infant. This crime has been heightened by the fact that until 1980 hundreds of thousands, even millions, of abortions were paid for by federal funds.[75]

This decision in *Roe v Wade* has become one of the most controversial decisions of the Court in its long history and has aroused public opposition to a far greater degree than any other in

[74] 410 U.S.113. For an excellent discussion of the issues before the court in this case, see "The Right to Abortion, the Scope of the Fourteenth Amendment Personhood, and the Supreme Court's Birth Requirement." *Southern Illinois University Law Journal*, 1979, Vol. 1 (John D. Gorby, author). See also Donald N. Regan, "Rewriting Roe v Wade," *Michigan Law Review*, August, 1979, Vol. 77, No. 7.

[75] This practice came to an end legally in September, 1980, when the Supreme Court refused to hear a case on appeal allowing the decision of a lower court to stand.

recent history with the possible exception of cases dealing with segregation. The opposition to the *Roe v Wade* decision arose in all sections of the country and brought forth demands that Congress remove the right of appeal to the Supreme Court in such cases. The irony in the position assumed by the Court in this case finds its basis in its 1967 decision to outlaw capital punishment as it was then provided for in the laws of most states. In both situations the court was ruling against the great biblical heritage of the nation and was introducing the principles of humanism into the very fabric of our legal system.

10

Conclusion

Whether we look at the Puritans and their fellow colonists of the seventeenth century, or their descendants of the eighteenth century, or those who framed the Declaration of Independence and the Constitution, we see that their political programs were the rather clear reflection of a consciously held political philosophy, and that the various political philosophies which emerged among the American people were intimately related to the theological developments which were taking place. Political philosophies are not created in a vacuum, but are in turn the product of systems of thought which find their inspiration and nurture in theology. What is true of colonial and Revolutionary America is no less true of the America of the nineteenth and twentieth centuries.

Because of this there appeared at an early date in the colonies a kind of political orthodoxy, a way of looking at government and its functions and of the proper relationship which should exist between the government and its citizens. A Christian world and life view furnished the basis for this early political thought which guided the American people for nearly two centuries and whose crowning lay in the writing of the Constitution of 1787. This Christian theism had so permeated the colonial mind that it continued to guide even those who had come to regard the Gospel with indifference or even hostility. The currents of this orthodoxy were too strong to be easily set aside by those who in their own thinking had come to a different conception of religion and hence of government also.

The history of this political orthodoxy during the nineteenth and twentieth centuries has been quite a different story. It has gradually lost its hold on the American mind to such an extent that there is very little evidence of its former power in our national life today. The old Puritan-colonial dream for America has been replaced by one which bears little resemblance to that which was dominant two hundred years ago. The reason for this decline is not to be found primarily in the vast social and economic changes which have taken place in the last two centuries, or in the new role which this country has been called upon to play in international affairs. These have had their effect on the American mind, but the developments themselves are the result of vast intellectual changes which have so transformed this nation that it would be virtually unrecognizable by those who lived here one hundred years ago; and they would have great difficulty in evaluating this nation in terms of the Puritan dream with which they were quite familiar.

If the disappearance of this Puritan vision for the new land is not to be laid at the door of those important social and economic changes which have characterized our development since 1860, how then is it to be explained? It is to be found in the great changes which have taken place in American theology since the latter part of the eighteenth century; as a result, Calvinism in particular and the older evangelical theology in general, have lost their hold on the American mind to such an extent that they are no longer the dominant forces in the formulation of our political, social and economic thought. They have yielded to various schools of theology, nearly all liberal in their outlook, which have been able to secure command over the intellectual life of the nation, a command as great as Calvinism once wielded over the American mind. These great changes in theology could not, and did not, fail to have a decisive and enduring effect on American thought.

While they differed in their intensity of rebellion from Calvinism and on some of their various doctrines, these liberal theologies had much more in common than they did of peculiarities distinctly their own. All rejected the Calvinistic view of the sovereign God. Deism looked to a God who was a captive of his own creation and its natural law, while Transcendentalism brought forth a god who was a part of creation. Unitarianism, the theology which accompanied both of these systems of thought, denied the doctrine of the Trinity and the deity of Jesus Christ. The god of these religious and philosophical systems was far different from the God revealed in the Scriptures. Political philosophy could not but suffer in the hands of those who looked for their frame of reference in the affairs of state.

The Darwinism and Social Gospel which came to dominate large segments of American theology after 1870 provided the inspiration and foundation for a new liberalism in theology which shared many of the attributes of previous schools. It also added some ingredients of its own, largely culled from the Darwinism to which it eagerly looked as a new oracle of infallibility to replace the discarded view of the infallibility of the Scriptures. This new liberalism gave even less of a place to the transcendent God of Deism or the immanent deity of Transcendentalism, and placed a greater emphasis upon human capabilities for progress, in alliance with the forces of nature which were now interpreted in the light of an evolutionary pattern of development. This new theological liberalism paved the way for a view of man which was more greatly determined by the new biology, the new psychology and the new sociology than it was by any reference to biblical doctrines. Ultimately the whole doctrine of human redemption would be so reinterpreted as to leave little room for the Christian view. The emphasis on the redemption of society would become so great that the salvation of the individual would all but be forgotten. Darwinism and the Social Gospel would then become the inspiration for the Utopianism which became such a prominent part of American thought in the latter years of the nineteenth and the early decades of the present century. There had been Utopian visions in previous eras, but they had lacked the all-embracing sweep of these later plans and the deterministic character which the reliance on Darwinism gave to those which appeared in this country with Lester Frank Ward and Jeremy Bellamy.

The development of liberalism in the twentieth century pushed the God of the Scriptures further into the background of human affairs and gave an increasingly important role to man himself so that God, to the extent to which he was considered at all, was benignly regarded as the ally of progress and democracy. He could cooperate with the human race should he desire to do so, but any refusal on his part would not be taken too seriously by those in control of the situation in this country and it certainly would impede America's realization of her historic destiny. Obviously those theological systems, or schools, which could give voice to such views can hardly be called theistic, and never Christian. For many leaders the very term "God" had ceased to symbolize much more than the vague yearning of humanity for a better life on earth and the realization of the "best that was in the human race."

Inevitably, political thought reflected this trend toward humanism and the secular character of American political movements after 1870 became more open. The revolt had become so momentous by 1900 that the political thought of Deism and Transcendentalism seemed almost evangelical in comparison to its offspring of the opening decades of the twentieth century. Theories of government and courses of political action were advocated which bore little resemblance to the thinking of the Founding Fathers and were little less than a gross distortion of the Puritan dream. The old ideals of a moral righteousness as the key to the national character were lost in a welter of secularism which demanded full employment, a rising tide of prosperity and an increasing degree of economic security as the enduring test of successful government. The older view that government existed to enforce the law of God in a nation was discarded as a relic of the Middle Ages, unsuited for a modern nation in an industrial era. There was, in short, a decided shift in emphasis from the older liberalism of the period from 1800 to 1850 which placed a great importance on individual freedom, and the prevention of war and drunkenness, along with certain other reforms, to a new position which insisted that it was the role of government to maintain by all the power at its command, an economic and social freedom for all peoples and classes while it actively entered into the economic life of the people to raise the standard of living, and bring about an economic and social equality by political means. A social and economic equalitarianism thus became the goal of this later political liberalism.

This development was not accidental nor did it take place without reference to the changes in the outlook of theological liberalism on social and economic matters. For the increasing radicalism of theological liberalism in these areas is one of the major intellectual forces at work in American society. Its roots are to be seen in the developments which took place between 1865 and 1900, but it reached its maturity in the first forty years of this century. There is a striking similarity between the position assumed by the Federal Council of Churches in its social pronouncements of 1908 and the Methodist Social Creed of that same year, and the general position assumed by the progressives in both of the major parties in the 1908 and 1912 campaigns. The position of both the Methodist Church and the Federal Council, as it was stated in 1908, was comparatively conservative in contrast to their pronouncements on economic and social issues after 1932. The shift to a more clearly defined radicalism was made possible, as we have seen, by the further departure of liberal theology from the biblical norm and by the coming of the Great Depression. In 1908 those who desired socialism as the best solution for the problems of the day were not able to gain a hearing in the final drafting of the two documents of that year.

But after 1932 the situation was quite different. Not only did leaders of the Methodist and other great denominations, as well as the Federal Council of Churches, condemn capitalism as contrary to the Gospel, but they also extolled socialism as the very essence of the Gospel message. Theological liberalism had taken a further step in its social creed and it found a much more widespread response in many of the larger denominations than it had previously received, including some which had generally been regarded as rather conservative in their political and economic outlook. A progressively liberal theology could only bring in its wake a progressively liberal social and economic outlook; and this development was obvious in many of the churches officially related to the Federal Council. Liberalism in the one area brought forth its counterpart in the area of social thought and action. Actually, many of the more vocal leaders within theological liberalism were in advance of the more practical politicians of the New Deal who were keenly aware of the state of public opinion at large and who had no desire to create a socialist state merely to please a small segment of American society if they could not gain the support of the great majority of people at large. The more radical leaders of the New Deal were keenly aware of the support which the liberals in the denominations were giving them, but they did not always set the policy of the administration in such matters. Political considerations took precedence over New Deal idealism and the demands for socialism and collectivism. In the third place, it must be noted that theological liberalism not only became increasingly radical in its political and social outlook, but it was generally, if not always, to be found in support of the democratic movement in this country; and in opposition to those forces which were conservative in their outlook and devoted to the maintenance of constitutional government as it had been brought forth by the Convention of 1787. This does not mean that all theological liberals accepted the logic of their position and became ardent champions of democracy any more than it implies that all those who favored the maintenance of the basic principles of the Constitution were always orthodox in their theology. There have been important and notable exceptions in both camps. It does mean, on the other hand that, in general, theological liberalism has been in sympathy with those men and movements who have sought to bring about a greater degree of political, economic and social democracy in this country. It has given its blessing to those programs which sought to bring more power to the people at large. It has pursued such a policy simply because theological liberalism has consistently placed a great deal of confidence in the people, their innate goodness and even their perfectibility. There is between the democratic philosophy and theological liberalism a basic affinity which has placed them in the same camp in many major political struggles.

This condition exists because theological liberalism shares the basic postulates of the democratic philosophy. It is true, of course, that as a political phenomenon in ancient Greece, democracy antedated Christian orthodoxy, but in its more modern development the two movements have often grown out of the same soil and in the same intellectual climate both in Europe and America. Theological liberalism at heart has been a continuing protest against Calvinism, particularly against its insistence on the sovereignty of God and the total depravity of the race. These two biblical doctrines have often proved to be a stumbling block to theologians within the church as well as to the unbelieving world at large; many attempts have been made since the Reformation to rewrite the creeds of the Reformation in such a way that some concession could be made to the ideas of human sovereignty and goodness. Most, if not all, of the evangelical movements since the Reformation which have denied Calvinism at these points have actually been attempts to democratize the Christian faith. Inevitably these efforts have resulted in a view of God which denies to him that full sovereignty which the Scriptures ascribe to him, and in a doctrine of man which places him on a pedestal to which he has no claim.[1] Many of the evangelical and pietistic movements since the Reformation in their denial of a full-orbed and fully biblical Calvinism have presented a theology which is the result of a desire to seek a *modus vivendi* between Calvinism and its democratic alternatives. Calvinism is the antithesis of the democratic philosophy with its insistence on human depravity and the denial of the innate goodness of man. In its insistence on the complete sovereignty of God in human affairs it is likewise the antithesis of that democratic conception of the state which finds its origins and inspiration in the writings of John Locke.

However, most of these evangelical movements have frequently found themselves the inspiration of, and in alliance with, democratic movements in American history. These "democratic evangelical theological systems" have also been the home of much of the theological liberalism of our day. Once they had departed from a strict biblical position on the sovereignty of God and total depravity, there was no logical stopping place short of a position which practically denied these scriptural truths. This does not mean that all of these movements followed the logic of their own position to these consequences and some of them have been miraculously preserved from this humanistic abyss. Neither can it be denied that this denial of Calvinism has taken its toll in many denominations and they have virtually lost their biblical moorings in favor of some form of philosophy to which they frequently add a religious coating with biblical quotations and

---

[1] This tendency can also be observed in the history of the Roman Catholic Church, both in the Middle Ages and since the Council of Trent, in the various departures from its Augustinian heritage. In fact, this "democratization" of Roman Catholic theology has not only produced the absolutism of the Papacy, but actually made such an absolutism highly necessary as a human safeguard against the logical conclusions of a "democratic" theology. Thomism in Roman Catholic circles and Arminianism in Protestant circles can only lead to the same logical conclusion unless checked by some ecclesiastical authority.

references to Jesus Christ as the Great Teacher, the Master of men. Thus theological liberalism is a further extension of this "democratic" philosophy which came to play such a dominant role in the life of many denominations after 1900. It gave its blessings to those assumptions of the Enlightenment, such as the innate goodness of man and the perfectibility of his society through a properly directed education. Thus modern democracy, growing out of the Enlightenment, found a natural ally in theological liberalism and this liberalism found in this political philosophy the extension of its own thought into the political life of the American people.

The ultimate result of this alliance between theological and political democracy was the further secularization of the state, of education and of American life in general. The very "democracy" of their theology made it rather easy for the liberals to accept the concept of popular sovereignty and the idea that government is responsible to people rather than to God and that law is little more than the embodiment or expression of the will of the majority. It is in this context that the recently successful efforts to remove the Bible and all Christian activity from the public schools, must be understood. The democratic philosophy is actually opposed to all Christian assumptions concerning God, man and the nature of the educational process. It is not merely a matter of the separation of church and state under the First Amendment, although it is that; it is much more than that. It is basically an attempt to separate public education, and ultimately the state itself, from every aspect of Christian theology. Although many theological liberals look on this with horror, for reasons of expedience, if no other, they all too often fail to realize that the present impasse is one of their own making. For many decades they have been presenting a set of religious teachings that could only have this result. They have unwittingly aided in the destruction of the Christian heritage of this nation, and of the ethical content which they wished to maintain to guide a secular democratic state in its quest for its governmentally achieved millennium.

It is at this point that theological liberalism not only betrayed the Founding Fathers but its own past as well. For, in its willingness to free itself from the last vestiges of its biblical restraints and to come to terms with a secular democratic philosophy, it necessarily accepted as its own the hopes and aspirations of this secularism. Many liberals by 1900 were willing to join forces with the Socialists in the creation of a democratic socialism in this country, in which the government would own and control the principal means of transportation and communication and have an increasing control over industry in general. After 1920, and even more so after 1930, many of them found it no more difficult to accept the Communist blueprint for American society. Although the exact number may never be known, there can be no doubt of the fact that a substantial element of the leadership of the Federal Council of Churches was in sympathy with the communist philosophy in the nineteen-thirties. Some of them actually held membership in the Communist movement[2] and, it is of more than passing significance, that the great majority of those liberal leaders who joined ranks with the Communists, in one way or another, were trained in those seminaries which had departed from the evangelical orthodoxy.[3] Very few of them came from the more conservative denominations, or from the seminaries which had remained true to the historic faith.

Thus, the final contribution of theological liberalism to the present dilemma confronting the American people has been an impetus toward the totalitarian type of government in which an economic collectivism becomes the order of the day. It would certainly seem ironical at first glance, that a theology which sought to emancipate man from the clutches of a sovereign God and a political philosophy which placed such a high value on human freedom and dignity should join in a subtle conspiracy to bring political freedom to an end in this country in the name of

---

[2] For an interesting verification of this position see an article by Reinhold Niebuhr in the *Christian Century*, August 19, 1953, pp. 936-937. He admits that this clerical Stalinism could not have existed if there had not been a considerable Marxist dogmatism in American liberalism.

[3] Nearly all come from the Methodist and Congregational Churches.

democracy. Yet this is exactly what has happened and while it may seem incongruous at first glance, this is not the case. The final negation of freedom in the name of democracy is the logical and almost necessary outcome of the rejection of the biblical insistence on the sovereignty of God. In its rejection of the sovereignty of God, liberalism was committing itself to a doctrine of abject slavery for the whole human race, and was severing itself from the source of all freedom, namely, God himself. This is the essential failure of all those philosophies of freedom which seek this precious commodity elsewhere than in man's subjection to the righteous and holy will of God. In rejecting Calvinism, the liberals were, in effect, denying the only true source of human freedom: political, social and economic, and in their alliance with the secular democratic philosophy, they were setting the stage for the disappearance of that freedom which had been safeguarded by the Puritan political tradition and the Constitution. The willingness of modern liberalism, both theological and political, to come to terms with totalitarianism and collectivism as that form of freedom most compatible with the needs of twentieth century man is a tragic commentary on the intellectual and moral emptiness of these philosophies. When theology rejected the Scriptures as the norm of all truth and accepted the dictum that man is the measure, then there was little left but to accept the idea that in democracy, the expressed will of the majority, there is the norm by which all truth is measured. Collective man thus becomes the measure of political truth, or rather political expediency and collectivism take over in the economic, social and political life of the state which is dedicated to this philosophy. A totalitarian state, virtually infallible, becomes as necessary in a democratic society as an infallible Papacy is for a church which rejected the Scriptures as the only rule of faith and practice. The totalitarian regime in the state must save a democracy from its own excesses even as the Papacy must keep the Semi-Pelagian trends in Roman Catholic theology from removing the last vestiges of biblical truth from that organization.

One last conclusion must be noted and this has to do with

the role of the ecumenical movement in the rise of liberal theology to political power. It would be both unhistorical and unfair to assert that the desire for Christian unity was born within the folds of liberal theology. This is not true, but there can be little doubt that the theological liberals soon claimed it as their own and that the evangelicals began to regard it with increasing doubt and dismay. Although it made some slight headway in this country as early as the eighteen-seventies, it did not have any real significance until after 1920 when the ecumenical movement picked up strength after World War I. It gained its first real victories in the United States in the early nineteen-thirties in the formation of the Congregational Christian and Evangelical and Reformed Churches. But in the unification of the Northern and Southern Methodist Churches along with the Methodist Protestant Church in 1939, the movement entered a new era; for, numerically, this represented the largest number of members yet brought within the fold of one denomination.

Agitation for church union became increasingly frequent and persistent during and after World War II; the movement received quite an impetus from the Amsterdam meeting of the recently formed World Council of Churches in 1948, and in the creation of the National Council of Churches out of the former Federal Council of Churches in 1950. It registered two more significant achievements in the union of the Presbyterian Church USA and the United Presbyterian Church of North America to form the United Presbyterian Church in the United States of America and in the creation of the United Church of Christ out of the Congregational Christian and the Evangelical and Reformed Churches in the closing years of this same decade.

Although the ecumenical movement did attract to its ranks some evangelicals, for the most part it was, and continues to be, a liberal movement designed for the accomplishment of liberal purposes. For a long time its real purposes were concealed by an insistence that an organic union of the Protestant Churches was necessary to counteract the great political strength of the Roman Catholic hierarchy, but this argument lost much of its force when the leaders of the ecumenical movement within Protestantism showed a great interest in the possibility of reconciliation with Rome, going so far as to send official representatives to the ecumenical council held at Rome in the autumn of 1962 under Pope John XXIII.

It is to be doubted that this appeal for unity on the grounds of the necessity of opposing Rome ever had a large part in the thinking of those who were pressing for Protestant unification. It was more of an argument used for the public defense and presentation of the cause than an actual reason for seeking such union.

After 1945 the architects of the ecumenical church were much more candid in their statements of hopes and purposes for Protestant unity and made more of the argument that such a unity was necessary for the realization of the social and economic aspects of the Gospel in the life of the nation. In short, liberal theology was in need of organizational strength for the promotion of its social program. Charles Clayton Morrison made this position very clear in the *Christian Century:*

> Protestantism has not learned to live in the modern world. It has carried over from the era of individualism its structures of organization and its simple procedures that seemed appropriate then. Everything around it has changed—the whole structure and psychology of society, but Protestantism proceeds as if it were still living in the middle eighties . . .[4]

> Protestantism cannot win America until it rids itself of the illusion that the American mentality is still individualistic, and that its churches are gaining because they are recruiting individuals into their membership. The American mind is now predominantly collectivistic in its structure. It is molded by a relatively few massive blocks of secular interest. . . Protestantism, on the other hand, is sectarianized, localized and individualized. It has neither organization nor techniques for gaining entrance into or commanding the respect of these collectivities.[5]

[4] *Christian Century,* May 15, 1946, p. 618.
[5] *Ibid.,* p. 619.

The one solution which he put forward to this alleged Protestant dilemma was the ecumenical church, by which he did not mean merely a unity of effort and strength from denominations as such, but a union of denominations into one big church which would be able to meet a secular collectivism with ecclesiastical collectivism.[6] There is much that can, and should, be said concerning the errors in this position outlined above—its lack of perception as to what the church really is, its lack of dependence upon the Holy Spirit in the proclamation of the Gospel, its lack of realization that the Gospel is always preached to individuals—and that only individuals can be saved—that society is never collectively saved, but only as the individuals comprising it are brought under its redeeming power and given newness of life as individuals. The blindness of liberalism in regard to American society and its problems becomes even more apparent in the insistence that the political collectivism can only be successfully met by a corresponding ecumenical collectivism. The creation of an ecclesiastical hierarchy of such a kind as the liberals seem to advocate, can only give a new impetus to further growth and development of the secular collectivism they wish to oppose.

Increasingly, after 1950, the leaders of the ecumenical movement have insisted that the creation of an ecumenical church is an absolute necessity so that the Christian forces of this nation may exert the right influence on the conduct of national affairs; by which they mean, a support of liberal policies both domestic and in the area of foreign policy. At home the ecumenicists have repeatedly declared themselves to be in favor of federal aid to education, the extension of the social security program to the inclusion of some form of medicare, the compulsory desegregation of all areas of American life, and the abolition of the House Committee on Un-American Activities. In regard to foreign policy, the weight of the ecumenical movement has always been on the side of those policies which are quite liberal and even

[6] *Christian Century*, May 22, 1946, pp. 650-653.

radical. Its leaders have supported the United Nations and its policies (even when that organization failed to maintain the peace, and chose to use warfare for the realization of that aim). Again and again they have rallied to the support of various proposals for world government and the drastic limitations of national sovereignty.[7] This same naive attitude toward Russia has led the ecumenical forces to call for the ending of tests on nuclear weapons and various kinds of disarmament plans; they have, on more than one occasion, criticized various administrations for refusing to accept Russian-sponsored plans which openly threatened our national security and actually invited the very nuclear wars which they professed to oppose.

It must be admitted that once again these liberal forces in their ecumenical pronouncements and protests have not used their influence in vain. For the liberal press and their allies in Congress and other public offices have assumed these positions and in their editorials and public statements have echoed all too often the same arguments found in the ecumenical journals and statements of councils of churches.[8]

The Orthodox Answer to the Dilemma Posed by the Rise of Liberalism

Does orthodoxy have a satisfactory answer to the dilemma which this nation faces? This is an important question and demands an answer. If liberalism has been such an influential

[7] See, for example, the articles in the *Christian Century,* January 14, 1948, pp. 38-40, in which the writer insisted that Russia should be invited to join such an organization and February 11, 1948, pp. 166-168.

[8] The perusal of the *Congressional Record* and such journals as *The Nation* and *The New Republic* for the years since 1945 will offer sufficient evidence for the truth of this statement. In fact, the evidence is so massive that it would be tedious to attempt to reproduce it, as the reader will soon discover for himself, should he go to these sources. Underlying all their arguments is the very dangerous and very erroneous assumption that there is not as much difference between Communism and the West as we imagine and that there is a common ground for both the East and West on which they can meet and achieve a workable understanding which will maintain world peace for the foreseeable future.

agency for the creation of a movement away from constitutional government and the traditional American freedom toward a collectivistic society and some kind of totalitarian regime, does Christian orthodoxy have a remedy for this situation? A thorough discussion of this question actually demands a volume in itself, but a short presentation is necessary as a capstone for this volume.

The answer is found in the biblical view of government. The Scriptures clearly teach that human government is of divine ordination and does not have its origin in any social compact or contract, as Hobbes and Locke taught, nor was it created by man himself to meet the needs of his society. Rather does Christian theism insist that government was ordained of God for man and that its just powers come from him and not from man. Government is not ordained primarily to defend human liberty, but to insure that kind of society necessary for man to carry out those duties which he owes to God alone. Thus, government has clearly defined powers and operates in a clearly defined sphere. The basic error of liberalism at this point has been its insistence that human government is a social institution, responsible to those men who created it and is primarily concerned with the preservation of human rights as they were defined by Jefferson and others of that day. This error is very popular among Christian people as well as the nation at large and it has been productive of great error for it has allowed the forces of political liberalism to extend the operations of government into those spheres where it has no right to be, and in so doing it has actually become a menace to the human liberty which the liberals insist that it must protect. But above and beyond this, when human government extends its powers and operations to those spheres of human life which God did not render subject to it, government then finds itself in opposition to its divinely bestowed purposes for it takes unto itself powers which were never bestowed upon it. It is this extension of power into these forbidden areas which has created the modern totalitarian state. When human government enters into the field of labor relations, education, mental and physical health, agriculture, housing, and those many other areas of legislation so characteristic of the federal government today, it leaves its proper functions and enters into those areas of life which God has either ordained that the church or the family should have as their particular sphere of responsibility, or that they should be the concern of some human institution which man may erect for his own civil purposes under God's common grace.

The real problem then, is not basically the reduction of governmental expenses (as important as that is), nor the proper relationship between the states and the federal government, or the victory of one political party over another. All of these have their place. But the basic issue is the reduction of the total scope of government, on both the federal and state level, to those spheres which are clearly conferred upon it by the Scriptures and the surrender of those extra-biblical powers which liberal political philosophy and practice have given to it during the last one hundred years or so. Only then will our government be truly Christian and freedom be restored to its former and proper place in the life of the American people.

Bibliography

Adams, Henry. *The Degradation of the Democratic Dogma*. New York: Peter Smith, 1949.

————. *The Education of Henry Adams*. Boston: Houghton Mifflin, 1918.

Armstrong, Maurice, and Loetscher, Lefferts. *The Presbyterian Enterprise*. Philadelphia: Westminster Press, 1955.

Becker, Carl. *The Heavenly City of the Eighteenth Century Philosophers*. Chicago: Quadrangle Books, 1960.

Beecher, Henry Ward. *Evolution and Religion*. New York: Harvard and Fullback, 1893.

Blau, Joseph. *Men and Movements in American Philosophy*. New York: Prentice-Hall, 1952.

Borstein, Daniel. *The Lost World of Thomas Jefferson*. New York, 1948.

Brisbane, Albert. *The Social Destiny of Man*. Philadelphia, 1940.

Bundy, Edgar. *Collectivism in the Churches*. Wheaton, Ill.: Church League of America, 1960.

Carroll, Jackson. *Religion in America, 1950 to the Present*. New York: Harper and Row, 1978.

Carter, Paul. *The Decline and Revival of the Social Gospel: Social and Political Liberalism in American Protestant Churches, 1920–1940*. Ithaca, N. Y.: Cornell University Press, 1956.

Cauthern, Kenneth. *The Impact of American Religious Liberalism*. New York: Harper, 1962.

Chugerman, Samuel. *Lester Frank Ward, The American Aristotle*. Durham, N. C.: Duke University Press, 1939.

Commager, Henry Steel. *The American Mind*. New Haven: Yale University Press, 1950.

Curti, Merle. *The Growth of American Thought*. New York: Harper, 1943.

Emerson, Ralph Waldo. *Complete Works* (Riverside Edition). Boston: 1883.

Forcy, Charles D. *Cross Roads of Liberalism: Croley, Weyland and Lippman, 1900–1925*. New York: Oxford University Press, 1961.

Frothingham, O. B. *Transcendentalism in New England*. Philadelphia: University of Pennsylvania Press, 1972.

Gabriel, Ralph. *The Course of American Democratic Thought*. New York: The Ronald Press, 1940.

Handy, Robert T. *The Social Gospel in America*. New York, 1966.

Hodge, Charles. *What Is Evolution?* New York: Scribner and Armstrong, 1874.

Hofstadter, Richard. *Social Darwinism in American Thought, 1860–1915*. New York: Oxford University Press, 1945.

Holmes, Oliver Wendell. *The Common Law*. Boston, 1881.

Hopkins, C. H. *The Rise of the Social Gospel in American Protestantism*. New York: Yale University Press, 1967.

Hutchinson, William. *The Modernistic Impulse in American Protestantism*. Cambridge, Mass.: Harvard University Press, 1976.

Jackson, Robert H. *The Struggle for Judicial Supremacy*. New York: Alfred Knopf, 1940.

Jameson, Franklin P. *The American Revolution Considered as a Social Movement*. Boston: Beacon Press, 1951.

Keller, A. G. *Reminiscences of William Graham Sumner*. New Haven: Yale University Press, 1933.

Keynes, John Maynard. *Essays in Persuasion*. New York: Nation, 1963.

————. *General Theory of Employment, Money and Interest*. New

York: Harcourt Brace, 1936.

————. *Treatise on Money*. New York: Macmillan, 1936.

Koch, Adrienne. *The American Enlightenment*. New York: Braziller, 1965.

Landis, Benson Y. *A Rauschenbusch Reader*. New York, 1957.

Manion, Clarence E. *Cancer in the Constitution*. Shepherdsville, Ky.: Victor Publishing Co., 1972.

McConnell, Francis J. *Democratic Christianity*. New York: Macmillan, 1919.

Methven, Eugene H. *The Rise of Radicalism*. New Rochelle,: N. Y.: Arlington House, 1973.

Miller, Perry. *The Life and the Mind in America: From the Revolution to the Civil War*. Harcourt Brace, 1965.

————. *The Puritan Mind*. Cambridge, Mass.: Harvard University Press, 1954.

Miller, Perry, and Johnson. *The Puritans*. New York: American Book Co., 1938.

Miller, Robert M. *American Protestantism and Social Issues, 1919–1939*. Chapel Hill: University of North Carolina Press, 1958.

Mosier, Richard. *The American Temper*. Berkeley: University of California Press, 1952.

National Council of Churches. *Pronouncements* Issued by the National Council of Churches of Christ in America, Through February, 1961. New York, 1961.

————. *Triennial Reports, 1954, 1957, 1960, 1966, 1969, 1972, 1975, 1978*.

————. *Minutes of the General Board* (Matthews Collection), unpublished. Montreat, N. C.: Presbyterian Historical Foundation.

Orr, John. *English Deism: Its Roots and Fruits*. Grand Rapids: Wm. B. Eerdmans, 1934.

Orton, W. A. *The Liberal Tradition*. New Haven: Yale University Press, 1945.

Parrington, Vernon L. *Main Currents in American Thought*, 3 vols. New York: Harcourt Brace, 1954.

Person, Stowe. *American Minds: A History of Ideas*. New York: Henry Hilt, 1958.

Porter, K., and Johnson, D. B. *National Party Platforms, 1840–1964*. Urbana: University of Illinois Press, 1966.

Rauschenbusch, Walter. *Christianity and the Social Crisis*. New York: Macmillan, 1907.

———. *Christianity and the Social Order*. New York: Macmillan, 1912.

———. *A Theology for the Social Gospel*. New York: Macmillan, 1917.

Roosevelt, Franklin D. *Public Papers, 1928–1932*. New York: Random House, 1938.

Schlesinger, Arthur M. *The Crisis of the Old Order*. Boston: Houghton-Mifflin, 1957.

Singer, C. Gregg. *The Unholy Alliance*. New Rochelle, N. Y.: Arlington House, 1976.

———. *From Rationalism to Irrationality*. Phillipsburg, N. J.: Presbyterian and Reformed Publishing Co., 1979.

Sumner, William Graham. *The Challenge of the Facts and Other Essays*. New Haven: Yale University Press, 1913.

———. *Folkways*. Boston: Ginn and Co., 1906.

———. *Selected Essays*, ed. A. G. Keller and M. B. Davies. New Haven: University Press, 1934.

Thornwell, James Henley. *Collected Writings* (particularly vol. 4). Carlisle, Pa.: Banner of Truth, 1973.

Turner, Frederick Jackson. *The Frontier in American History*. New York: Henry Holt, 1958

Tyler, Alice Felt. *Freedom's Ferment*. Minneapolis: University of Minnesota Press, 1944.

Wallace, Henry. *Statesmanship and Religion*. London: Williams and Norgate, 1934.

Wallas, Graham, *The Great Society*. New York: Macmillan, 1914.

Ward, Harry F. *In Place of Profit*. New York: Scribner Press, 1933.

Ward, Lester Frank. *The Psychic Factors in Civilization*. Boston: Ginn and Co., 1893.

———. *Pure Sociology*. New York: Macmillan, 1903.

Wells, David, and Woodbridge, John. *The Evangelicals, What They Believe—Who They Are, Where They Are, Where They Are Changing*. Grand Rapids: Baker Book House, 1977.

Wilson, R. J. *Darwinism and the Intellectual*. Homewood, Ill.: Dorsey Press, 1967.

Young, William. *God's Messenger, Religious Leadership in Colonial New England*. Baltimore: Johns Hopkins Press, 1976.

Index